MW01702215

MAPPING MEMORY

First published in 2006
Second edition published in 2007 by David Krut Publishing

Copyright © Constitution Hill 2006

All rights reserved
The moral right of the authors has been asserted

This book was initially developed with a grant from Atlantic Philanthropies and the Conference Workshop Cultural Initiative Fund (CWCI). The Mapping Memory Project was managed by the Johannesburg Development Agency.

ISBN 978-0-620-36819-3

No part of this publication may be reproduced, stored in a retrieval system or transmitted in any form or by any means, electronic, mechanical, photocopying, recording or otherwise without prior written permission of Constitution Hill

Editors and curators: Lauren Segal and Clive van den Berg
Design and typesetting: Carina Comrie from Bon-Bon*
Photographers: Fati Moalusi and John Hodgkiss
Proofreaders: Sheila Steinberg and Di Stuart
Workshop leader and collections curator: Churchill Madikida
Workshop facilitators: Thandokhazi Mashiya, Thenjiwe Mchunu and Lebogang Mokgalaka
Workshop assistant: Vido Madikida
Printing and binding: Mortimer Offset

David Krut Publishing
140 Jan Smuts Avenue
Parkwood
2193 South Africa
www.davidkrutpublishing.com

DAVID KRUT PUBLISHING

CONSTITUTION HILL

CONTENTS

INTRODUCTION

by Lauren Segal
Clive van den Berg
Churchill Madikida

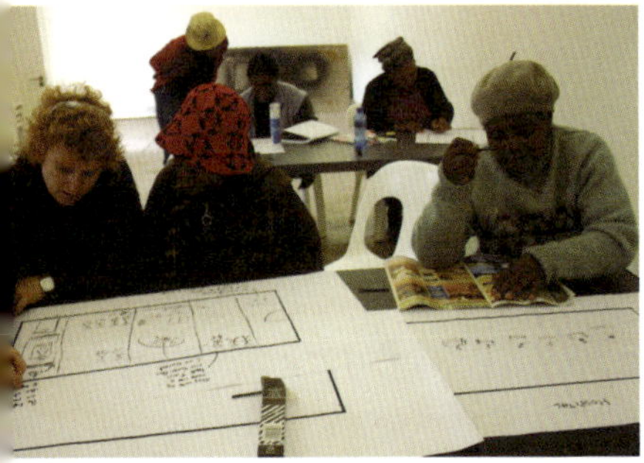

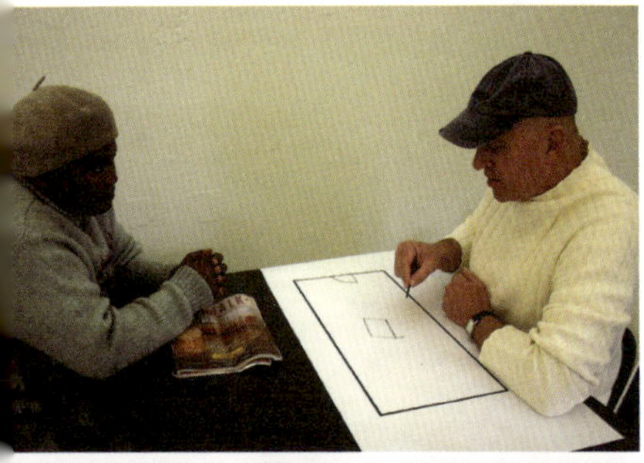

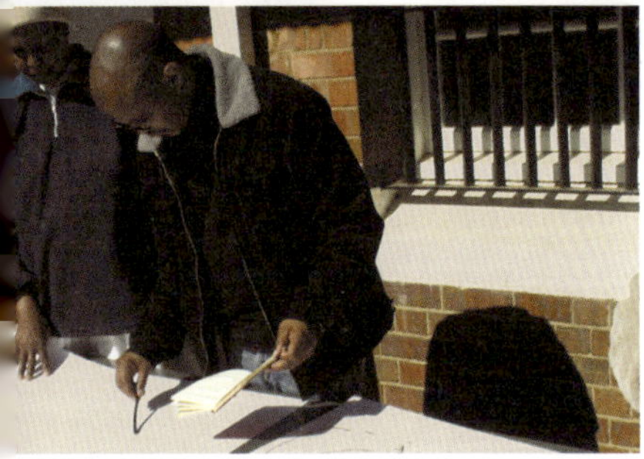

CURATORS OF THE MAPPING MEMORY PROJECT EXPLORING NEW LANGUAGES OF EXPRESSING MEMORIES WITH FORMER PRISONERS.
TOP: LAUREN SEGAL
MIDDLE: CLIVE VAN DEN BERG
BOTTOM: CHURHILL MADIKIDA

When we sat down as a team to conceive the Mapping Memory project, we had already run many workshops with both men and women former prisoners over the past three years at Number Four. Our main intentions in these previous workshops were to ensure that the former prisoners played a key role in the development of the new heritage site of Constitution Hill and to try and understand the history of the jails on site. So much of this history had neither been recorded nor archived when Number Four still functioned as a prison. The prisoners who had been held in one of the four prison buildings on site were not allowed to record their surroundings in any way. There are only three archival photographs of Number Four taken while it was still in operation and a couple of paintings of the Women's Jail that were done in secret by Fatima Meer.

As curators, we relied on former warder and prisoner testimonies to understand the rhythms and workings of these places that had occupied such a central place in the psyche of mainly black people living in Johannesburg under apartheid. So we began to bring back those who had been imprisoned here to afford them the opportunity to give material form to memories made fragile by the passage of time. We wanted to try and understand the changes that have taken place in the physical environment of their incarceration and to help them explore the difficult process of remembering. The vast majority of prisoners had been in the jail simply because the colour of their skin meant that they had transgressed one of the many discriminatory laws of the day. There were others who were thrown into jail for directly participating in political activities against apartheid. And then there were those who had committed crimes, although we were soon to learn that the line between political prisoners and so-called 'criminals' was sometimes difficult to draw, given the nature of the criminal justice system under apartheid.

There were several challenges in these initial workshops. The first was to locate the former prisoners because there was no register of prisoners to which we could be referred. Once we had found groups of former prisoners - mainly political prisoners to begin with - many were reluctant to dredge up the extremely painful memories that the jails evoked. Some refused to participate because of the horror of their experiences. We ended up working with specific groups of former prisoners – women political prisoners from the 1970s and men from the early 1980s, for example – and through oral history and life history processes the story of the jail slowly and painfully began to emerge. The exhibitions that opened Number Four and the Women's Jail in 2003 and 2005 respectively, relied on these prisoner testimonies to give visitors a sense of the history of the buildings and the horrific conditions that prisoners of all races, but especially black people, were forced to endure.

From the inception of Constitution Hill, it has been our curatorial intention for the exhibitions to grow and develop as new layers of information emerge and more memories surface. After the first phase of workshops and the opening of the site to the public, we set about finding new ways to expand the reservoir of memory with the former prisoners. Given that we now had a basic understanding of how the prisons had functioned, we wanted the process to become more intimately focused on the prisoners' experiences and to be directed as much as possible by the prisoners' themselves. We had to find mechanisms through which memories that have been deeply suppressed or erased or perverted could be legitimated in the public realm with the former prisoners in charge of the process. We were keen to explore new languages and new material forms in which to express memories of this place.

We discussed various avenues for implementing the workshops. We decided on asking former prisoners to take photographs of the jail and to draw their experiences. They would also continue recording oral testimonies to accompany the photographs and drawings. The material that was generated in the workshops would form the basis of an exhibition and a book. It would also provide the springboard for public seminars and discussions on human rights issues at Constitution Hill. We hoped that the exhibitions and publications resulting from the workshops would be powerful physical prompts facilitating the exchange of knowledge and empathy. We also hoped that the material would allow former prisoners to take pride in sharing and legitimating their memories within the new political context. We anticipated that, through this process, memory would be given a unique form, determined by a strongly autographic process.

Many former prisoners had never considered using drawing as a means of recording and unearthing memory. Some were apprehensive about participating in this activity because they feared a lack of 'talent' and ability. But as the process went along, the participants realised that the drawing process could be an effective way to understand the past for themselves as individuals, as well as for the group. A plan of a cell or the prison complex often stimulated debate and facilitated memory through the push and pull of lines on paper. The drawings have become valuable recordings that increased our understanding of buildings that have disappeared, patterns of punishment and humiliation in the prisons, as well as other deeply complex tissues of memory whose recall gives dignity to the past.

Several people in the group had lost loved ones while they were in prison. They were left bereft and traumatized, not only by the loss of a father, mother or child whom they were unable to bury, but also by not having a memento of the dead. Drawing provided a means for an image to be made that served as this memento. The experience was also gratifiying for the facilitators. Their training as artists was put to a use that was unique, serving as a conduit to memories that otherwise had no representation. Joyce Dipale, like many others, had been tortured at John Vorster Square. One day she asked one of the facilitators to draw that torture (see fig 1). She directed this drawing with great particularity, speaking determinedly as she explained the wall socket, the placement of the electrodes, the black hood over her head. This confrontation through visualization seemed to mark a milestone for her, causing a re-living of trauma as well as some degree of completion. As a nation we have become used to stories of torture and abuse. To some extent we achieve collective catharsis by hearing these stories, but this process made apparent once again the importance for each individual to confront the devils of their memory.

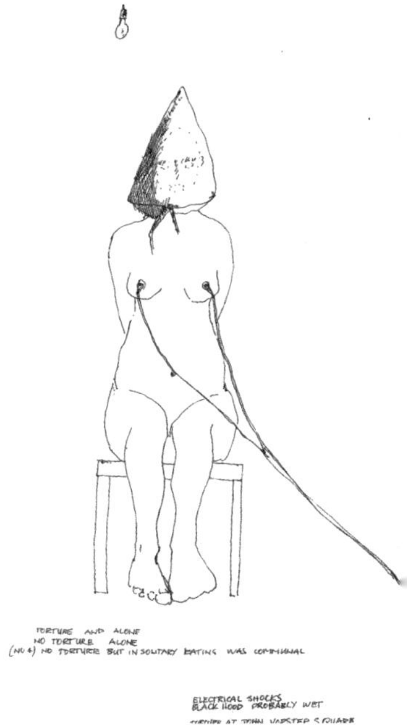

FIG 1

Courage in the workshops took many forms and found many expressions, sometimes in the connections between individuals, sometimes through group solidarity. It was interesting to see that it was the small strategies devised to cope with everyday challenges to dignity that brought the most courageous acts to the fore. It was these acts that defined the women's narratives and were retained as positive memories of the prison. Nikiwe Deborah Matshoba's concern for her fellow comrades was expressed in her determined act to send money and food to those held on the other side of a high wall. The comrades on the other side were not allowed to receive these items as they were being held under a different act (see fig 2). Communication among prisoners had many prohibitions. The workshops revealed the manifold strategies designed to overcome the barriers that the authorities enforced.

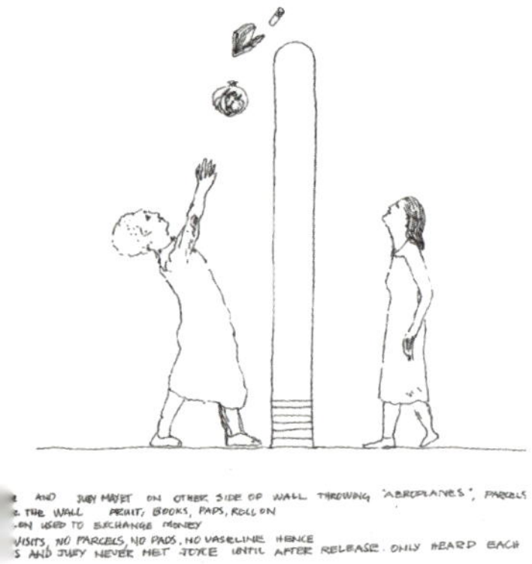

FIG 2

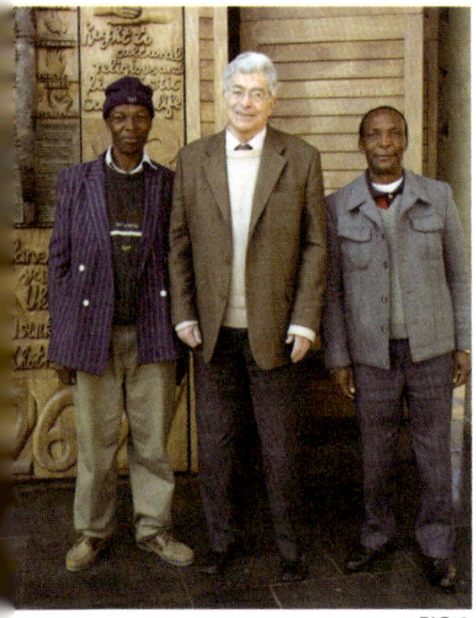

FIG 3

For many of the male participants, courage was defined through their political association and beliefs and the ways that they maintained their identity as a group thoughout their imprisonment. John Mahapa describes how he would communicate with comrades by attaching a message to a piece of string and throwing it to comrades in other cells in order to share information and stay in touch. Another striking characteristic of the group of Pan Africanist Congress (PAC) men was the cohesion of collective memory that matched the cohesion of the group of people who had been comrades in arms under the banner of the PAC. The similarity of their memories in prison spoke to the discipline and collective strength of their behaviour in the face of prison indignities. Their expectation of the workshops was that at last they had a chance to tell their poltical story that they felt had been marginalised by the dominance of African National Congress (ANC) history. Interestingly, over the course of the workshops, their stories became more and more biographic and smaller, more intimate details started to emerge from the collective narratives of their political past.

One of the great moments for the PAC men was meeting Justice Arthur Chaskalson, then advocate whom Napoleon Mazabane Letsoko and Sipho Victor Nkabinde described repeatedly in their stories as the man who saved them from the death penalty. The meeting took place on the steps of the Constitutional Court, itself an emblem of the achievements of their struggle. The photograph that was taken that day will forever remind these men of the great road that has been travelled since 1963 (see fig 3).

The so-called criminal participants did not bring with them a cohesive ideological identity. Neither did they enjoy the support that this kind of identity gave to the political prisoners. Their stories were about the battles against the vagaries of prison life and the domination of the cells by gangs. Sexual practices in prisons are seldom articulated outside of prison with any candour.
The taboos that restrict their expression ensures that these practices are not given the chance to be reframed. The workshops provided a safe forum in which to speak and hear of experiences that were the cause of trauma and which had remained suppressed and unspoken for decades. Zolile Mgweba has made a skirt from a prison blanket resembling one that he had been made to wear as the 'wife of a prison boss'. This emblematic object speaks to the sexual life of many who have been in Number Four.

One of the other participants, Khaya Isaac Magi, had dropped off a painting of a cell at the Constitution Hill archive a few weeks before the project began. We invited him into the workshops to continue the journey of remembering his experiences at Number Four through the medium of painting (see fig 4). This resulted in four new painitngs that give a vivid sense of his memories at the jail. The perspective that Khaya adopts is one of looking down on a scene from above, as if able to see all that went on in the cell simultaneously. Each tableau is recorded with a need to assemble multiple aspects of memory, a palimpsest of recall (see fig 5).

Using drawing, painting or sculpture to explore memory gave both connection and distance, connection because these were memories closely known and distance because the act of learning a new language diverted attention away from what was being said to how it was said. Making something, the physical in this way functioned both as defence and means of exposition. The unfamiliarity of the medium acted as a kind of buffer between the traumamatic experience and its confrontation.

In the previous workshops, a great deal of trauma surfaced during the process of exploring memories of the jails. As a result of these experiences, we made provision in this project for a psychologist to be on hand if required by the former prisoners. In fact, this service proved not to be necessary. It appears that, because many of the participants have been part of the workshop processes from the beginning of the development of the site, this has allowed them to begin a healing process. In this set of workshops they were able, in general, to engage in the process without the very raw emotions of their first encounters with the prisons. What is significant is that these workshops have consolidated and deepened the healing process.

Ultimately, the process of mapping memory is central to building a human rights culture in South Africa. Our rights today acquire a particular value through explorations and physical memorials to the past. Because Constitution Hill is a heritage site that has at its core issues of democracy, human rights and gender, we feel it to be our responsibility to also allow for a group of former prisoners to contribute to the great process of reconciliation in South Africa outside of the legal and political languages and the official discourse of the Truth and Reconciliation Commission (TRC).

It is significant that the exhibition of both the men and women former prisoners will have its opening on Women's Day, the 9th August 2006 - the 50th anniversary of the women's march to Pretoria. The women's work is on display in the Women's Jail and, like the women's march of 50 years ago, it will stand as a celebration to the strength and resilience of women in the struggle for democracy. The Women's Jail is one of the few memorials to the contributions of women to the struggle for democracy in South Africa and this exhibition, in the 50th anniversary year of the march to Pretoria, is a particularly important homage to the struggles of previous generations of women.

The men's exhibition in Number Four also pays homage to the contributions of men to our freedom.

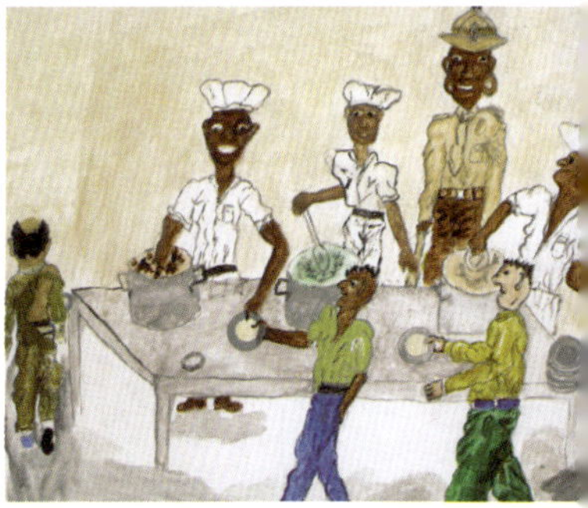

FIG 4

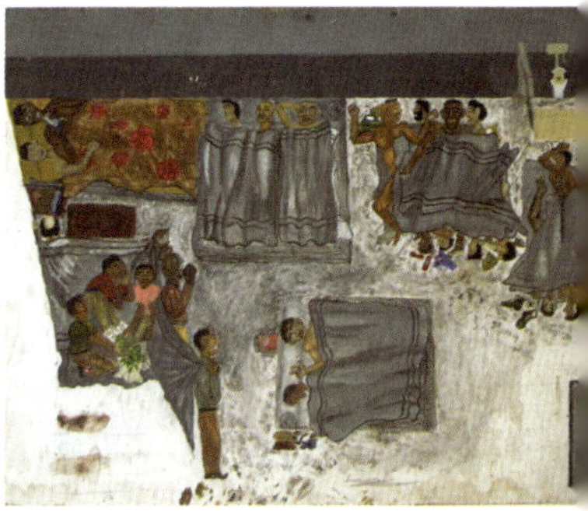

FIG 5

AUDIENCES

Our intention for Mapping Memories was to reach a broad audience. The following are the primary audiences that we hope to reach.

FORMER PRISONERS

Former prisoners are a primary constituency at Constitution Hill. Many are growing old and it is important to capture the memories that may otherwise be taken with them to their graves.

LEARNERS

Heritage sites in South Africa remain at a crossroads, serving as effective tools of memory that bridge the gaps in experiences from generation to generation. The challenge for many sites is in defining the role that they can play within the educational curriculum. This project offers a highly relevant example of how learning areas that are intrinsic to the new curriculum – such as oral history - can be brought to life in an imaginative way. One of the primary aims of the new democracy is to give people the skills to represent histories that were previously silenced and suppressed, and this project will showcase this endeavour.

In addition, learners in schools are often disconcertingly ignorant of aspects of the apartheid and colonial past. A project of this nature will not only inform them of the struggles which have resulted in the human rights culture in which they live, but also of the tremendous sacrificies that their parents and grandparents made to bring democracy to this country.

TEACHERS

Special projects and exhibitions of this kind are of particular interest to teachers. This exhibition will present avenues for storytelling about the past that then can be simulated in classrooms with the learners themselves. The public programmes manager will write up this project into materials that will be shared with teachers at workshops to be conducted at Constitution Hill. The materials will enhance the strategies and methodologies around heritage studies that are currently available in the classroom.

NEW AUDIENCES

There is a growing interest internationally in self-representation by survivors of torture and abuse, both physical and psychological. A similar project, for example, has been conducted by former prisoners who were incarcerated in the Maze prison in Northern Ireland and has raised much interest from scholars in history, cultural anthropolgy and the arts. Current discourses around reconciliation, human rights and democracy have particular currency in South Africa, and indeed the world, right now. The fact that the exhibition coincides with one of the biggest political celebrations of 2006 will add a resonance and cogency to the exhibition.

SPECIALIST AUDIENCES

A project of this nature will attract specialised audiences to the Hill, particularly those who are interested in expanding the means of representation of the past beyond the linguistic and other conventional forms of recording history.

INTRODUCTION TO THE MEN'S WORKHOPS

by John Moeketsi Mahapa

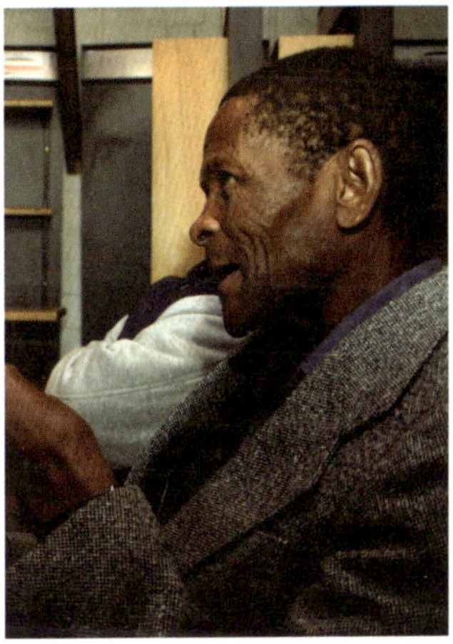

It has always been my wish to share my experience with the people around me. I had thought of writing a book but due to the lack of experience of doing so I abandoned the idea. I was happy to be invited to the workshop where I could relate my experience at the Fort. I received a call from Lauren Segal and I knew that here was an opportunity where I would be able to share my life experiences as well as those of my comrades. Fortunately, I have kept a list of political prisoners from the 1960s that Lauren asked me to furnish her with. This list tries to keep a record of what has happened to all of the people in the PAC who I rose up in struggle with and it records when one of my comrades passed away. The list always brings back sad and happy memories of the Fort and other prisoners.

The workshops were pleasant especially when you listen to various members relating their stories that you have never heard before, either because they were not at the same place as you were held or else they were here at a different time. The sad part about this workshop is that we are an endangered species. Almost half of the people I have been with are no more and what we fought for all those years ago has not been achieved. Our people still live in appalling poverty, there are no jobs, people have no houses and worst of all, many of our people are landless.

INTRODUCTION TO THE WOMEN'S WORKHOPS

by Juby Mayet

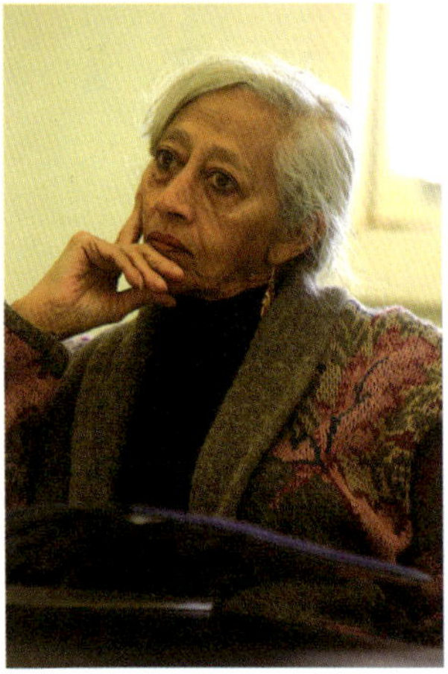

"Oh no!" I thought. "Not again!" It was late April/early May 2006 when Lauren Segal loomed, aided and abetted by Churchill Madikida, to ask if I would participate in a series of workshops sponsored by the Conference Workshop Cultural Initiative Fund (CWCI). (I had already been a part of the first round of workshops for the making of the exhibitions, hence my reaction.) I was attending my regular Tuesday meeting with other members of Sizoya Sibuye's (SiSi) committee (a group formed to carry on the work of women former prisoners). We were all invited to participate and to suggest the names of a few more women former prisoners of Number Four. Naturally, the prospect of receiving a small stipend helped us make up our minds that we would do it.

So there we were – Nikiwe Deborah Matshoba, Lilian Keagile, Yvonne Ntonto Mhlauli, Sibongile Tshabalala, Johana Tikie Mthimunye, Joyce Dipale, Bella Dlamini, Patricia Alarm, Assienah Mnisi and myself – all talking up a storm at virtually every workshop. We drew pictures, enacted some jail scenes, sang, danced, laughed. And some of us cried... again.

Much to my amazement, I found myself enjoying the CWCI workshops. I found myself remembering stuff I didn't even know I had stored in what passes for my mind. After 28 years I guess my memory is a bit wobbly, but discussion and interaction with the SiSi group helped me to recall my life in detention in 1978 with greater clarity.

There were obviously deeper emotions and issues at play during those five months, but I decided to treat the whole thing as a free holiday at the state's expense... A sometimes boring holiday; at times lonely and often frustrating and anger making. But a holiday nevertheless.

This process of going way back over so many years, I think, changed all of us in some way or another. I know that many of us did not, at first, want any part of this "going back and remembering" thing... Whether we were conscious of it or not, we all felt, or knew, that remembering was going to be somewhat more – much more – than just that. Remembering.

It was going to bring back pain, the re-living of the humiliation, the suffering and often the sheer horror of those times in prison. It was also going to bring a new sense of camaraderie, a feeling of having shared a universal experience, of understanding one another, a need to reach out and touch and care – not only for ourselves but for others. Not that we may have lacked this need before, but this experience made it manifest and real.

In the beginning it may have seemed strange, a bit surreal even, that a group of women from such diverse backgrounds could actually get together to share, vent, laugh and cry about their jail experiences. I mean, the group consisted of political prisoners (one of whom was, at least, a slightly mad journalist), a couple of illicit beer-brewers, a shoplifter or two and even a-would-be model/actress who had been charged under that good old cornerstone of apartheid, the Immorality Act.

As Assienah said to me, during the penultimate workshop, "I am happy that I am a part of this group. It has made me feel better, as a woman, to be able to talk to all of you about my experiences of jail, and to hear your stories also..."

Me, being me, – I laugh at everything. Life is too short to bear grudges, to agonise over what might have been, to get angry about stuff that one would like to have changed but couldn't. But even I almost shed a tear or two a couple of times during the workshops, when the emotions of one or other of the group got too much for them as they re-lived the sadness of an instance during their imprisonment.

And Debs was suddenly reduced to tears when she focused her memories on the late Gladys Manzi, who was a fellow detainee in Number Four. I remember Auntie Gladys being very disapproving because Debs and I both smoked. And she was even more disapproving when I decided that we were going to have a drink (or two or three) to commemorate the first anniversary of 'Black Wednesday' on 19 October 1978. This was the day, the previous year when the Nationalist government stomped its Nazi-like boot and shut down various publications and organisations, among them *The World* newspaper, SASO (South African Students' Organisation), BPC (Black People's Convention), UBJ (Union of Black Journalists), Pro Veritate (a Christian publication) and so on.

We did have a drink or two or three – vodka spiked with Sprite, right inside our cells in Number Four! However, the details hereof shall remain my secret, for the time being at any rate.

All of us being individuals, it goes without saying that all the women interviewed for this book have their own different takes on their experiences in and of Number Four. But it all makes for quite riveting and thought-provoking reading. For instance, here's Debs Matshoba telling us how her then three-year-old son was left parentless when both she and her husband were detained. And here's Sibongile Tshabalala saying how she was arrested and locked up at age 14... And there's Yvonne Ntonto Mhlauli informing us why to this day she hates baked beans. And all the other women, colouring in the blanks...

In case you're wondering about Sizoya Sibuye (SiSi), this is a women's forum that was born out of a luncheon held at Number Four Women's Jail on 15 July 2005. One of SiSi's chief aims is to make Number Four as famous as Robben Island, because it seems that the world at large forgets that many women played an important part in achieving democracy for our country. We should not downplay the roles of such stalwarts as Jeanne Noel, Vesta Smith, Fatima Meer, Sally Motlana, Esther Barsel, Rita Ndzanga, Joyce Seroke, Winnie Madikizela-Mandela, Cecilie Palmer, the late Ellen Khuzwayo, Lillian Ngoyi and Gladys Manzi, who all contributed in various ways to the liberation struggle. We salute them all.

009-
010

ASSIENAH MNISI

I was born in Pimville in 1946 in a backroom that my parents were renting. We later got our own house in Jabulani, which is where I grew up. I used to play this ball game as a little girl. It was my favourite childhood game. When I came home I was so dirty, I was like a boy.

I used to accompany my mom to the train station near Denver where she used to sell food to the commuters. We also sold dagga but we kept it in a nearby factory and whenever a customer wanted it, I would go to this factory to fetch it. One day the police arrived and they arrested one of the factory workers who then told them that I was the one selling dagga, not him.

I was arrested and sentenced to five years in jail. The usual sentence was 18 to 24 months. This was the first time that such a long sentence was given for dagga selling especially considering I was eight months pregnant at the time. But the government had just announced tougher laws to control the spread of dagga so I got that sentence.

I gave birth to my son in Number Four. It was terrible to have a baby in this jail. His name is Clement. It has affected him forever.

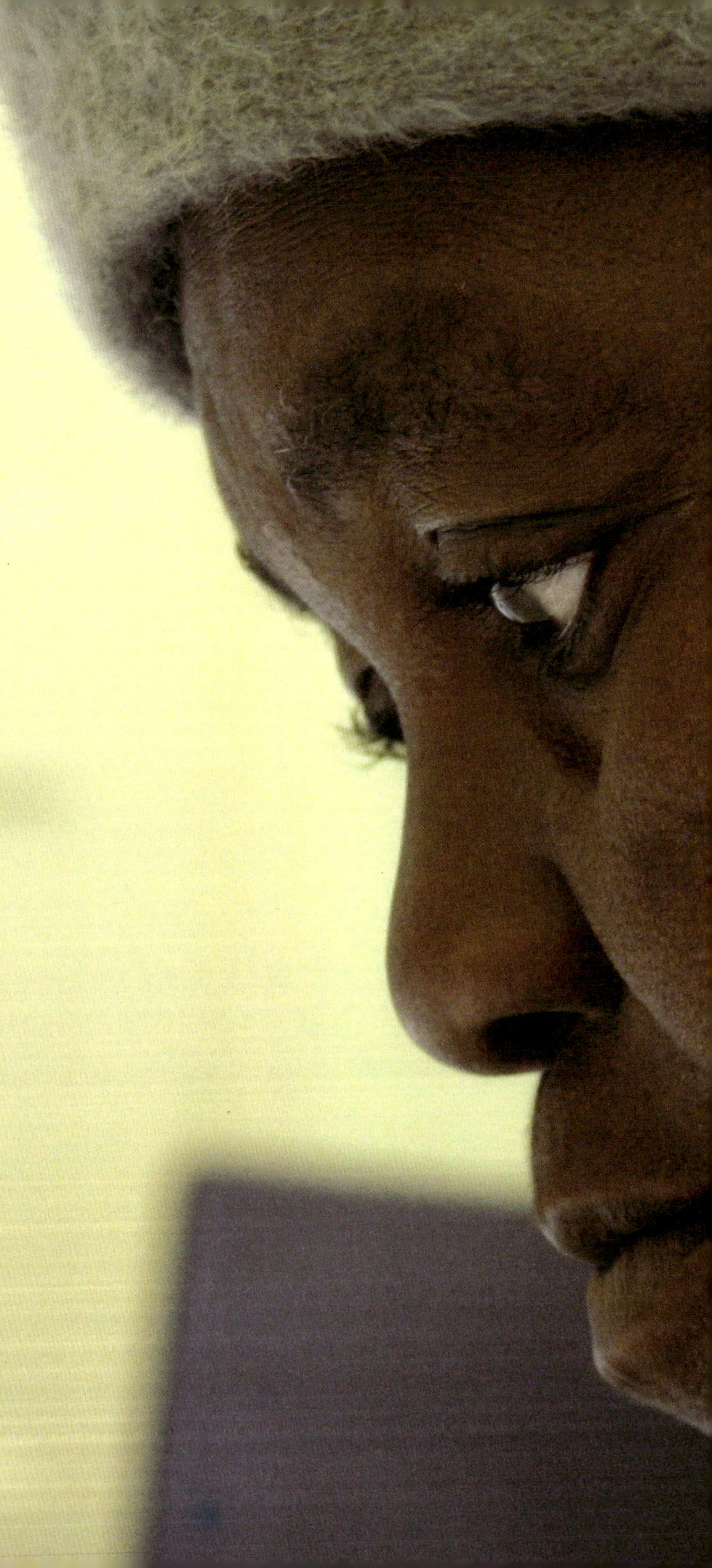

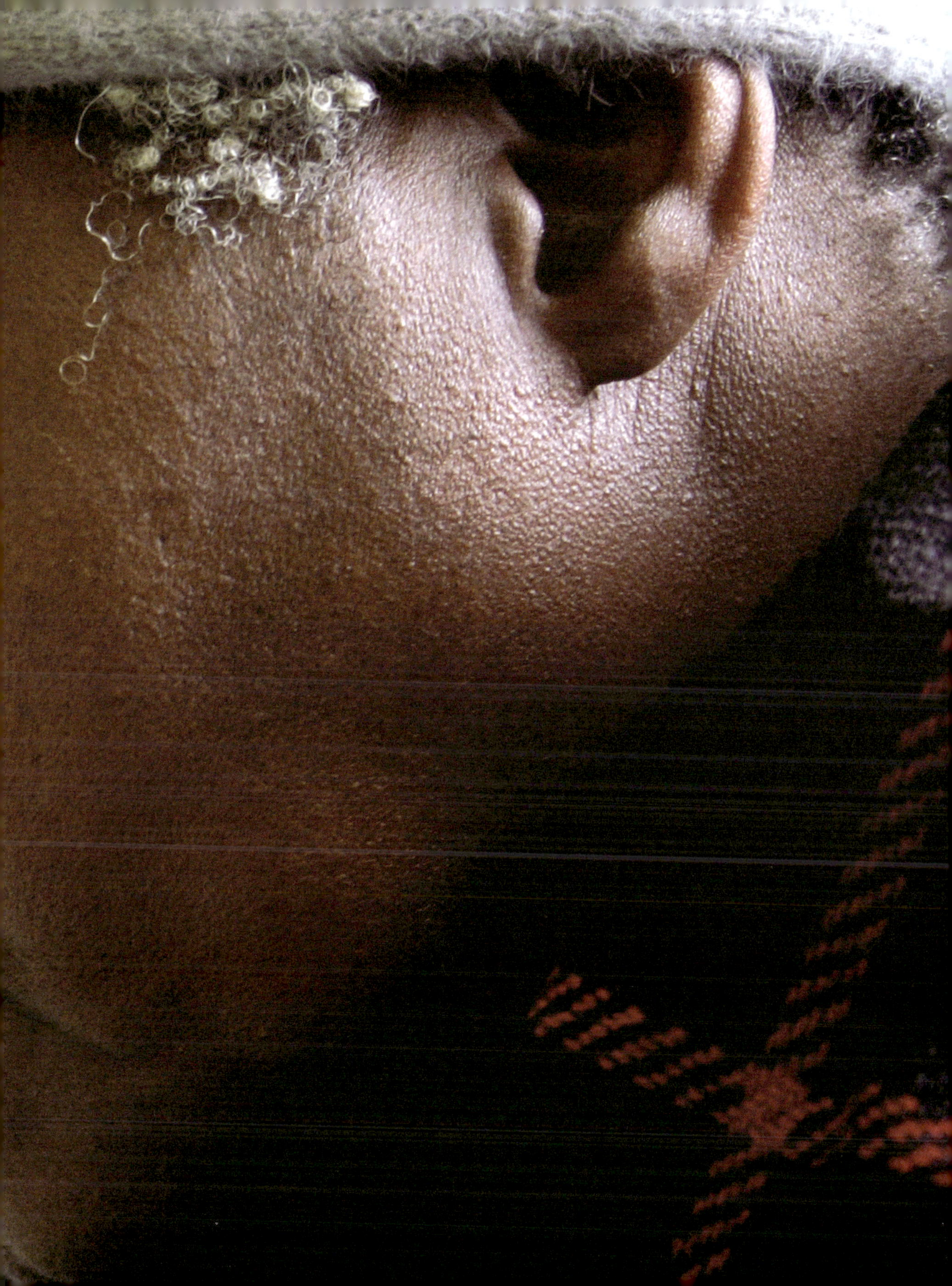

BELLA DLAMINI

I was born in 1954 in Orlando West, Soweto. I grew up in the same area where Albertina Sisulu and Winnie Mandela were staying. One of my earliest childhood memories is of these women. They used to arrange milk and peanut butter sandwiches for the poor children. I was six years old at the time and so enjoyed the food that they brought.

My other vivid memory is of when I was 11 years old. My uncle had come to visit my mother from Daggakraal, which is a rural area. My sister and I would sleep on the kitchen floor, as space was very limited in our house. On the third night of his visit, a 'Blackjack' (council policeman) arrived to arrest him. There was a lot of shouting and screaming and shoving. I remember being so afraid because I did not know what it was he had done wrong. I found out he was arrested because he had not reported his presence in the city to the officials and therefore was considered a 'trespasser'. His pass did not have the stamp allowing him into the city. That is when I first began to be politically aware.

The other important memory was when my parents were late with the rent payments. The council did not give a warning letter of their intention to lock you out of your home. I remember coming home from school to find this big padlock on our door. I sat outside until my parents came home. But it was too late for them to do anything, as the council offices were already closed for the day. We relied on neighbours to take us in and we spent the night there. My parents tried to do all they could to pay the overdue rent the next day even if it meant borrowing from people.

I was arrested in 1969 or 1970 for 'failure to produce a pass'. I served five days. Upon arrival, the warders instructed us to write a letter home telling them where we were. I was amused to find that the letter only reached my family after I had finished serving my time and was back home already.

My second arrest was for housebreaking and theft. I was a domestic worker earning very little money so I would take the old sheets and blankets, which were stored away because they were no longer being used, to my family back home. Having taken the linen I went home to leave it there but while I was away my employer must have seen they were missing and they called the police. I was arrested and sentenced to three years imprisonment.

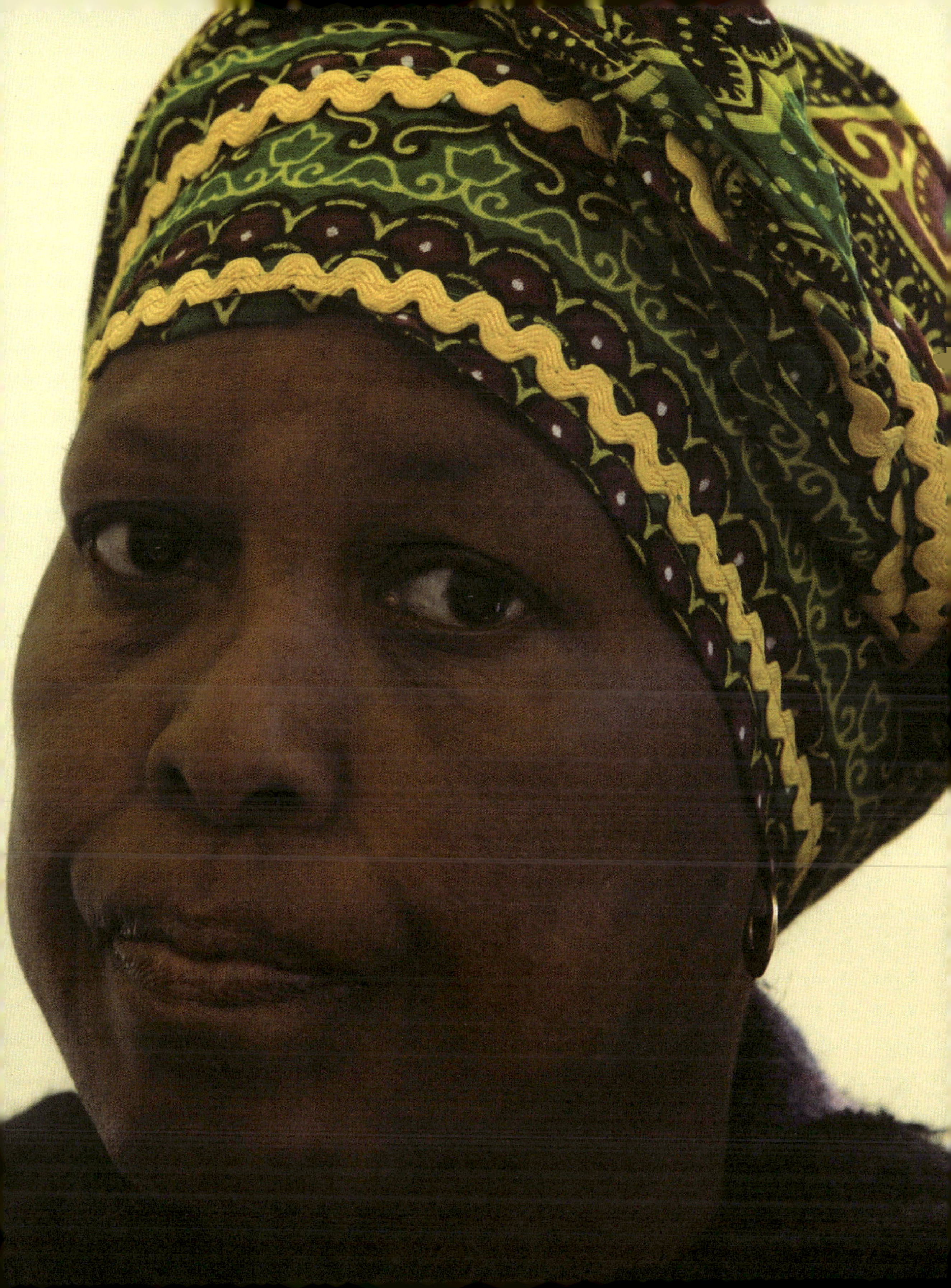

013-014

NIKIWE DEBORAH MATSHOBA

My name is Nikiwe Deborah Matshoba. I was born and bred in Munsieville. Later my family and other residents were forcefully removed and we resettled in Kagiso in Krugersdorp. One vivid memory I have of my childhood was when my friends from the neighbourhood were loaded into trucks and moved to Vuka (now known as Kagiso). Immediately their homes were razed into dust and nothingness.

I completed my matric at Inanda Seminary in 1968, and then proceeded to study radiography at Baragwaneth College of Radiology. My first job was as a radiographer at the Krugersdorp General Hospital.

My early politicisation dates as far back as sitting and listening to my parents discussing the newly banned *New Age*, an African National Congress (ANC) newspaper. My father's shop sold these. I remember Peter Keetse always delivering hidden papers shouting, "Africa!" and we shouted back "*Mayibuye*!" (Come back), with our thumbs up.

I was arrested in July 1976. I was, at the time, the literacy director of the South Africa Students Organisation (SASO) and Teen President of the Young Women's Christian Association (YWCA). I was held under Section Six of the Terrorism Act and held at the Women's Jail. After my release I was again arrested and brought back to the Women's Jail. While I was in detention, my husband, Gilbert Mabale, was also detained, leaving my thirteen month old son without his parents. After my release, I served a five-year banning order, which confined me to the Krugersdorp magisterial district.

I have worked on the team of the Women's Jail exhibition since the start of the Constitution Hill development.

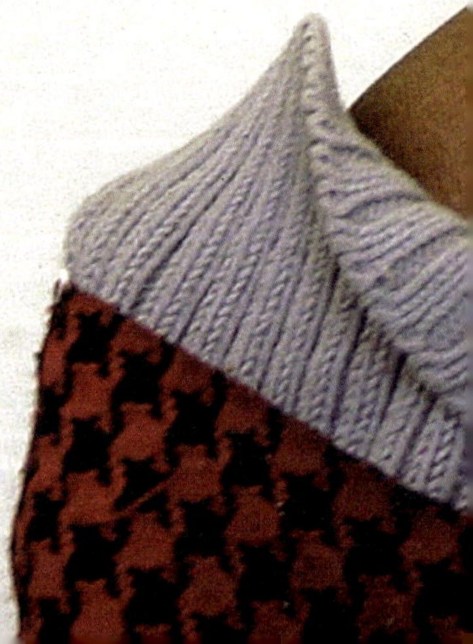

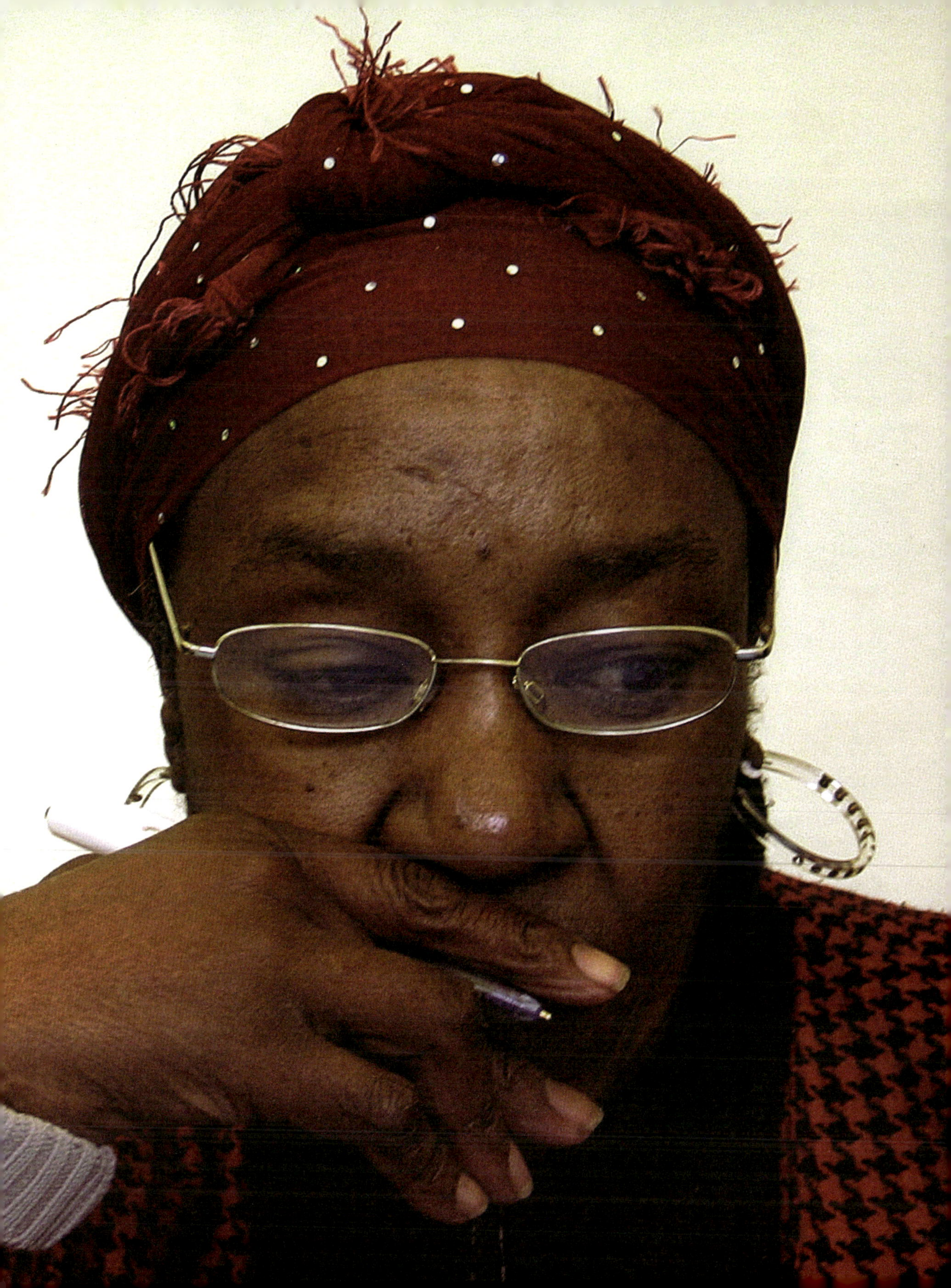

JOYCE DIPALE

I was born in Dube in Soweto, the second child of seven children. I learnt politics from my mother. After school, I wanted to be a radiographer but I was refused entry for health reasons. That made my family and me angry. I went to work as a cashier in Braamfontein at OK Bazaars. Braamfontein was the hub of political organisations at the time. I got involved in South African Council of Churches (SACC). This led me to work with the students. In September 1976, I was detained at a meeting in Dobsonville with some of the student leaders.

I was kept in different prisons around the country. All this time I was kept in solitary confinement and tortured for refusing to co-operate. When they took me out of my cell in Bloemfontein I was told that I was to be released to go home. Unfortunately my home was to be Number Four. During all of this time, my parents never knew where I was, so no one ever visited me or brought me clothes or food. I was in prison for two and a half years.

When Baby Tjawa and I were released from Number Four we were disorientated after being in prison for so long. We suddenly just ran and found ourselves in Braamfontein and only then did we realise how to get home. My younger brother, Moabi Dipale, who later died at John Vorster Square, was playing football in the street. He was the first to see me. He was shocked and ran up and hugged me. We went home. He was screaming, "*Ous* Joyce is here".

The police carried on harassing me after I was home, so about three months later, I left for Botswana with the ANC. There, my house was bombed and I was shot at four times. I ended up in Zambia and then in 1989, I moved to Canada to work for the South African Council of Churches (SACC). That was where I had my stroke. Nobody knows why, but it was probably from the stress I had suffered. I was in a coma. I recovered slowly and was in a wheelchair. But I lost my speech. I was completely blank and I lost all eight of the languages that I could speak. The SACC helped my mother to get to Canada to visit me. She thought I was going to die. But I recovered.

I came back to South Africa in 1998. Here I am, unemployed but going to therapy for my aphasia and slowly getting better. Now I can speak a bit, slowly, but at least people can understand me.

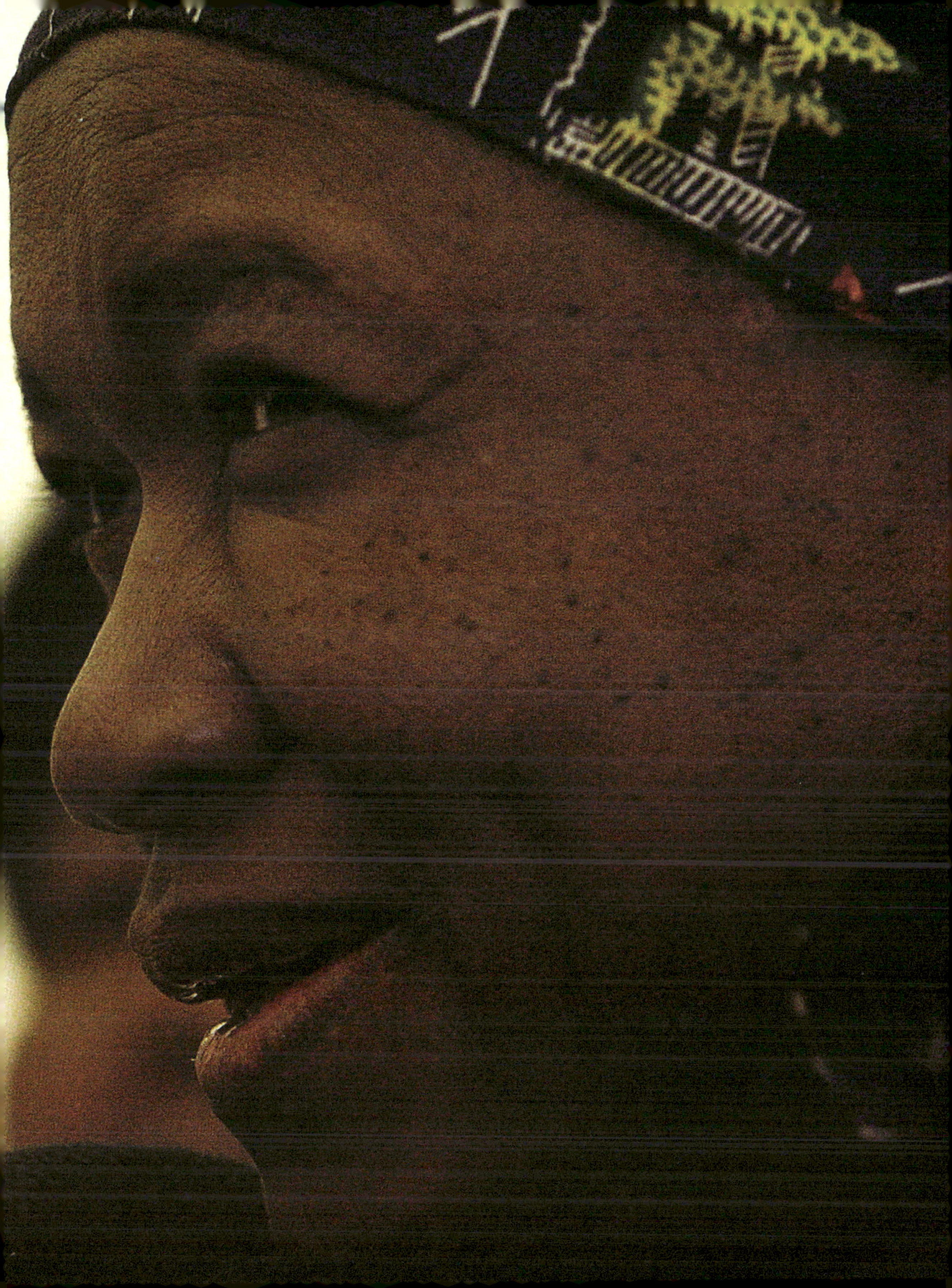

JUBY MAYET

I was born on 27 December 1937 in Fietas (Vrededorp). One of my earliest childhood memories is riding one of my daddy's carthorses in my granny's backyard in 15th Street, Fietas.

When I was a young woman, I worked on *Drum* magazine as a reporter, feature writer, columnist, agony aunt etc. I also did the typesetting and proofreading, as well as the stripping. After *Drum* magazine I worked on *The Voice* newspaper doing similar work. I was also a founder member of the Union of Black Journalists (UBJ).

I was arrested on 29 May 1978 at the offices of *The Voice* newspaper in Braamfontein under Section 10 of the Internal Security Act. I was detained at Number Four for five months. I guess all my work had something to do with my detention in May 1978 and my subsequent banning in December the same year.

As you will see from a letter given under his hand in Cape Town on 20 May 1978, the Minister of Justice – JT Kruger – was "satisfied" that I engaged in "activities which endanger or are calculated to endanger the state"!

I am now forcibly 'retired' because of arthritis and trying to write my autobiography – 'memoirs' sounds much too grand!

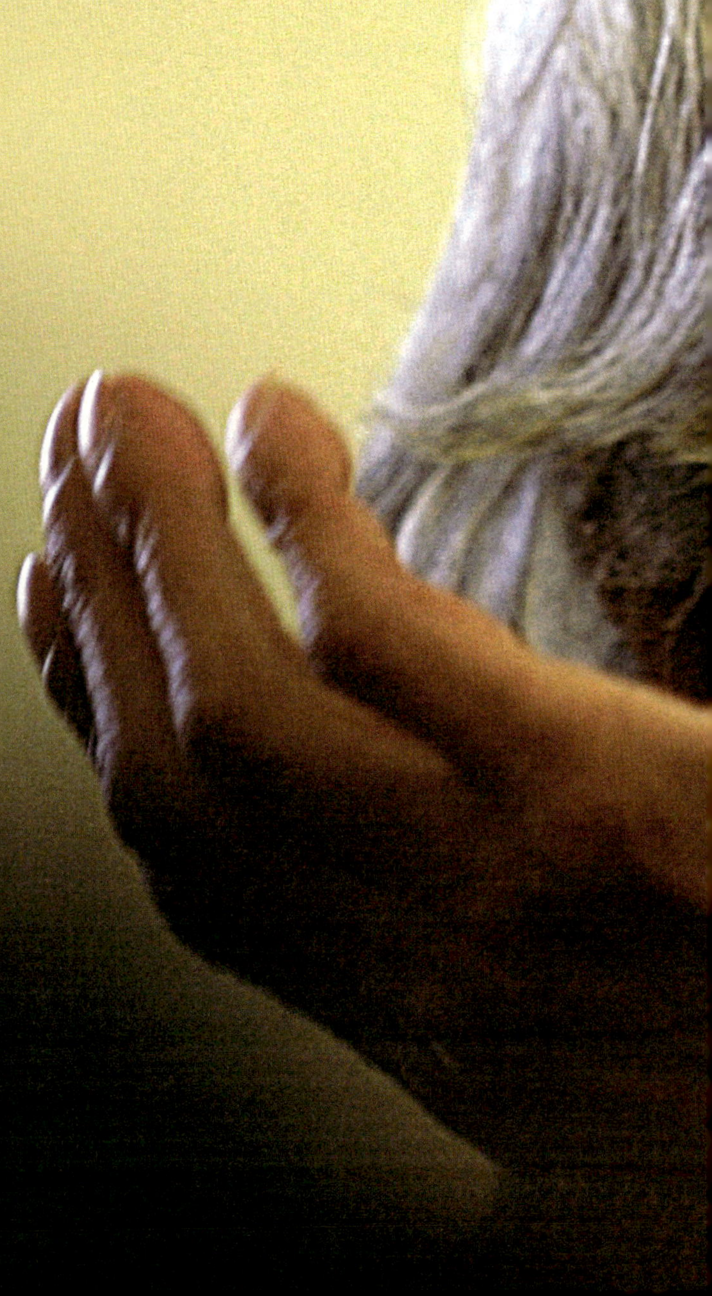

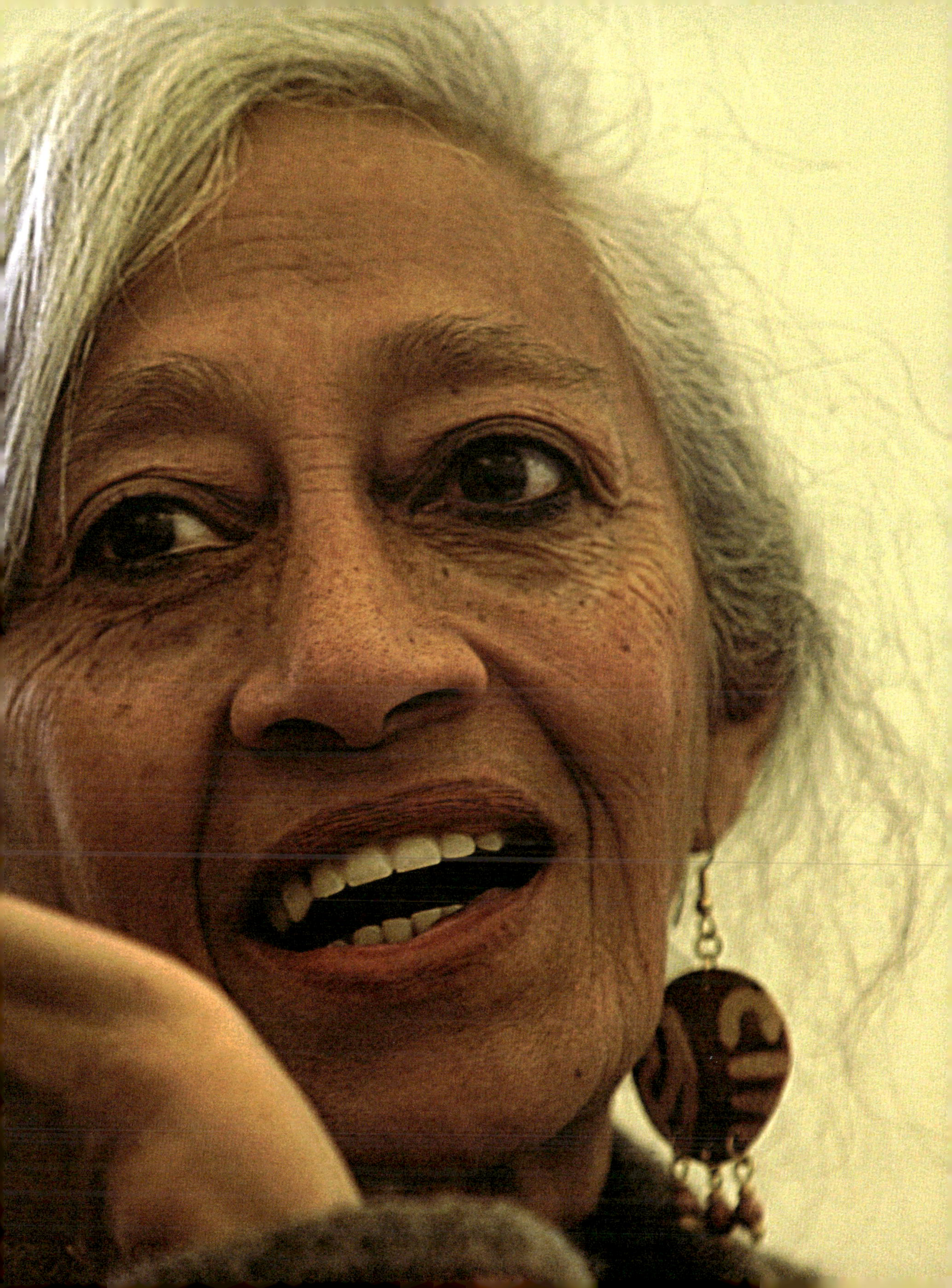

LILIAN KEAGILE

I grew up in Soweto where all of the houses looked the same. There were no playgrounds in my area and children played in the street. The railway line is not far from my home and we would go and play just near where the trains passed by. Parents were forever worried about us children.

Later, as I grew up, I realised the difference between whites and blacks living in suburbs. I used to go to these whites-only suburbs with my aunt who was visiting other family members who worked in the suburbs as domestics. I became politically aware. Then Onkgopotse Tiro was killed in 1974. It was the talk of my family. My brother Mpho Keagile spoke a lot about him and I had lots of questions. Later Snuki Zikalala and Kgalema Motlanthe were charged. Oh, the anger we felt. My mother, Mampho, and Mpho discussed that daily. I learned a lot. The Soweto Uprising was the crown of my knowledge. I was not at school anymore because I had had a child at the age of 18, but I read a lot of the books that my brother gave me and I later joined the students.

In 1976, my cousin's sister Joyce Dipale was detained. Now the arrest was in the family. My aunt and my mother and brother Mpho went to John Vorster to look for her. They found her only when she was released two years after she had been in detention without trial, as it was called. I became fully politically aware now and much more angry. Ha!

Then I got involved myself with the ANC and was arrested in November 1981, just 13 days after getting married to Martin Sere. I was first detained and tortured at John Vorster Square. Later I was brought to the Fort and kept in solitary confinement for nine months before I was sentenced to ten years for furthering the aims of the ANC. But I only served six years because four years were a concurrent sentence.

After I was released, I worked for the Committee Against Political Imprisonment and the National Peace Secretariat. At the moment, I am self-employed. I do embroidery and silk-screening.

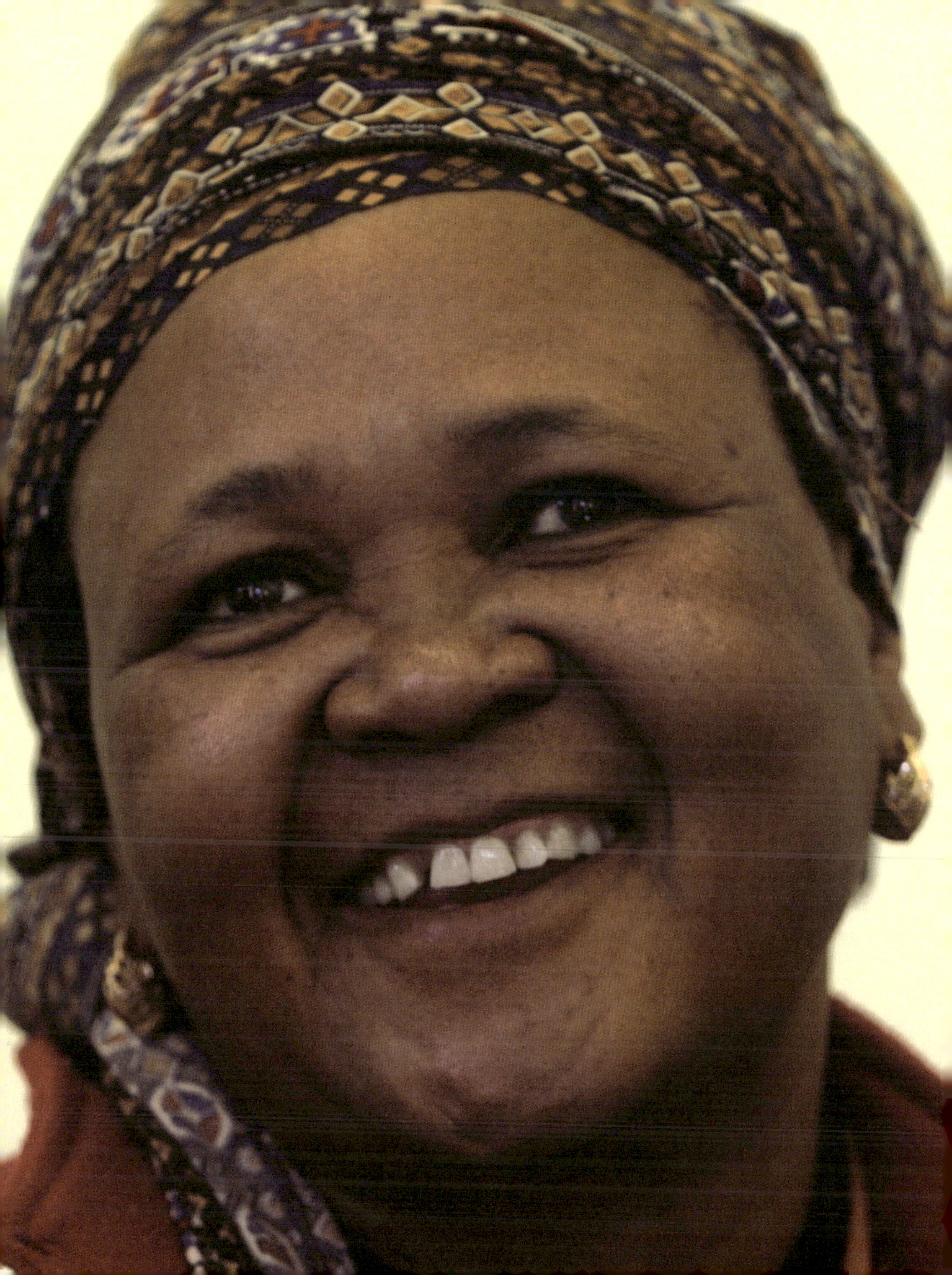

PATRICIA ALARM

I was born in 1932 in Alexandra Township. I lived with both my parents under hard conditions. My parents were both working but we only had enough for the basics. I had ten other siblings, all sleeping in the lounge, as my house had only three rooms – one bedroom, a kitchen and a lounge. My father started feeling sick when I was 13 years old and he died when I was 15 years old. I had to drop out of school to help my mother and to support my other siblings. I got married at the age of 19 and my husband died eight years after that and left me with four children.

In 1956, I marched to Pretoria with women from different political groups. We were marching against the pass laws. In 1976, as I was coming back from work, I found shops and government buildings burned down by the youth of Alexander. The next day, I couldn't go to work so I joined the other youth in the fight against the police. I instigated them to rebel. One evening, the police kicked my door down and found the petrol bombs that I was storing and all the supplies to make the bombs. They beat me up and arrested me and took me to Bramley Police Station. I was considered a danger to the maintenance of law and order. I pleaded guilty as I didn't want to be held under awaiting trial. I was sentenced to eleven years.

I was released in 1987. I never had a job. I started receiving pension in 1989. Even today, I still earn pension money from the government and I also earn money from projects like this one.

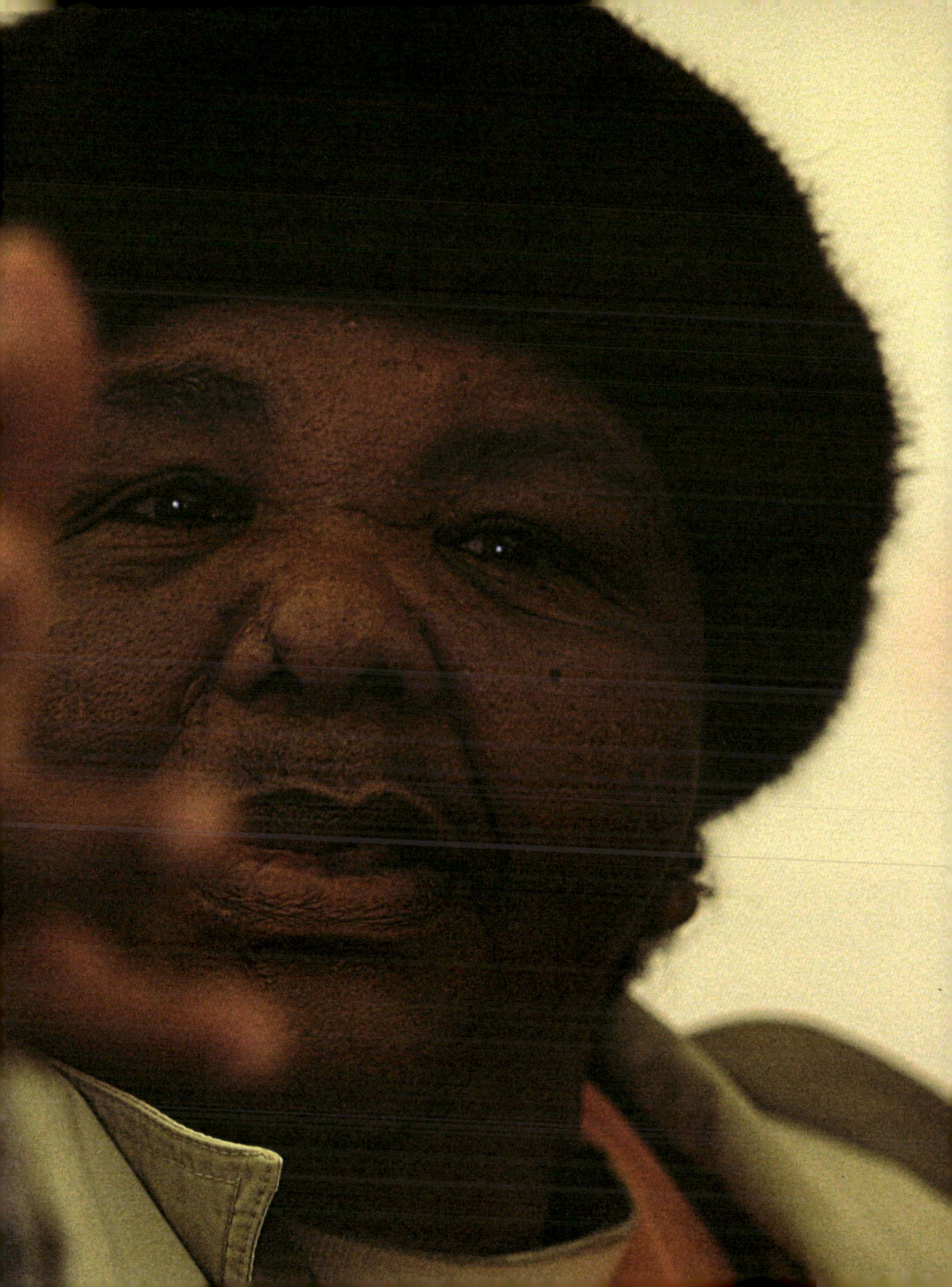

023-
024

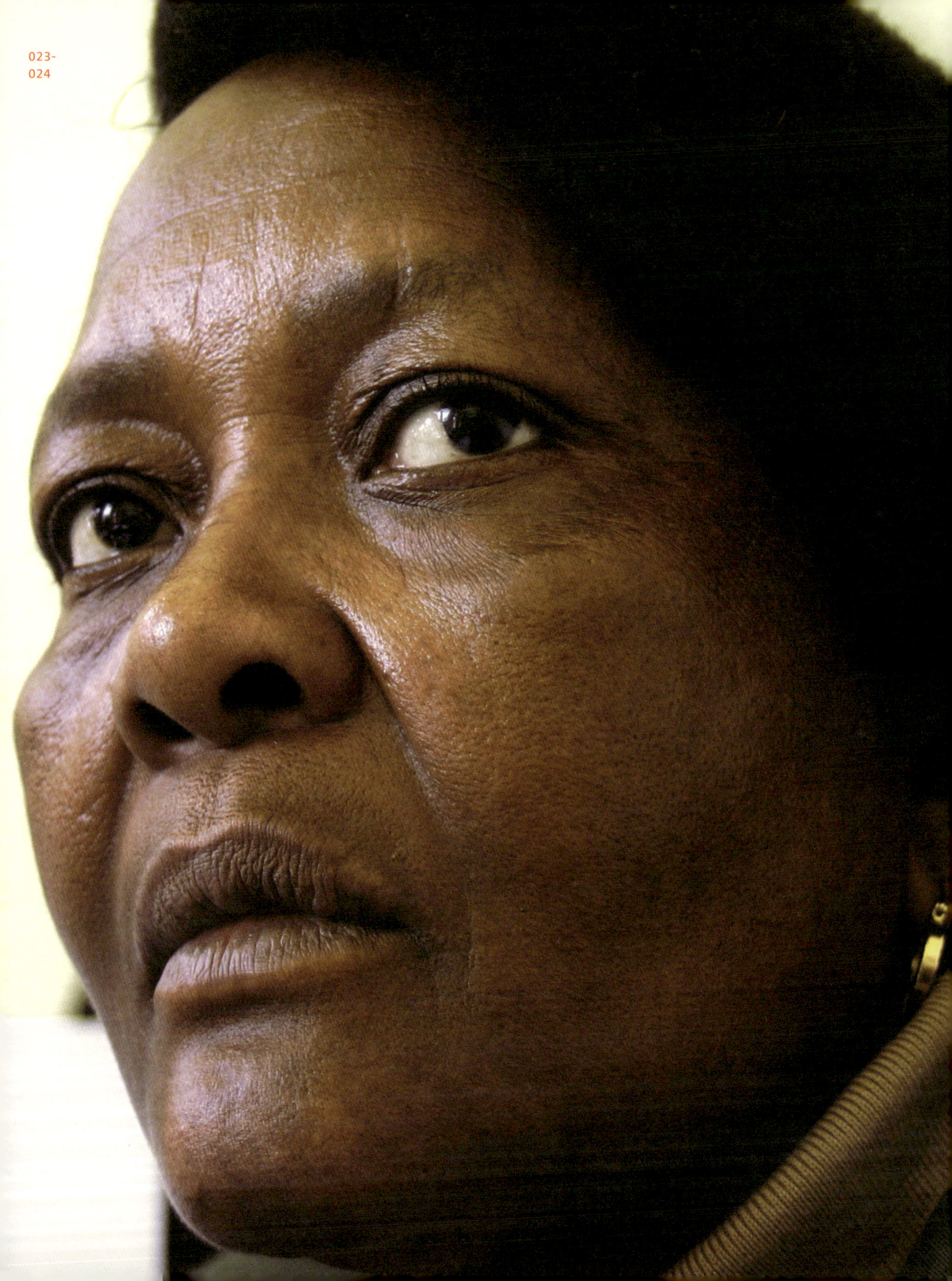

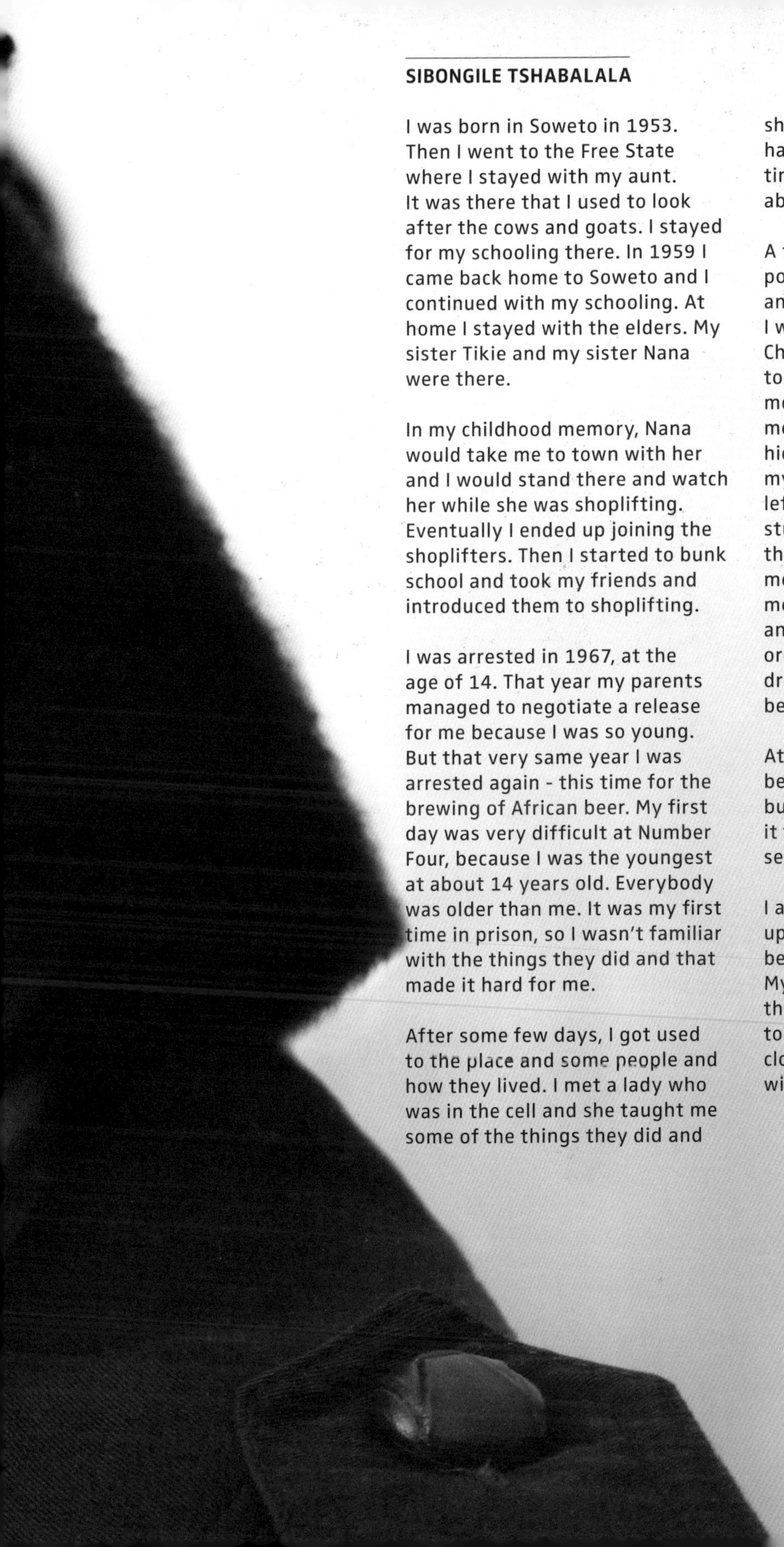

SIBONGILE TSHABALALA

I was born in Soweto in 1953. Then I went to the Free State where I stayed with my aunt. It was there that I used to look after the cows and goats. I stayed for my schooling there. In 1959 I came back home to Soweto and I continued with my schooling. At home I stayed with the elders. My sister Tikie and my sister Nana were there.

In my childhood memory, Nana would take me to town with her and I would stand there and watch her while she was shoplifting. Eventually I ended up joining the shoplifters. Then I started to bunk school and took my friends and introduced them to shoplifting.

I was arrested in 1967, at the age of 14. That year my parents managed to negotiate a release for me because I was so young. But that very same year I was arrested again - this time for the brewing of African beer. My first day was very difficult at Number Four, because I was the youngest at about 14 years old. Everybody was older than me. It was my first time in prison, so I wasn't familiar with the things they did and that made it hard for me.

After some few days, I got used to the place and some people and how they lived. I met a lady who was in the cell and she taught me some of the things they did and showed me around, because she has been in prison for quite some time and she knew a lot of things about the place.

A few days after my arrest, the police then arrested my mother and that is how my mother and I were reunited and we had our Christmas in Number Four prison together. On Christmas day, my mother had candy and buns for me as my gift. She had safely hidden them away. Just after that my mother was released and I was left in prison. I could not finish my studies because I was afraid that the other children would tease me. Number Four had traumatised me a lot. In general I couldn't and I didn't do the things that an ordinary child of my age did. My dreams were shattered as a child because of Number Four.

At the moment I am still brewing beer, I did not give up on this business. However, I have taken it to the next level and I am now selling even modern beers.

I am glad that I am able to keep up with my mother's business because we have come a long way. My family has suffered because of this business and today I am able to feed my family and children, clothe them and educate them with the profit.

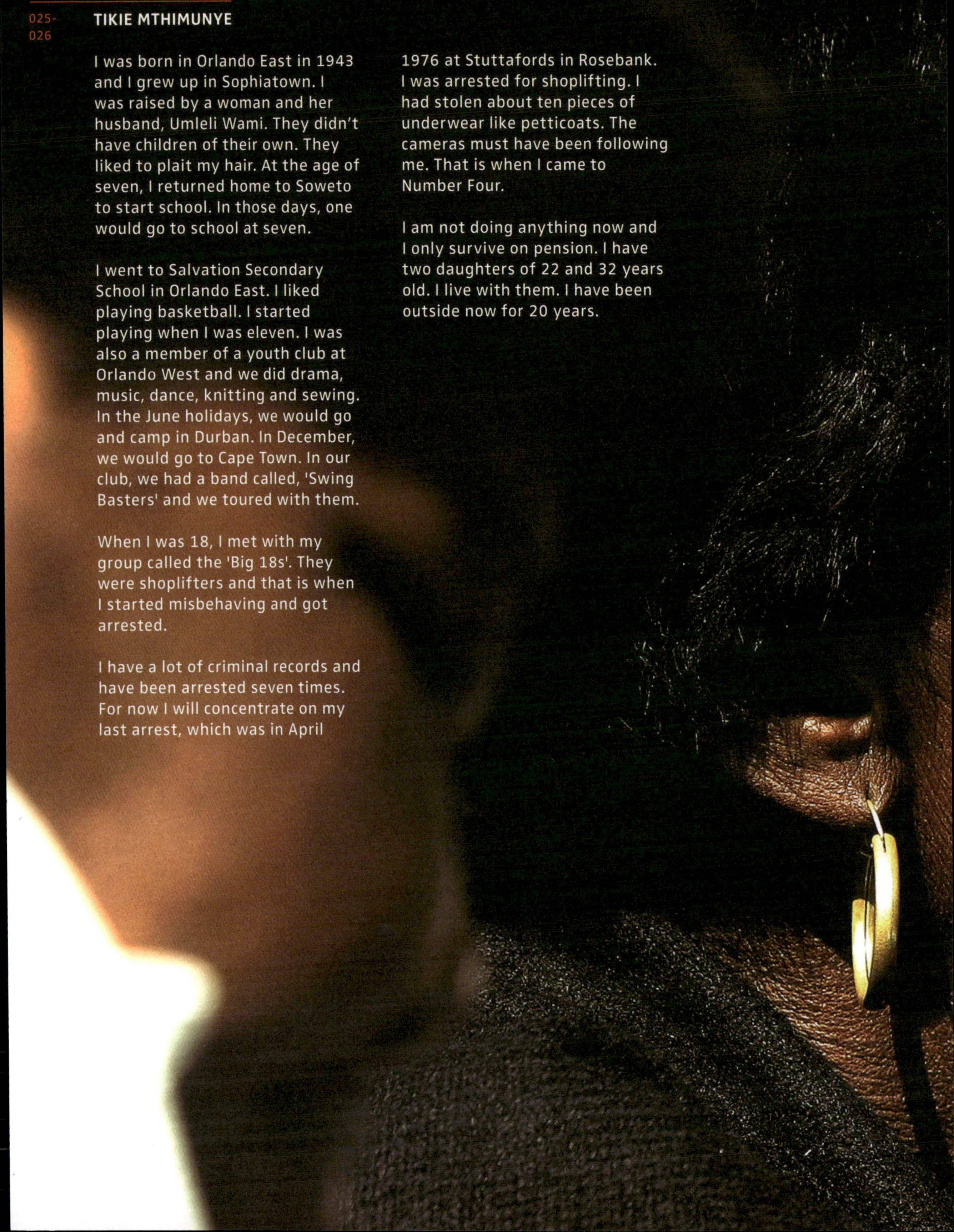

TIKIE MTHIMUNYE

I was born in Orlando East in 1943 and I grew up in Sophiatown. I was raised by a woman and her husband, Umleli Wami. They didn't have children of their own. They liked to plait my hair. At the age of seven, I returned home to Soweto to start school. In those days, one would go to school at seven.

I went to Salvation Secondary School in Orlando East. I liked playing basketball. I started playing when I was eleven. I was also a member of a youth club at Orlando West and we did drama, music, dance, knitting and sewing. In the June holidays, we would go and camp in Durban. In December, we would go to Cape Town. In our club, we had a band called, 'Swing Basters' and we toured with them.

When I was 18, I met with my group called the 'Big 18s'. They were shoplifters and that is when I started misbehaving and got arrested.

I have a lot of criminal records and have been arrested seven times. For now I will concentrate on my last arrest, which was in April 1976 at Stuttafords in Rosebank. I was arrested for shoplifting. I had stolen about ten pieces of underwear like petticoats. The cameras must have been following me. That is when I came to Number Four.

I am not doing anything now and I only survive on pension. I have two daughters of 22 and 32 years old. I live with them. I have been outside now for 20 years.

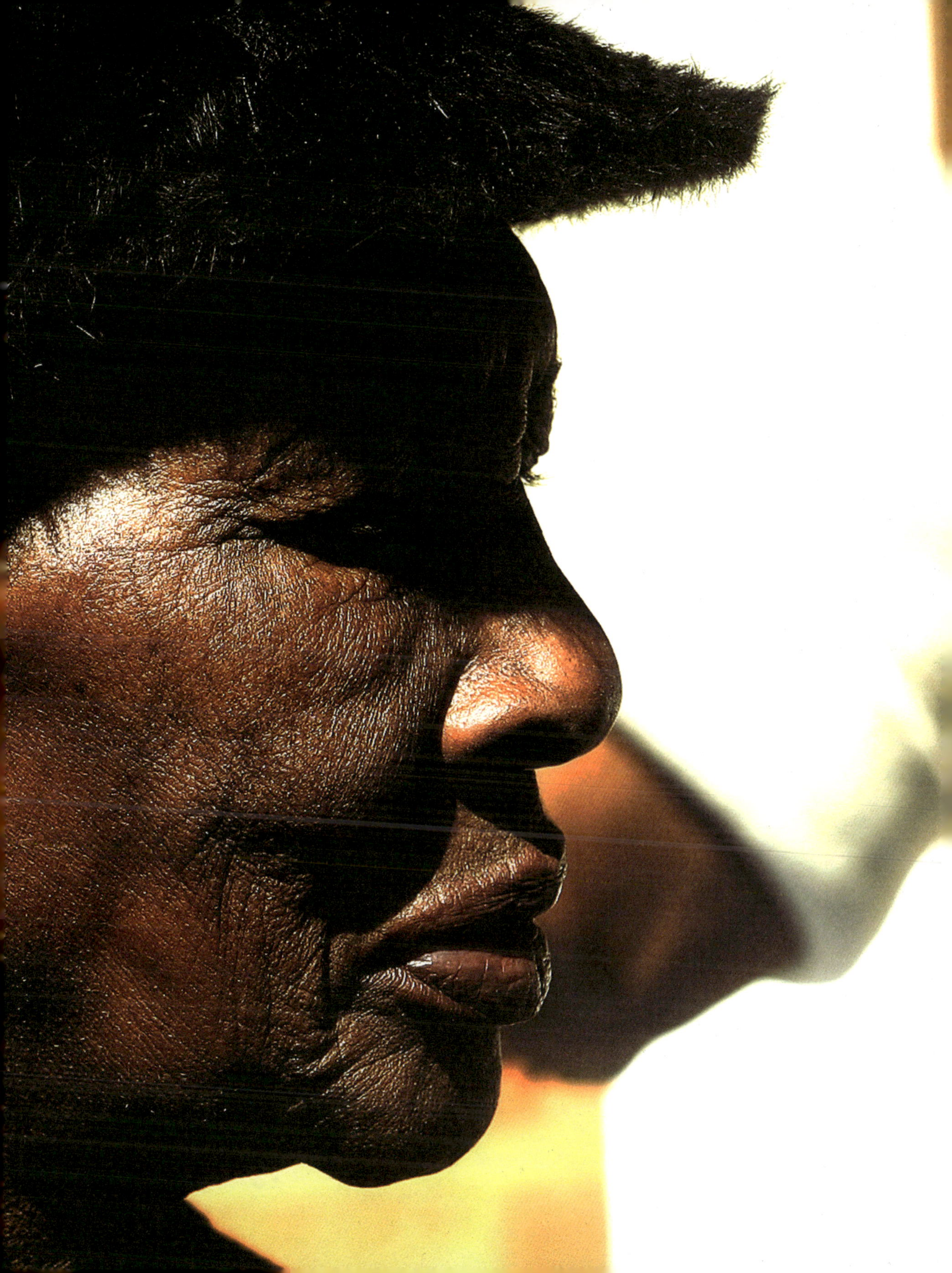

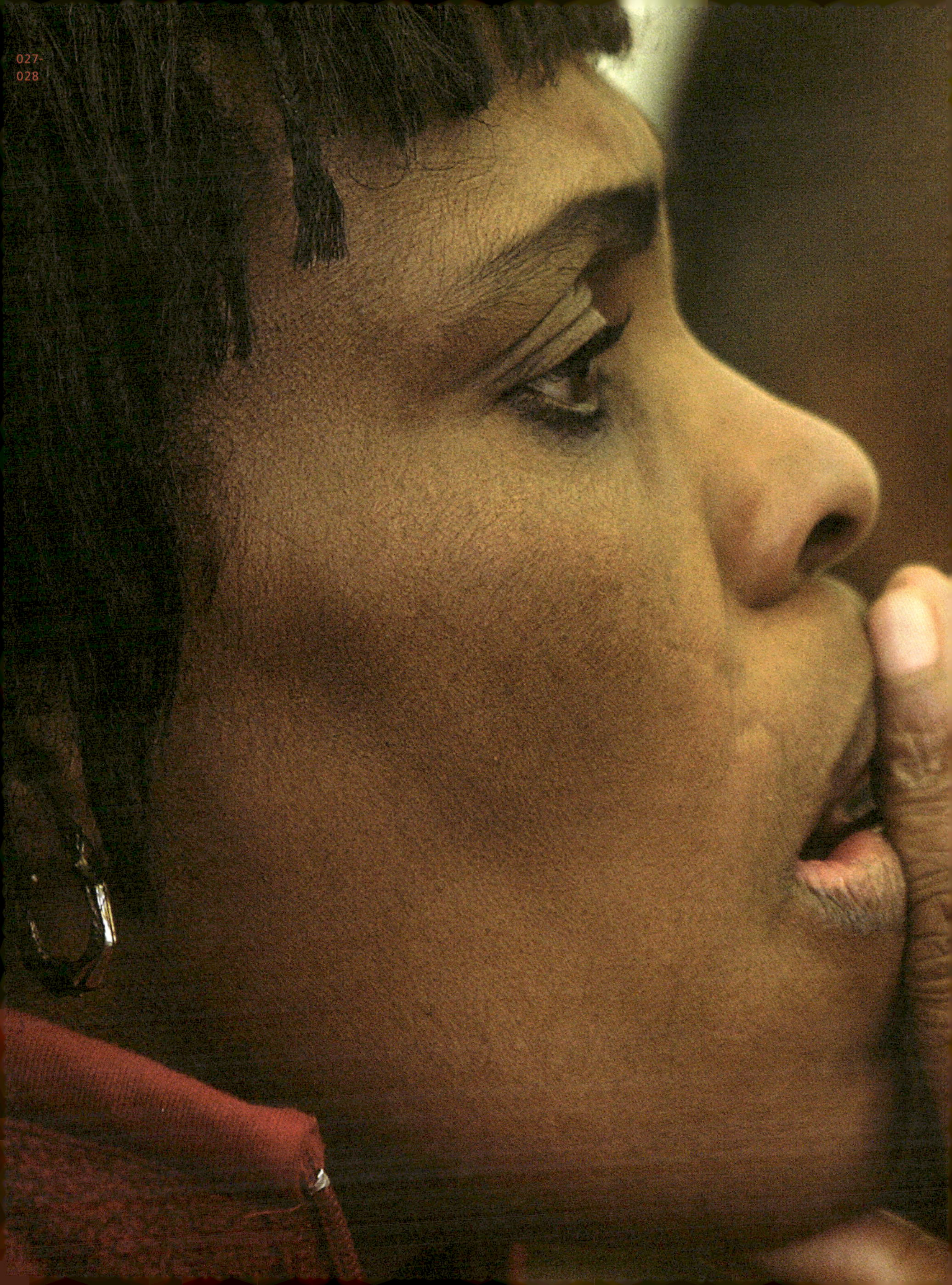

YVONNE NTONTO MHLAULI

I was born and grew up in the Eastern Cape in Tsomo Village. I am from a family of people who were members of *uPoqo* (the Xhosa name for the Pan Africanist Congress). My father was a member of *uPoqo* and went to Langa Township in Cape Town to participate in the protest there when I was still young. Some of my relatives were also part of the protests in Langa. So my father used to tell me about how he hated the pass laws.

As I was growing up I started to have my own attitude towards the apartheid laws that were dividing South Africans according to Bantu standards/racial categories.

In 1980 I went to Johannesburg to pursue my dreams in modelling and acting. Firstly I stayed in Soweto and then moved to Hillbrow, near Fontana Inn. I was arrested for resisting pass laws and, under the Group Areas Act for trespassing in town, as no blacks were allowed to stay in the inner city. Then in 1981 I ended up in Number Four, the Women's Jail. All I can say is that I had a bad time in the Women's Jail. I was here in and out until I was moved to Sun City – the new Diepkloof prison – in January 1983.

I am now a founder of the community project that deals with street children, senior citizens, sex workers and people infected and affected with HIV/AIDS. I have two daughters, one is my brother's and one is my biological daughter, Precious Lindelwa Mhlauli, who is in grade four in Woodmead Primary School.

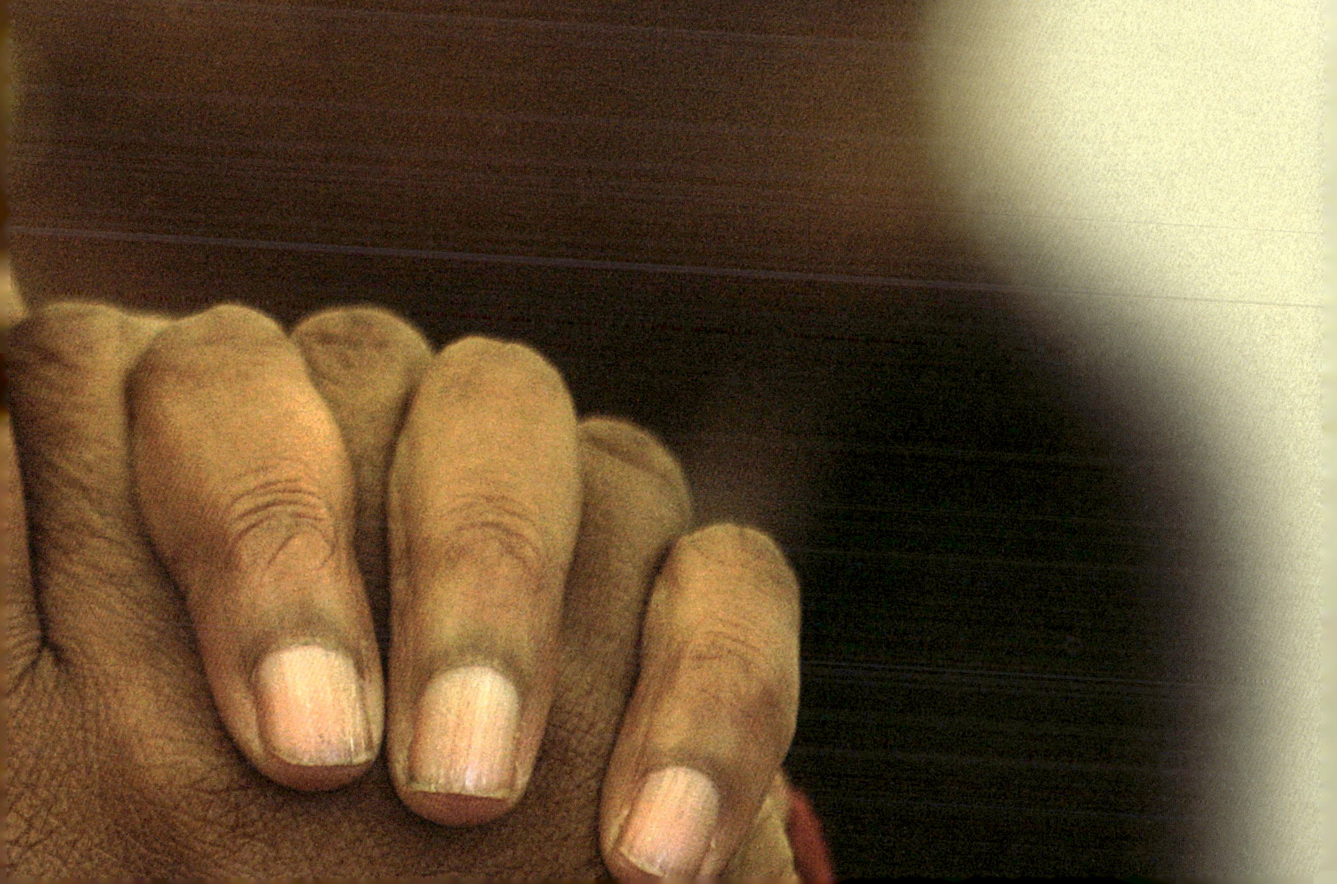

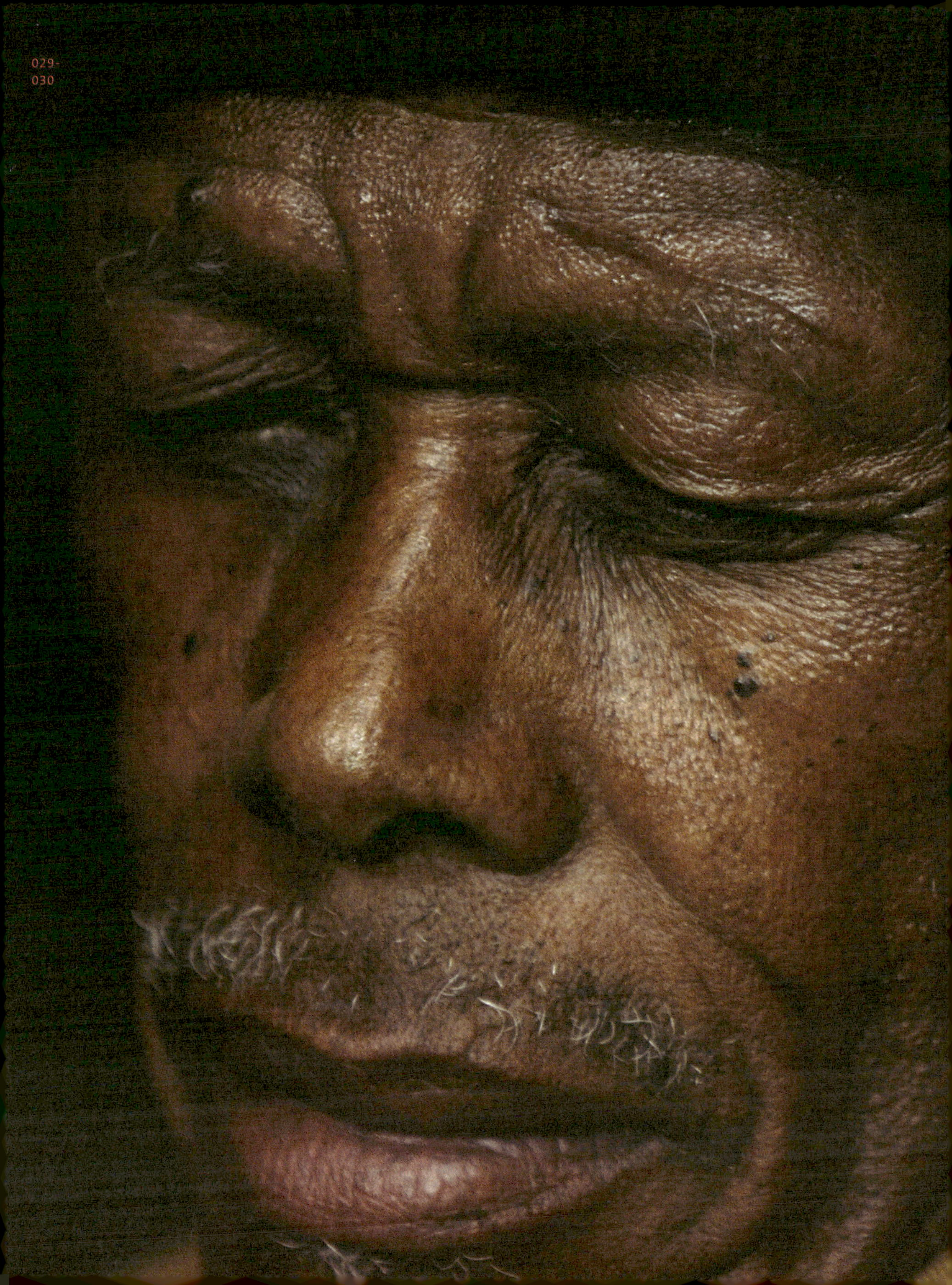

CORNELIUS MPSHE MANOTO

I was born on the 2nd of August in 1938, the third child of Magdeline and Shadrack Manoto. I stayed at the place called Orlando East. I grew up in Orlando and also schooled in the same place. I started my primary schooling in 1952, finished my primary in 1956. I then started my high school in 1957 and continued to 1959.

My childhood memory is that I was a very active person. I liked study and sport activities. After becoming involved in politics, we used to meet at Orlando Library during school holidays. That was where we would share our ideas, some concerning our curriculum. Mostly we would dwell on politics. That is how I came to be involved in politics whole-heartedly.

In 1959 I joined the PAC. In 1960 we embarked on a campaign to eradicate the pass system of the regime. We surrendered ourselves at the police station in Orlando under the leadership of Robert Mangaliso Sobukwe. We were moved from Orlando and brought to the Fort. Then we had to be taken to Braamfontein pass law court. We were duly charged under the Suppression of Communism Act. We were sentenced to three years in prison, which I served fully. Ever since I have been very operational in the PAC.

Presently there is not much that I am doing. I am a pensioner and staying alone. I lost my wife on the 27th of November 2000.

EDWARD SONNYBOY BHENGU

I was born on the 8th of November 1934 in Sophiatown at number 10 Gerty Street. The yard was big because my grandfather, Mr Mattera, owned and ran a bus company called Morosina bus services. He was a white man from Italy. His son Grower was my father. In 1948 when the nationalist (*Boer*) government took over from the General Smuts regime, they classified me as 'coloured'. I was recruited by Mr Nelson Mandela to the ANC youth league in the early fifties.

I applied for the *dompas* (stupid pass book) but the white official who sat in the office urged me to take a coloured certificate – the ID card for coloured people. I took a *dompas* because of my political association with the ANC Youth League. I was one of the ones who pulled out of ANC in 1958 to form a PAC under the leadership of Professor Robert Mangaliso Sobukwe. On Sharpeville Day, 21 March 1960, the professor had called on the African masses to protest against the pass laws. We were arrested on that fateful Sharpeville day. The next day we were taken to the Bantu Affairs Magistrates Court in Fordsburg. The charge was contravening the Suppression of Communism Act. The case was postponed to a later date. That's when we were taken to Number Four.

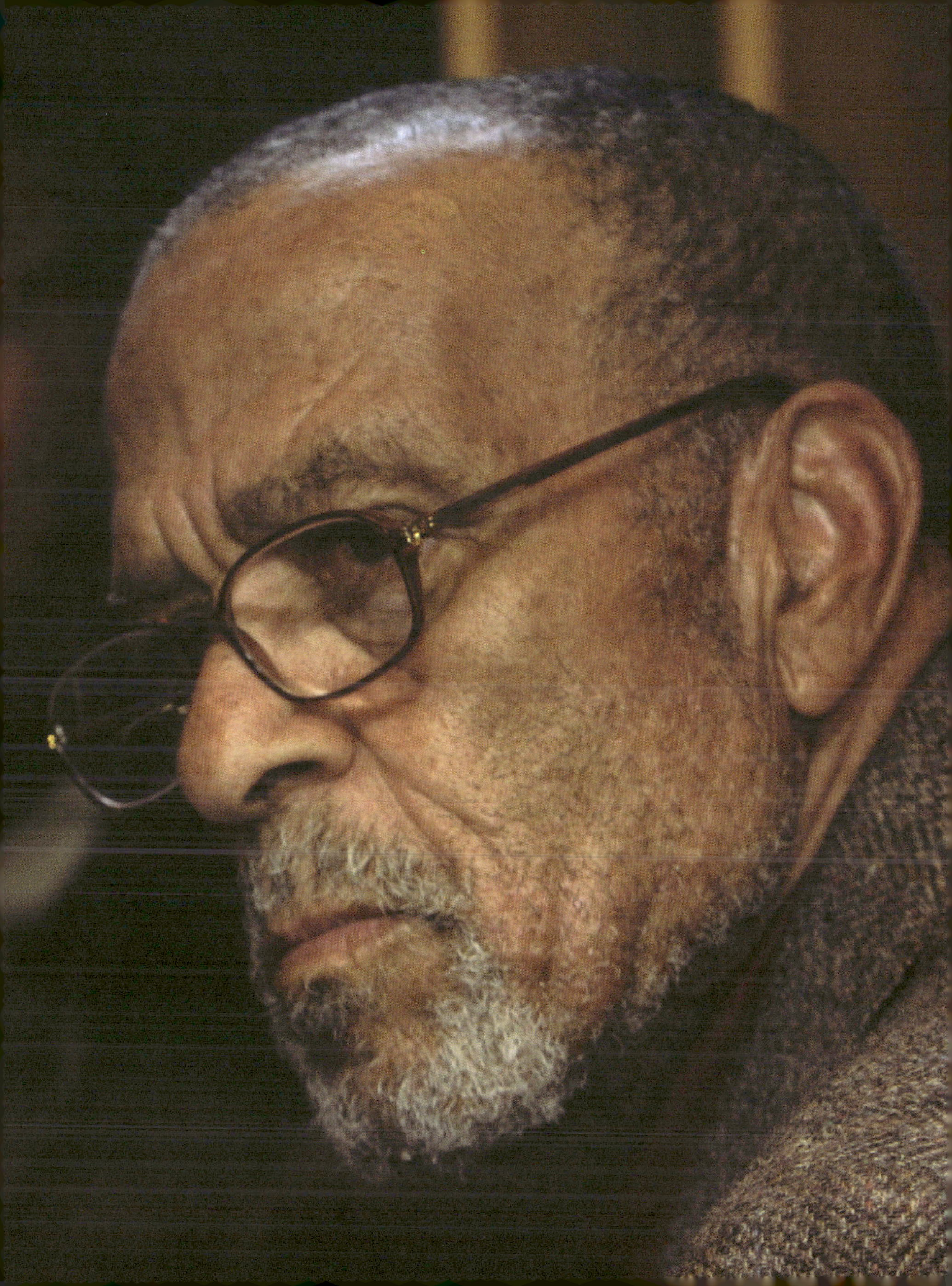

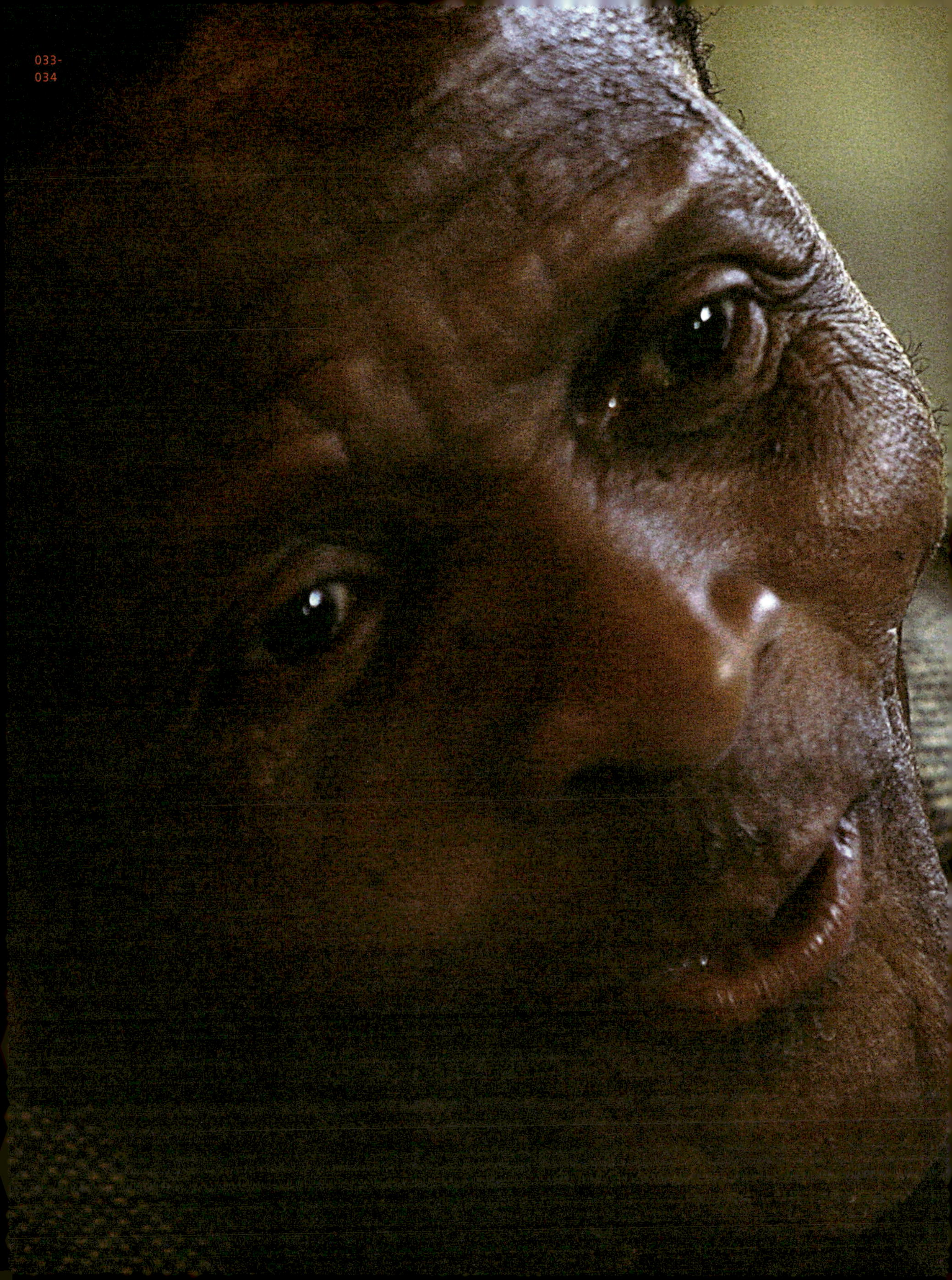

JOHN MOEKETSI MAHAPA

I am the son of my mother and Titus Mahapa. I was born on the 6th of April 1940, at number 2001 Orlando East. I was the third child. The first was Florence, the second Miriam and then Paulos, Moses and Ernest.

I started my schooling in 1946 at Bantu Methodist Mission School. I then went to Selope Thema, finished my matric at Orlando High School. It was at Orlando High School where I got into real politics.

I had been previously influenced by the *Drum* publications, especially their African editions, which gave prominence to the growing fights for liberation in various African countries in the middle 1950s, like Ghana, Nigeria and Kenya.

In 1958, I learned about the Africanist movement within the African National Congress Youth League. They were demanding that the programme of action resolutions be implemented. When it became evident that this was not going to be forthcoming and there was also much disgruntlement around the adoption of the Freedom Charter in 1955, the Africanists formed their own organisation in December 1959 and called it the Pan Africanist Congress of Azania, under the leadership of Robert Mangaliso Sobukwe.

In 1960, only 11 months after the inception of the PAC, the organisation started with the status campaign and demanded that African people be treated with respect. The days of calling our parents 'boys & girls' were to be done away with. Our second campaign was the pass campaign. The most trying moment of my life was when I and four of my colleagues were given the task of leaving the country in 1962 to go and explore the safest routes to Tanzania, where I successfully underwent military training and come back to liberate our people. I was one of the first five people from the then Transvaal to undertake such a mission. My colleagues were Moses Bosakwe, Olef Mthimkhulu, Danzig Masigo and Daniel Skosana.

Of the five, two made it to the then Southern Rhodesia where they got arrested, convicted, served three months, and were deported back to the country. I proceeded to Southern Rhodesia and landed in Malawi. I got arrested and sent back to South Africa. I was awaiting trial for four weeks. I applied for bail, got bail, skipped the country in 72 hours and found myself in Botswana. I was off again to Zimbabwe, arrested again, thrown back to South Africa. This time, my bail was set at R5000. I decided this time to hang around and get sentenced. That is when I got three years for leaving the country, three and a half years for furthering the aims of a banned organisation. I landed on Robben Island in December 1963. I was released in December 1971.

I then got a job and worked for various companies. The last was Edgars where I worked until I retired. I am still a hard nut to crack with my politics and a dedicated member of the PAC. We had envisaged true liberation where everybody, irrespective of colour or creed, will be happy thereafter. We have not got that. Our people are still in squatter camps, unemployed and we are still paying for our education.

JOSEPH GOGO KHOZA

I was born in the township Prospect in the year 1934 on the 15th of January. My mother worked for an Afrikaner man in Booysens who named me Gogo because I used to cry so much. There were nine of us siblings in my family. Four survived and two passed on and so I ended up occupying the position of first born. My parents acquired a house in Orlando in 1937 and we have been there ever since. My siblings looked to me for guidance in our formative years and they loved and respected me. I did not ask them to follow me into politics. They took the stance that "if it is good enough for Buti then it is good enough for us". Hence my family's total involvement in the struggle for liberation.

As a child growing up, my father, who had no education at all, was jealous of my mother who had a standard six. My education suffered because my unemployed mother could not keep up with school fees payments. Consequently I left school and went to seek a job and that was the beginning of my manhood. I was politically conscious in my teens and joined the PAC. To this day I am quite happy with the choice I made.

I was arrested – correction, I surrendered myself to the police during a PAC campaign in 1960. I was imprisoned again in 1964 and this time I landed on Robben Island for 12 years.

I have been a street snapshot photographer over the years and now at the age of 70 I no longer take photos because the younger generation has priced us out of the market.

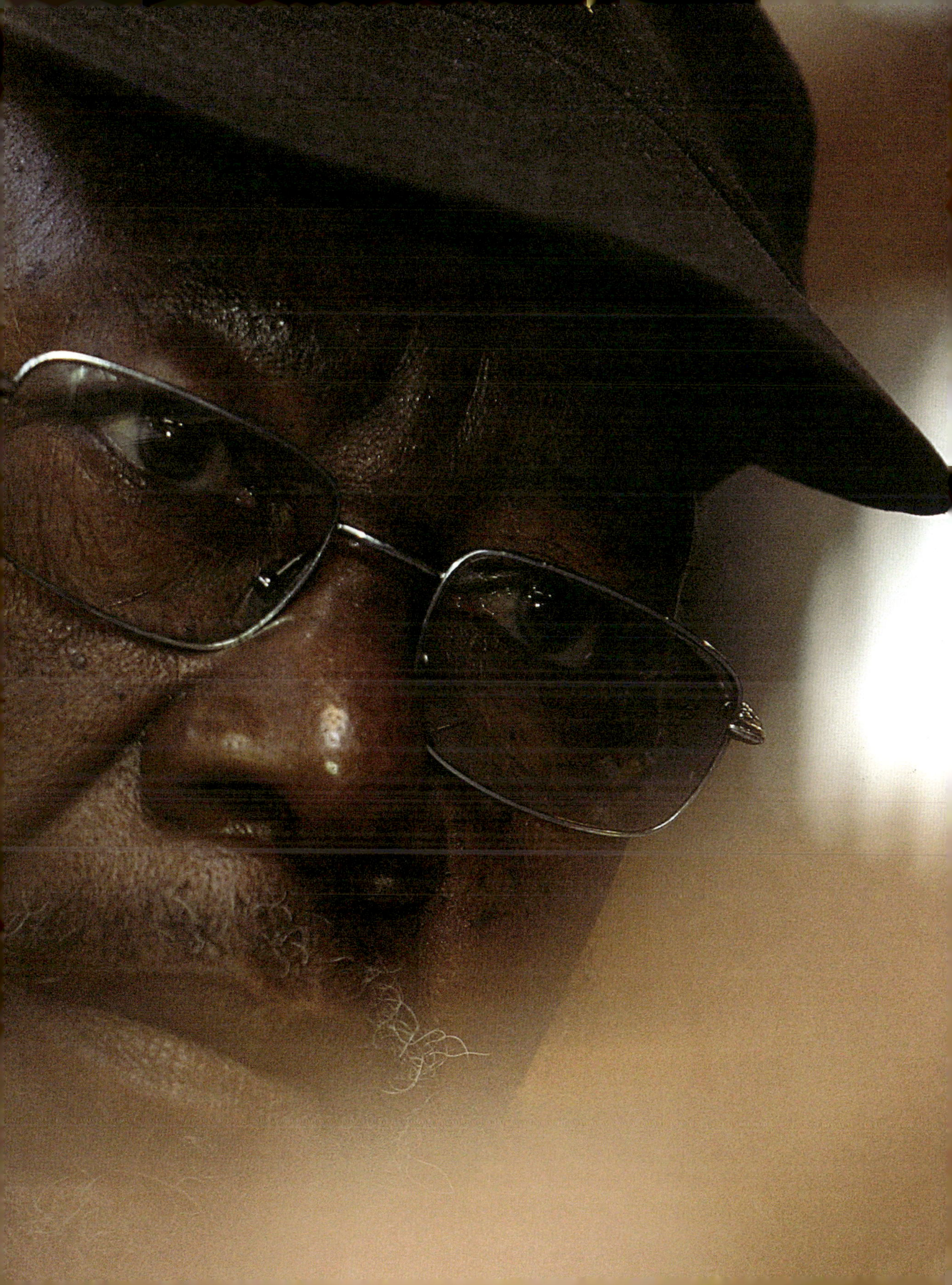

37-38

KHAYA ISAAC MAGI

My name is Khaya Isaac Magi. I live in Orlando East, 3555 Msimang Street. I was born on the 22nd of January 1953. I was living with my mother and my younger brother. The second time I was arrested for stealing because we were suffering at home, we had no father and my two other brothers were staying in different places from our home. I was in favour of the ANC so much.

Presently I am doing visual art (welding and wood work). I have been doing other work but not anymore.

I first got arrested around 1968 or 1969 by the municipal police whom we referred to as Black Jacks or *Gqoka Sihamber* (dress up and let's go). These were responsible for carrying out the eviction orders when we failed to pay our rates for three months or more. They would come and take you to the relevant office for negotiation of payment.

On this particular day that they came for me, I was so ill-treated that I lost my temper and hit the policeman, so instead of going to the office I was brought to Number Four. After spending three weeks at Number Four, I was taken to court in Orlando East where I was acquitted.

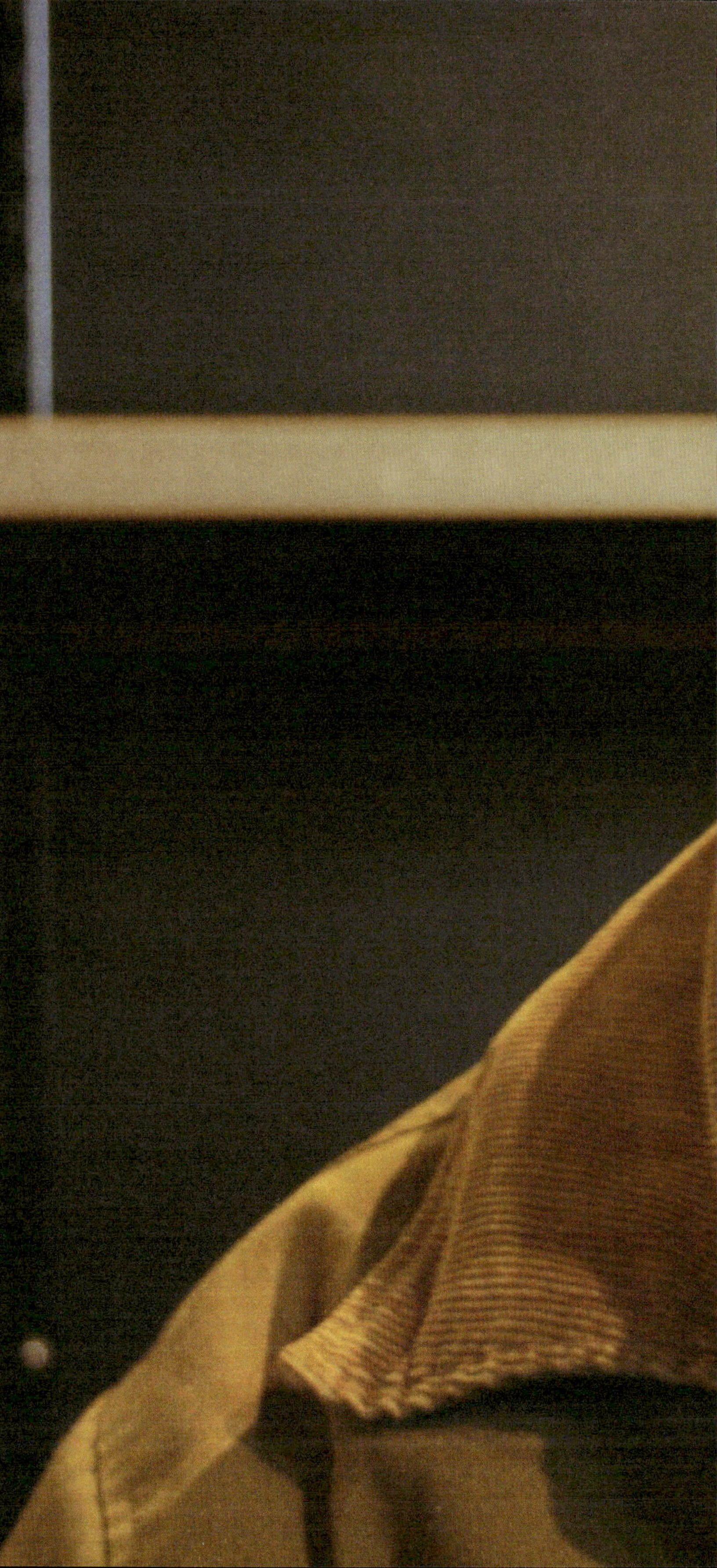

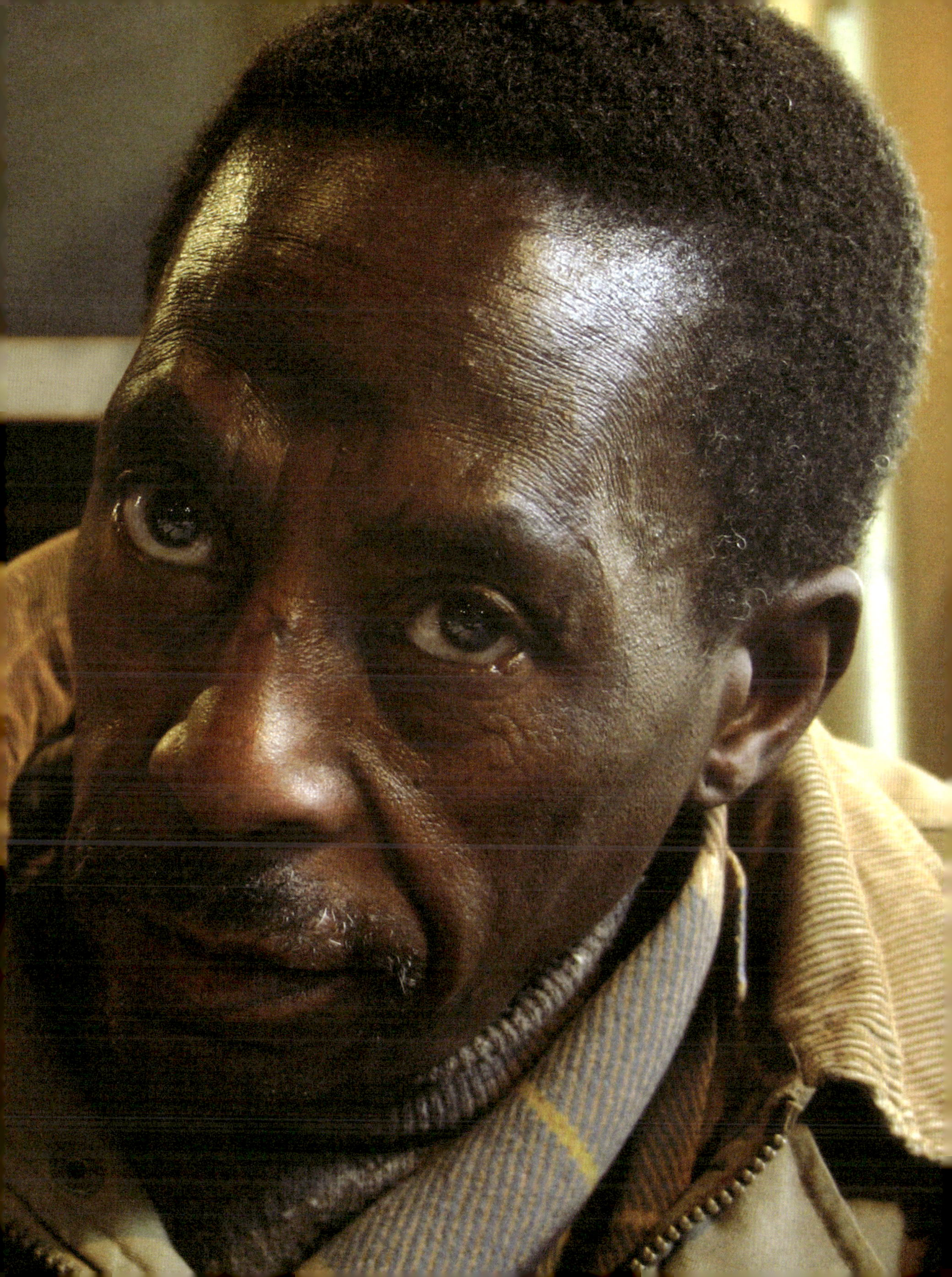

MABENA RAYMOND NENE

I was born on the 13th January 1954 in Soweto, Johannesburg. I am the third child at home. In 1971, I impregnated a young girl called Sheila Vilakazi. Because of this new responsibility, over and above everything else, I needed money.

I had to seek something to do. I was unemployed at the time. I then joined my friend who made a living in dagga dealing. I was arrested and brought to Number Four. That was in 1974, just before Easter holidays.

I spent three months as an awaiting trial prisoner and after my release in the same year, I told my friends that it was horrible in jail and they advised me to stop dagga. From then I started selling vegetables. After about two to three years selling vegetables my wife was robbed and everything was taken and we decided to stop our domestic business.

From then I have been working as a casual worker until today.

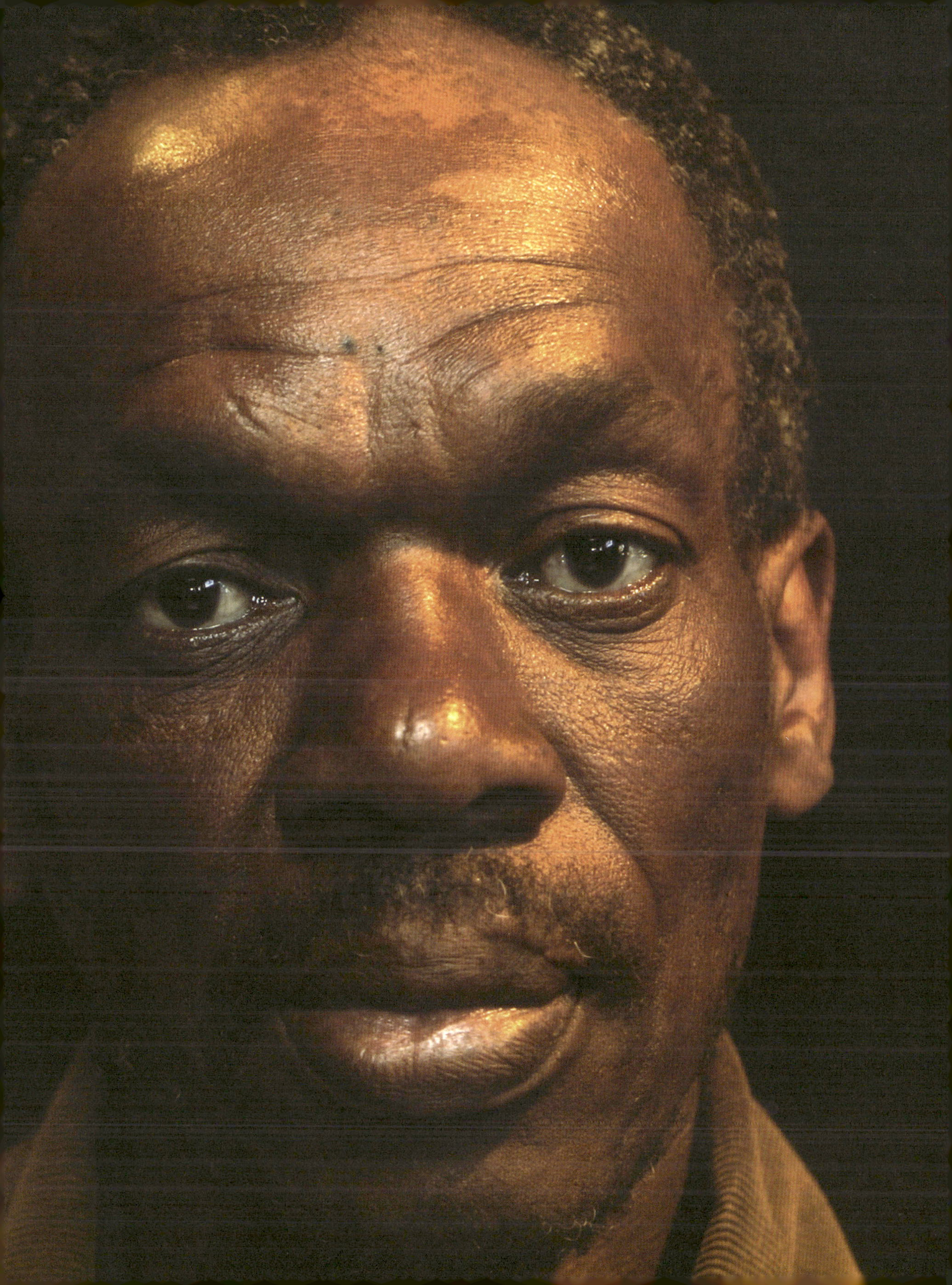

041-
042

MEHLOKAZULU LUKHELE

I was born in KwaZulu-Natal in an area called eDumbe in 1925. We moved to eMikondo, which is where I grew up. I worked on a white man's farm in Piet Retief from when I was about ten years old for 12 years. My parents were poor and there was no money for me to go to school. I woke very early in the morning to start work on Mr Kemp's farm. I had no shoes so my feet would be cracked and bleeding by the time I was finished working. I would fill the cracks with candle wax to ease the pain.

I was arrested in 1959 after surrendering myself to the police as part of the PAC's anti-pass campaign.

I now live at home with my son Sipho Lukhele. After the death of my wife, life was very difficult for me. I couldn't get work and I was summonsed to the municipal office as a rent defaulter. I even struggled to have something to eat. I don't work but I used to landscape people's gardens. I was so good. I have won some prizes. From time to time people come asking me to improve their gardens. As long as they pick me up and bring me back again I don't mind. Getting into the garden was the only solace after my wife passed away.

So I am grateful to the fellow Africans who used to console me and keep me informed of what is happening around me. Of all those who came to assist me, Mr John Moeketsi Mahapa is the man who is behind me.

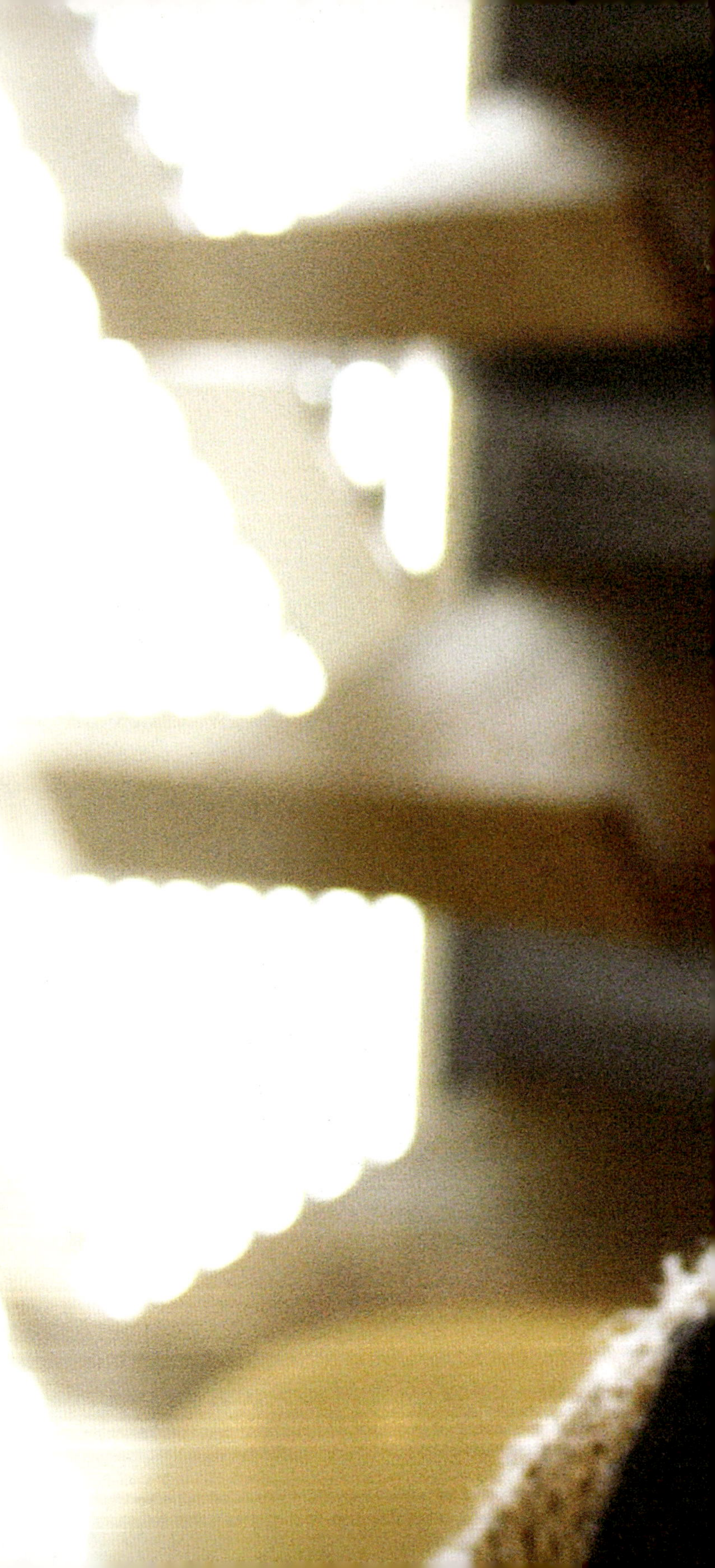

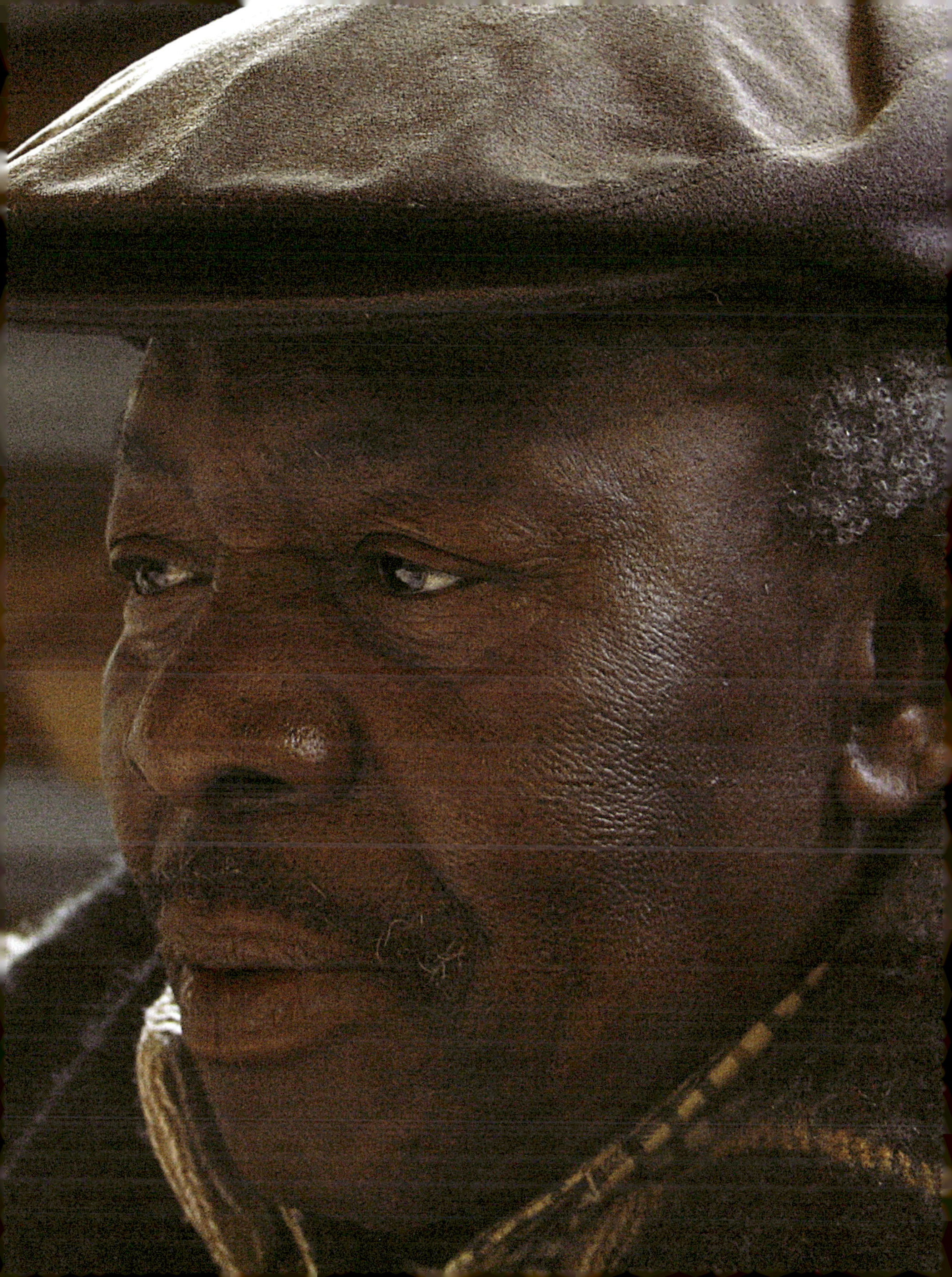

MUTHUPHEI PATRICK MUDAU

I was born in Louis Trichardt on the 6th of April 1956. I grew up there, staying with my aunt. My parents passed away very early. We used to help her after school, collecting wood and water. I am the second child in my family. After the death of my parents, I ended up staying with my aunt full time. I liked sport, particularly high jump. One other activity I liked was making cars of wire. Sometimes I would fix watches and radios. I passed my standard seven in 1972.

I started to look for a job in the city of Johannesburg in 1979 and I was arrested for failing to produce a *dompas*. The one that I produced did not have a Section 10 and they said that my pass is not allowed when looking for a job.

I was taken to Mothabi prison, where I was sold to a farmer to dig potatoes in Benoni. I was then released after three months. Within one week of my release I was arrested again and given 72 hours to disappear out of Johannesburg. Life was very hard during that time because you had to run away when you saw the police vehicle. Before you enter the van, they will kick you from behind and that van was very stinky, just like the cell of prison. We would call them '*basi*' (bus).

As I have mentioned, before that I was a person who liked fixing watches and radios. I am an entrepreneur, fixing radios, television and watches. I survive on the money that I make from my business.

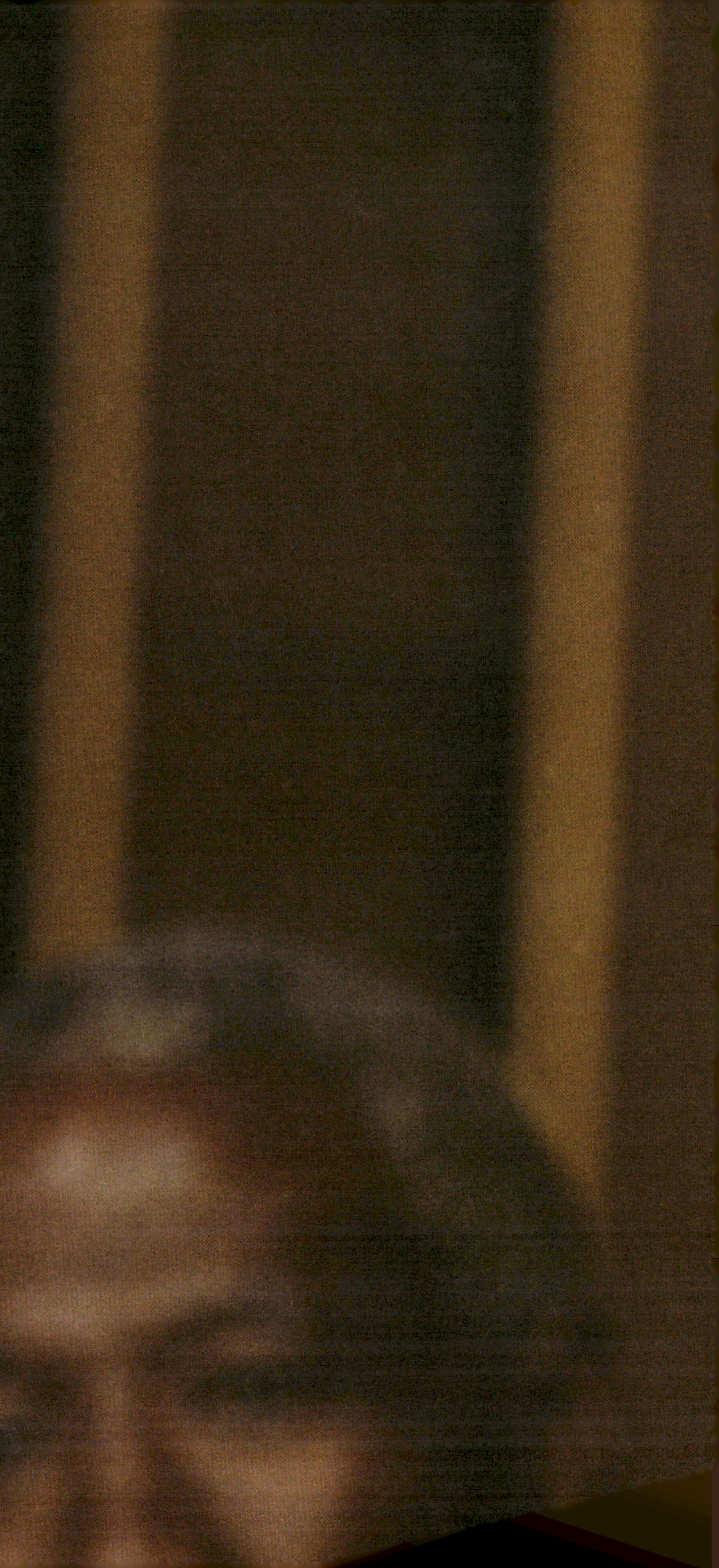

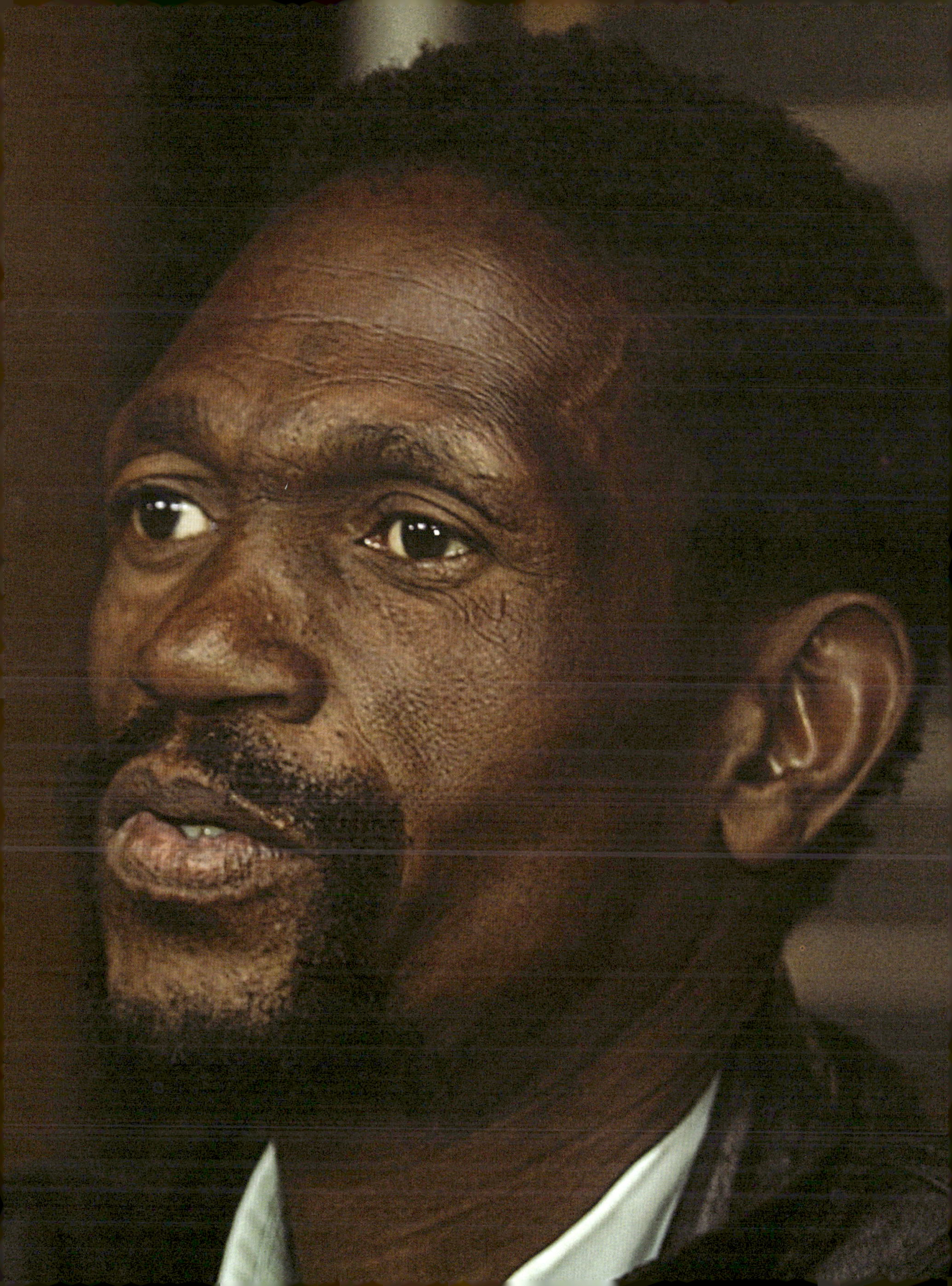

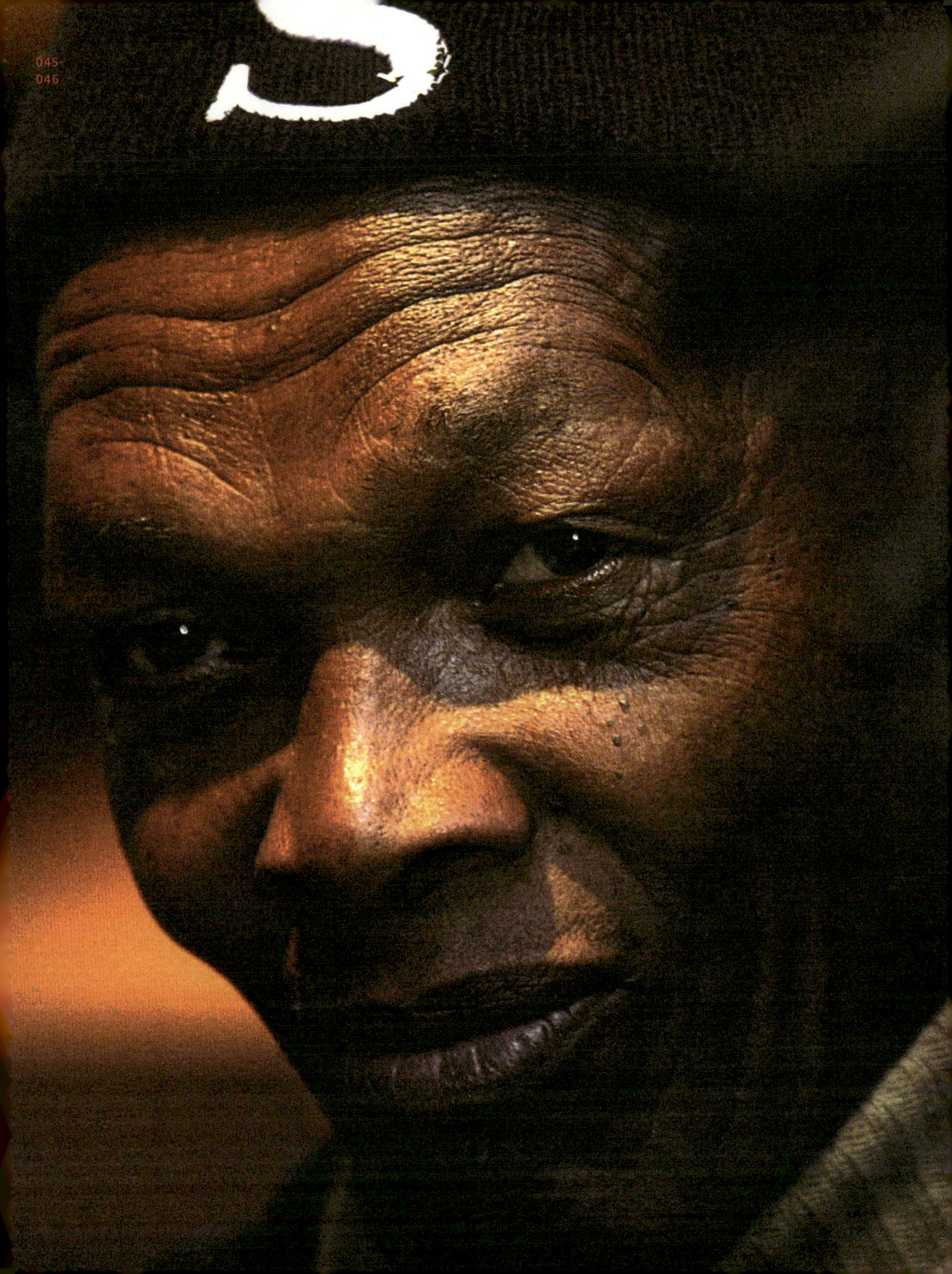

NAPOLEON MAZABANE LETSOKO

I am Napoleon Mazabane Letsoko. I am the third child of Mr and Mrs Bandi. We use the maternal name and surname of my mother because we were brought up at my maternal mother's place. In the course of time, we so got used to the maternal surname that we used it even at school. I was born at Bridgeman Memorial Hospital in Brixton, now known as Garden City. I attended school at Lopalma Memorial School. I only went as far as standard five. Due to the absence of my father, my mama was not in a position to pay for school fees for us, nor buy us school uniforms, for we had no source of income. The only source of income at home was a concoction of African beer that my mother sold to people. We survived out of this. And later, at the age of 14, I had to start fending for myself and my younger siblings. At the age of 21 I got my *dompas*. With a *dompas* I was obliged morally and legally to seek work and be employed. But there was something very inhumane about this *dompas*. Policemen would come and ask you for it. When you produced it, they looked for a permit to allow you to be in the area of Johannesburg to work there and so on. There were different ways of pinning you down even if you had the *dompas*.

Whilst I was still working a certain gentleman by the name of Selby Temba Ngendane, called me to get into a meeting. I asked him what type of meeting is this. He said that he wanted to organise some men to play football. He told me that the meeting would be held on the railway lines between two schools. I was interested in playing football so I went there. The most striking thing was that we were many there. It was a dark place, it was night. We couldn't recognise each other. He started to tell us the purpose of this meeting. He explained about the *dompas* once more, how inhumane it was. We kept on meeting twice a week.

It was through him that I became politically involved. One day, I led a group of PAC men to blow up a petrol station and rob a firearm shop in town. After a night of hiding, we were caught on the early morning train back to Soweto.

I was awaiting trial at Marshall Plein and then at the Fort. I served my sentence at Robben Island from August 1963. I was released in August 1980. When I came out, I wanted to leave the country to do military training, but the conditions at home were very pathetic. My father, my elder brother, my younger brothers and my younger sister passed away while I was in prison. My mother was left with five of my siblings. It was difficult to get a job because I was just from prison. I went to Lesotho to get military training with the help of the Lesotho Defence Force. In 1984, a friend of mine got me a job as a Messenger of the Court. I was serving legal documents to the defendants only to discover that my employer knew exactly who I was. He started discussing politics with me. I tried to elevate my family, take them to school and so on. I got married in 1984. I had three children with my wife. After 1994, there was a new dispensation at the courts and I left. I have had piece jobs since then – brick laying, plumbing, plastering. I have never worked regularly since 1994. It has been tough and difficult, living on pension. I am still a member of PAC.

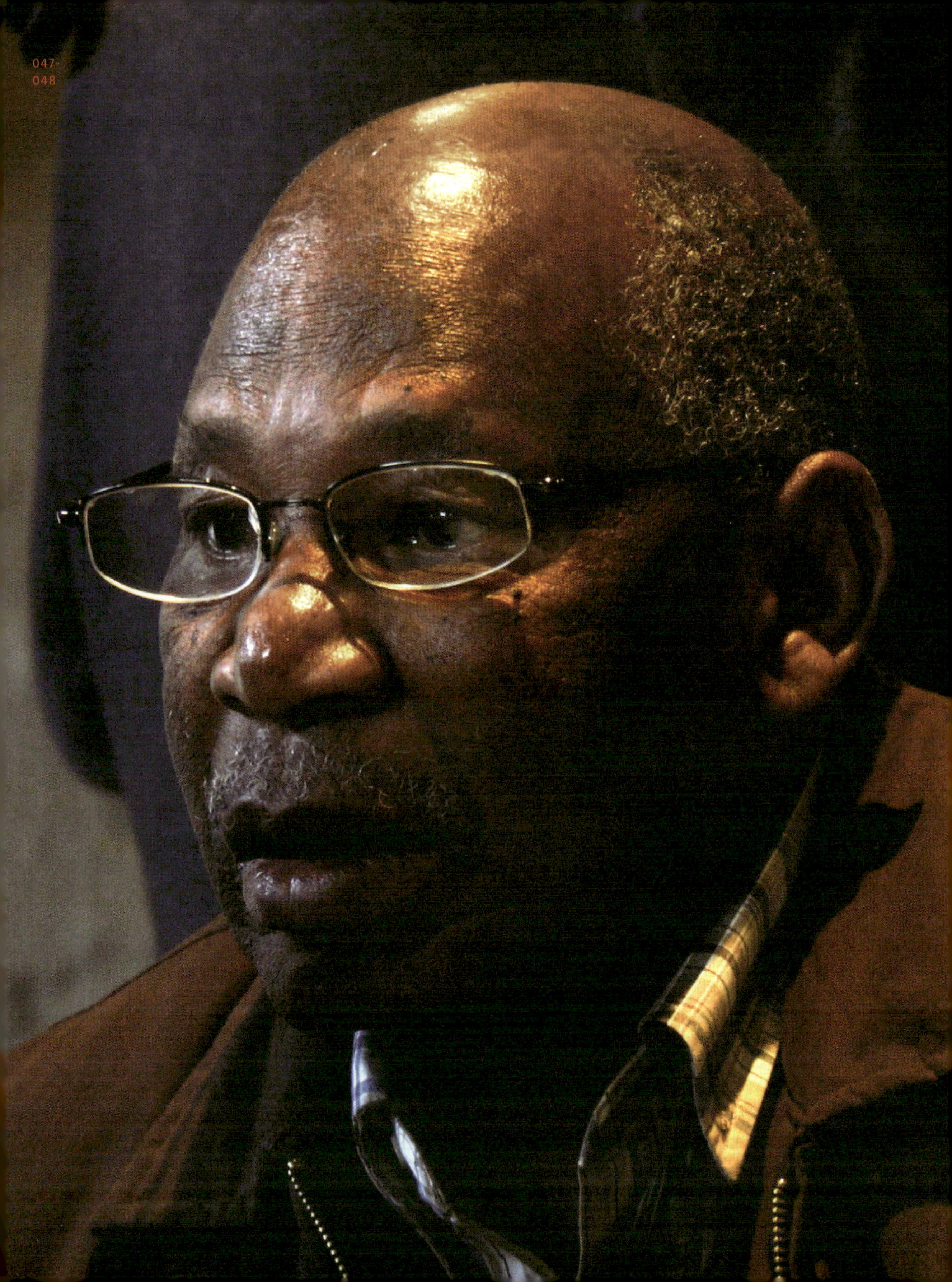

RASELEPE GIDEON NTHELEDI

I was born on the 3rd December 1930 on a farm known as Kwariefontein in the district of Groot Marico. I came to Johannesburg at the age of 18. I attended St. Cyprian in Sophiatown. After my primary schooling, I proceeded to Western Bantu High. After my secondary education, I started working for the YMCA at Baragwanath Hospital. Whilst working there, I moved to Orlando East because of lack of accommodation. I got married to Caroline Mokone whom I later divorced. I then moved to Dube where I am still residing. I got married again in 1966 to Mankosana Selina Ntheledi (nee Dlamini). We have four children.

In Dube I met a friend known as Rakhetla Tsehlana who was a member of the ANC Youth League. We used to discuss politics but I never formally joined the ANC. In 1958 we attended the ANC Congress. That was when the Africanists moved out of Congress and declared their independence from the ANC. We then moved to 142 Orlando East, where PK Leballo (the leader of the PAC) used to stay. The real bone of contention was the adoption of the Freedom Charter in 1955 that stated that the land belonged to those who lived in it. The Africanists said the land belonged to the African people. In 1959, the Africanists then held a conference that decided to form the PAC on 6 April 1959. It was also at this Congress that it was decided to take a stand against the pass laws. In November 1959, the pass campaign was launched and on 21 March 1960, the PAC marched against passes. A group from Mofolo, Dube and White City marched to Orlando police station. At the police station, we informed the police that we don't have our passes and formally asked them to arrest us. It was about three or four o'clock when they decided to arrest us. We slept at Orlando police station. On 22 April 1960, we appeared at the Fordsburg Bantu Commissioner's Court. We were remanded to the Fort, commonly known as Number Four. We were loaded in a big enclosed truck. When we got to Number Four, the truck reversed through the big wooden doors and into the long passage.

We were then led to the reception area where we were registered and led to a cell. It was during the Easter weekend and we received visitors who brought us food. We lined up and received our food and tried to pass a message to those outside. After several appearances, we were sentenced to a term of three years, with no fine.

After serving my sentence, I did several jobs. I also continued to do organisational work like helping those who wanted to go and do military training out of the country. I organised accommodation for those who were known to be politically active. In 1963, I was collected with several members of the PAC under the 90 days detention law. I was again detained under the 180 days detention law. I was detained in several police stations like Newlands, Rosettenville and Mondeor.

049-050 **SIPHO VICTOR NKABINDE**

I am Sipho Victor Nkabinde. I was born on the 9th of February 1940 in Orlando East. I am the third child of Leonard Nkabinde and Miriam Nkabinde. I am from a religious home. My home was really a warm home and that is why even now my own house is warm and friendly. In 1956 I started to look at life in a different way. The reason was that we were Africans and we were not looked at as human beings. That pushed me to be involved in politics at the time that I was still a student.

I joined the PAC in 1960. The reason I joined the PAC was to overthrow the government of the racist white minority. That led me to be arrested on 9th April 1963. Me and my other freedom fighting comrades were kept at Marshall Square for a period of four months.

When we arrived here at Number Four from the court, I really felt sad. It was really not a place that was good for human beings. Even the people at the reception were not having human feelings for other people. The other sad thing that I will never forget is the cry of a common-law prisoner who was killed. The last thing is the walk on the crushed stones, which we had to walk on. It made cuts on our feet. I was later sent to Robben Island.

At present I am not employed. I am struggling to start my small business due to lack of funds.

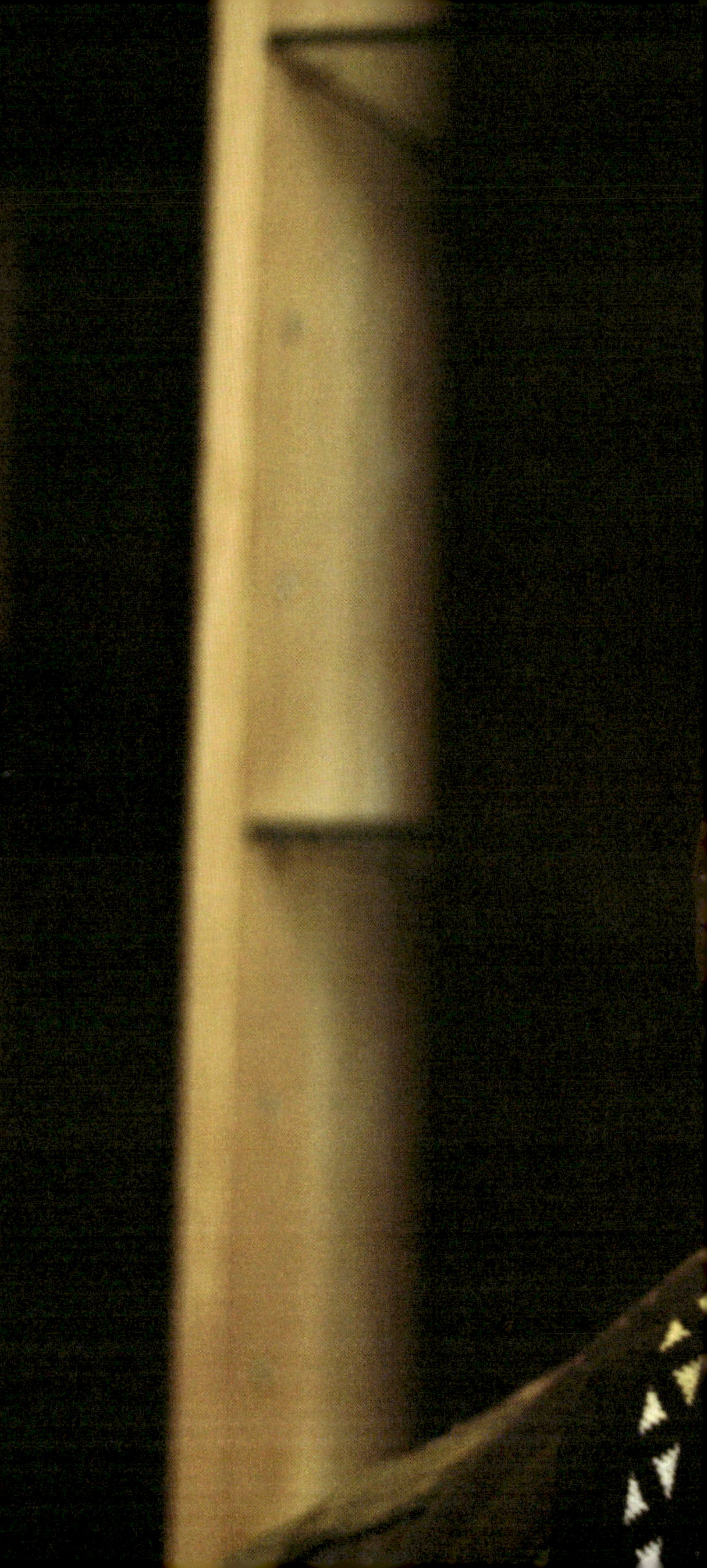

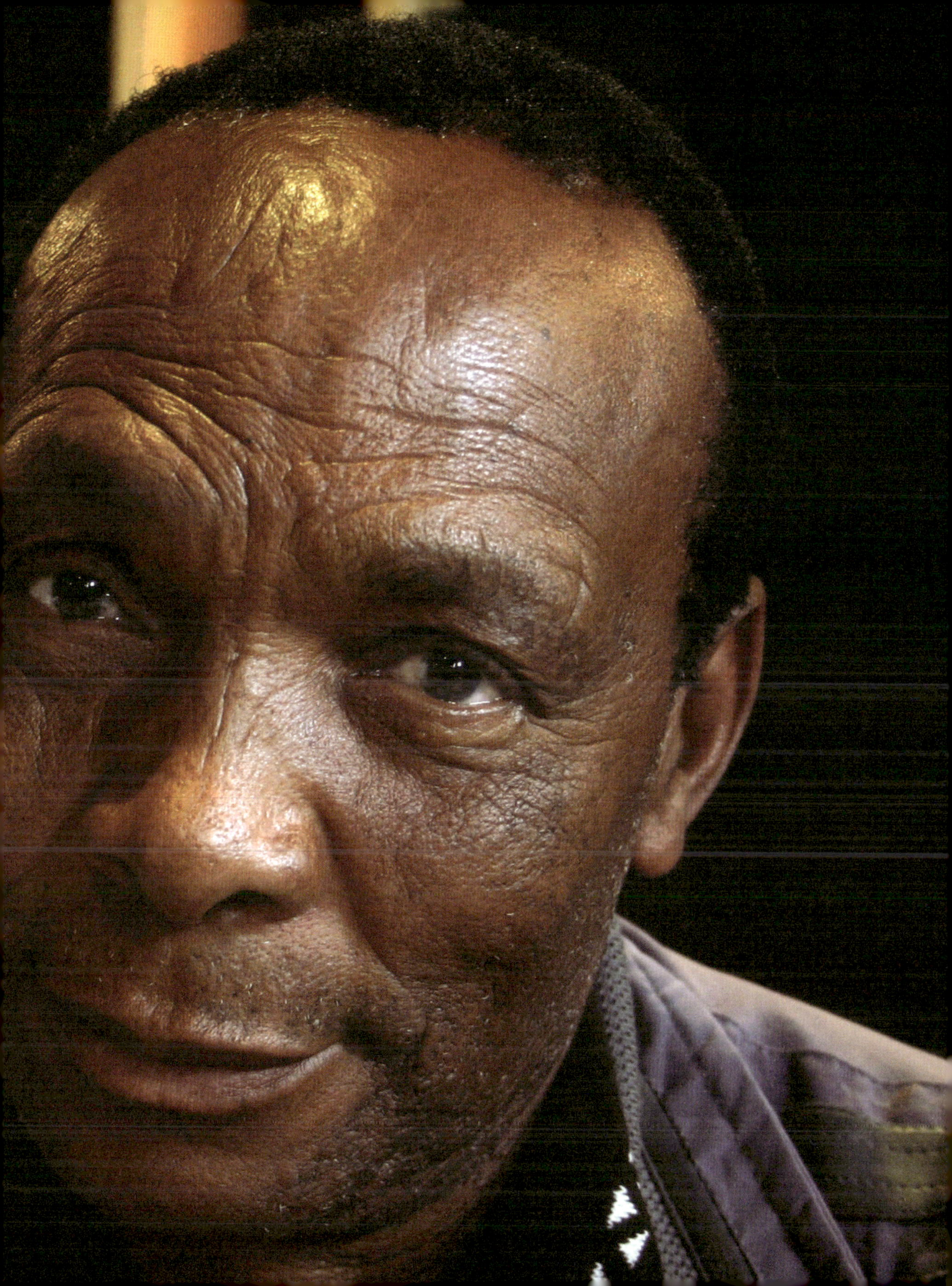

WHITE SESINYI

I was born in the Krugersdorp Old Location in 1939. This township was later demolished to make way for a white suburb known as Quelleriepark. I was the third child of Mr Neo Khoza and Dipugiso Grace Sesinyi. We are six children in the family. The present township where I live is Munsieville, in Krugersdorp. We were first housed in a one-roomed house where life was unbearable. This apartment served as a bedroom, dining room, sitting room, kitchen and bathroom. We slept on the floor and under the tables and put the chairs on top of the table. Thereafter we were relocated to a three-roomed house.

I was arrested in 1963 for "being a member and furthering the aims of a banned organisation" known as the Pan Africanist Congress of Azania. I was picked up by the security police where I worked as a filing clerk.

Presently I make a living by selling sweets, snacks and cold drinks.

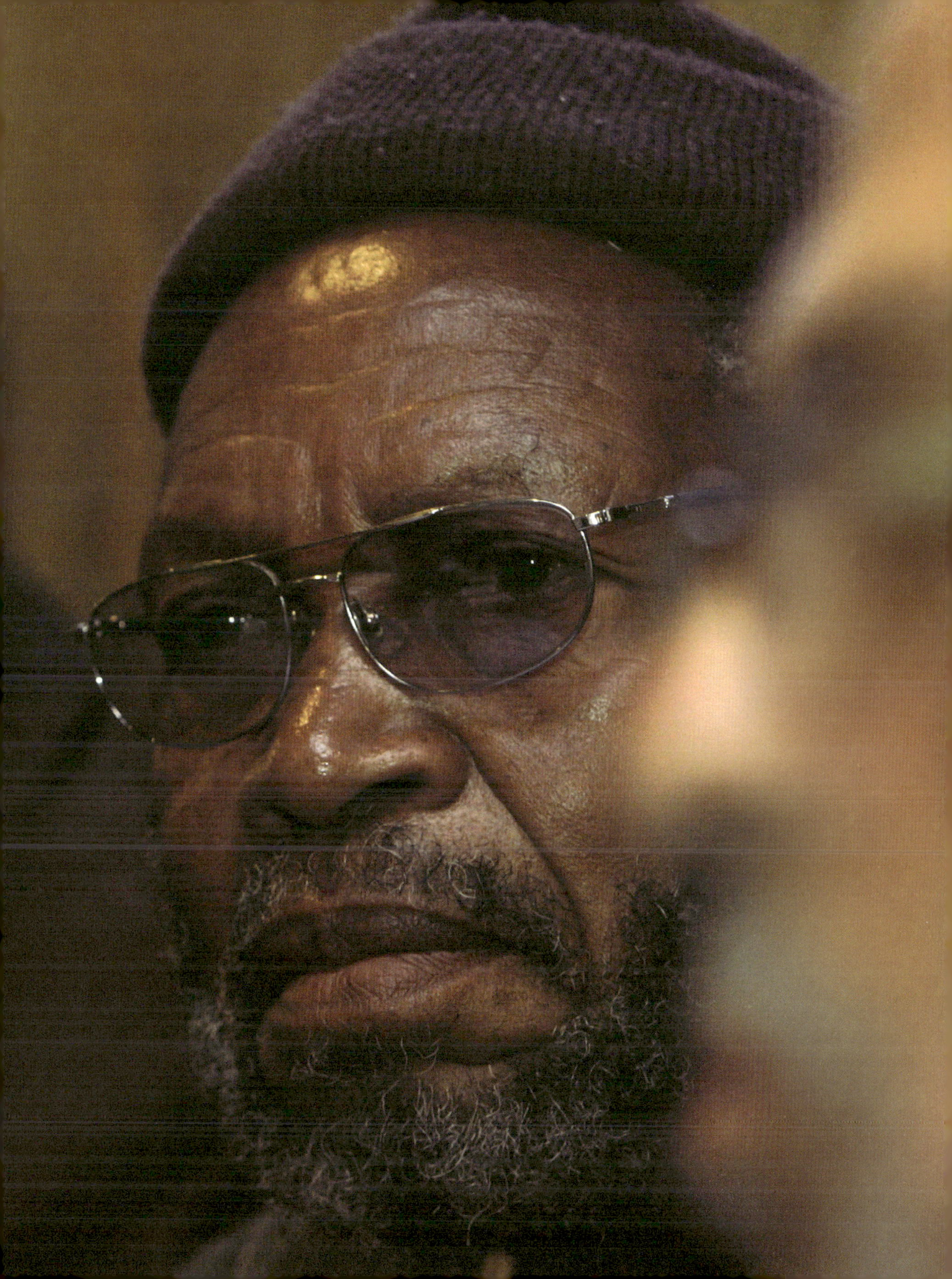

ZOLILE WILLIAM MGWEBA

My name is William. At home they call me Zolile. Every Saturday I liked going to the Zoo for temporary work because my mother was busy raising eight children. I am the first born, the eldest at home. My father was mining at Crown Mines. Sometimes he did not come home. He stayed at Westgate hostel in town. That day school closed for the holidays, me and my friend Bheki from Natal decided to look for work at the Zoo. On the Saturday, my friend and I who knew nothing about Johannesburg, waited at the gates of the Zoo hoping to get a job.

While waiting at the gates of the Zoo there were a few people selling things that can make money – like apples, oranges and even loose cigarettes. After an hour of waiting at the Zoo gate, this white man walked past and sat next to us. He was talking a good *tsotsi taal* and he said, *"Jitas ek soek 'n lekker zol"* (Brothers, can I have a skyf of dagga). I said, "No we don't have it and we don't smoke so please leave us alone." He persistently asked where he can get some zol (dagga) until my friend told him that there was a boy selling apples and stuff like that.

He gave Bheki five pounds (R10) to go and buy dagga for him. Bheki went and bought dagga for R10. As soon as he was back, to our surprise, this man was a policeman. He produced a police identity card and told us that we were arrested. We tried to explain to him that the seller was over there and he called other policemen and we were arrested and taken to John Vorster Square. We spent Saturday and Sunday night in jail, and on Monday we went to court. We saw the magistrate, and he charged Bheki for possession of dagga and me for bad company. That is when I was sent to Number Four for three weeks.

I was told that I am supposed to spend five days there and that on the following Monday I had to go back to court. After three weeks I heard them say *pikinini* (me, Zolile) was dead. I was surprised. They discovered that I was still alive when I had a visitor come to see me. They made a search in all the cells and they found me. I went back to court and was sentenced for six months in *stout* (naughty) school where I spent the rest of my sentence.

I have been self-employed as a jack-of-all-trades. Cleaning everybody's yard in Lenasia and even the Indian community around the settlement. I also collect cans and sell them in the scrap yard.

Then I met Mr Churchill Madikida, who inspired most of the things. He introduced me to Mr Clive van Berg. They taught me about the former prisoners' workshop. Those memories will never be erased from my mind. Now that I am talking about this, I might forgive myself and the apartheid regime that brought me the horrible memories of Number Four. I hated this place.

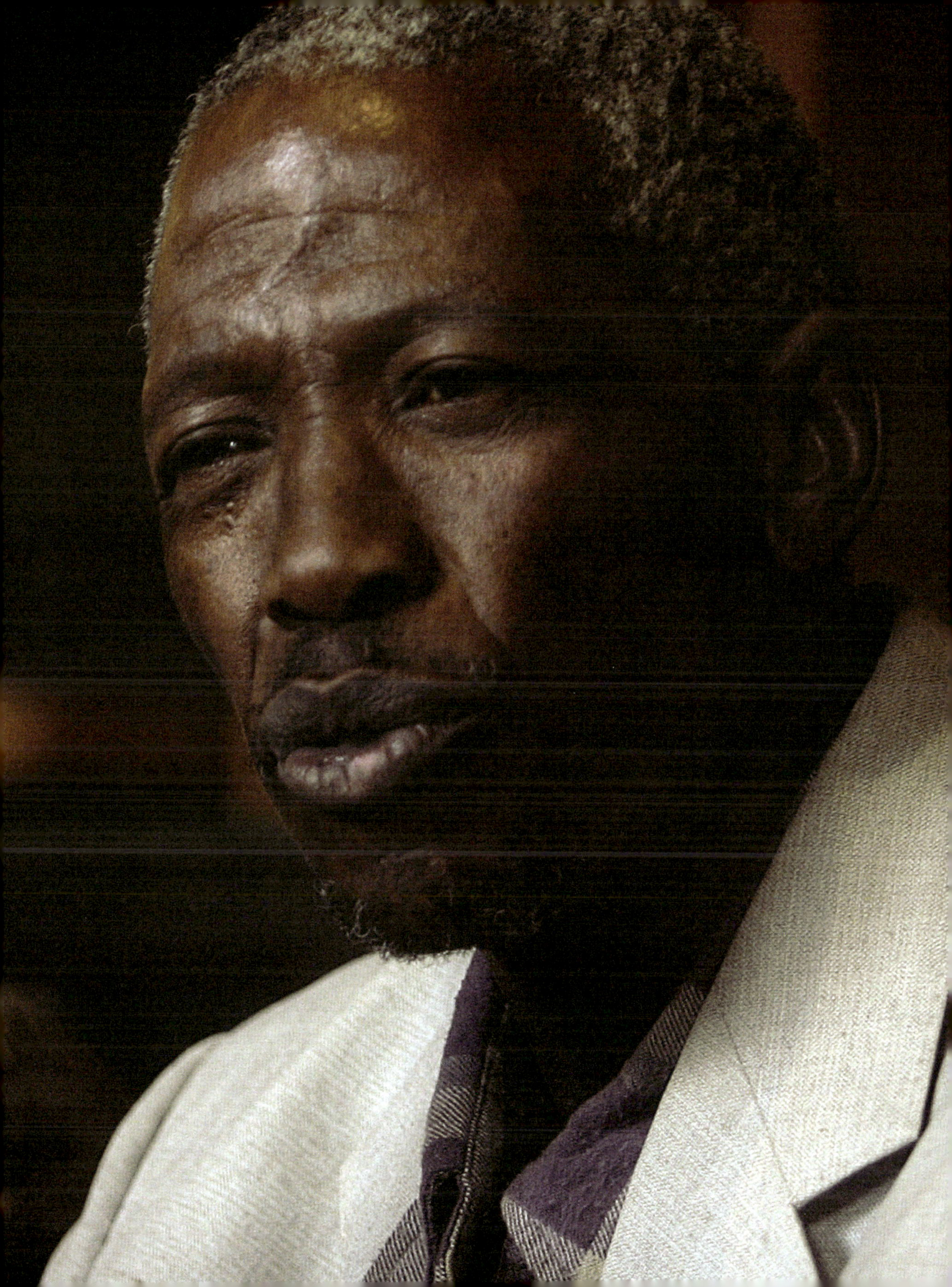

MAPPING MEMORY

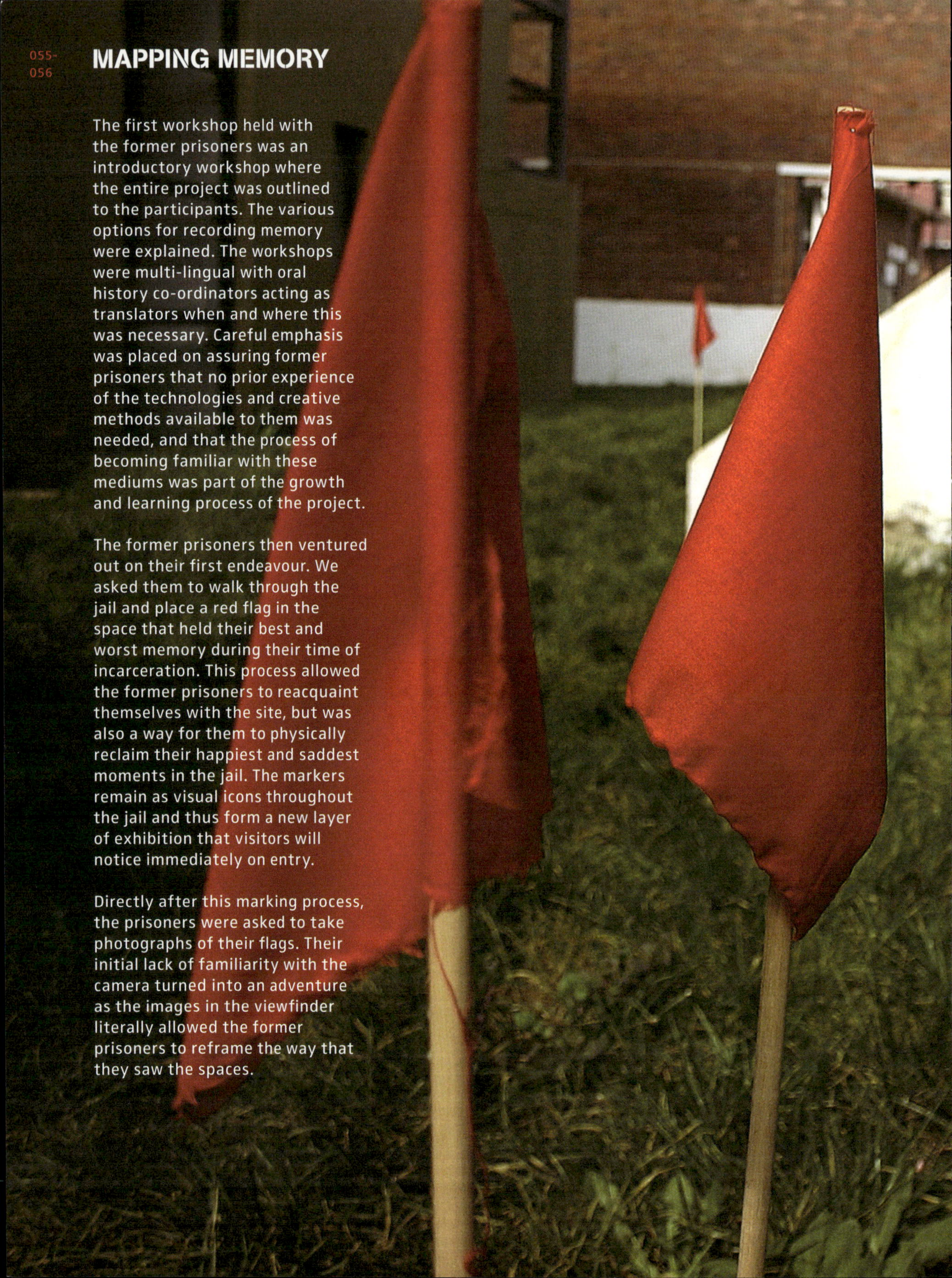

The first workshop held with the former prisoners was an introductory workshop where the entire project was outlined to the participants. The various options for recording memory were explained. The workshops were multi-lingual with oral history co-ordinators acting as translators when and where this was necessary. Careful emphasis was placed on assuring former prisoners that no prior experience of the technologies and creative methods available to them was needed, and that the process of becoming familiar with these mediums was part of the growth and learning process of the project.

The former prisoners then ventured out on their first endeavour. We asked them to walk through the jail and place a red flag in the space that held their best and worst memory during their time of incarceration. This process allowed the former prisoners to reacquaint themselves with the site, but was also a way for them to physically reclaim their happiest and saddest moments in the jail. The markers remain as visual icons throughout the jail and thus form a new layer of exhibition that visitors will notice immediately on entry.

Directly after this marking process, the prisoners were asked to take photographs of their flags. Their initial lack of familiarity with the camera turned into an adventure as the images in the viewfinder literally allowed the former prisoners to reframe the way that they saw the spaces.

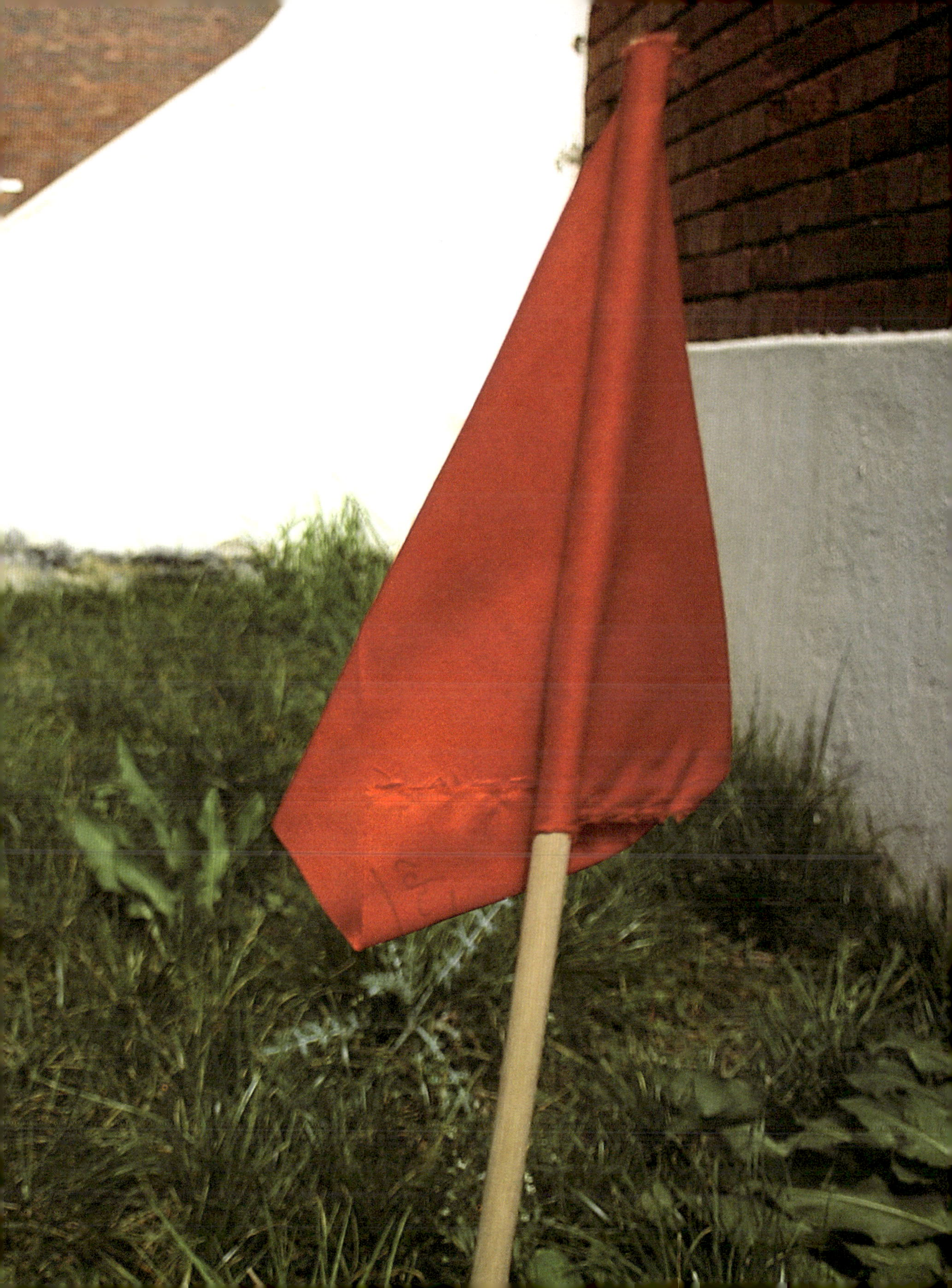

ASSIENAH MNISI

Best Memory

My best memory whilst I was imprisoned here was when I was to be moved to Kroonstad prison because I had once visited a friend there and she had told me of how well looked after they were. There was a crèche where the children were kept during the day.

Worst Memory

My worst memory is of all of the nights that my baby would be crying and the other inmates would shout and swear at me saying, "*Thulisa umntwana sigwetyiwe thina, sifuna ukulala.*" (Keep your baby quiet, we are sentenced prisoners and we do not need a crying baby, we need to sleep.)

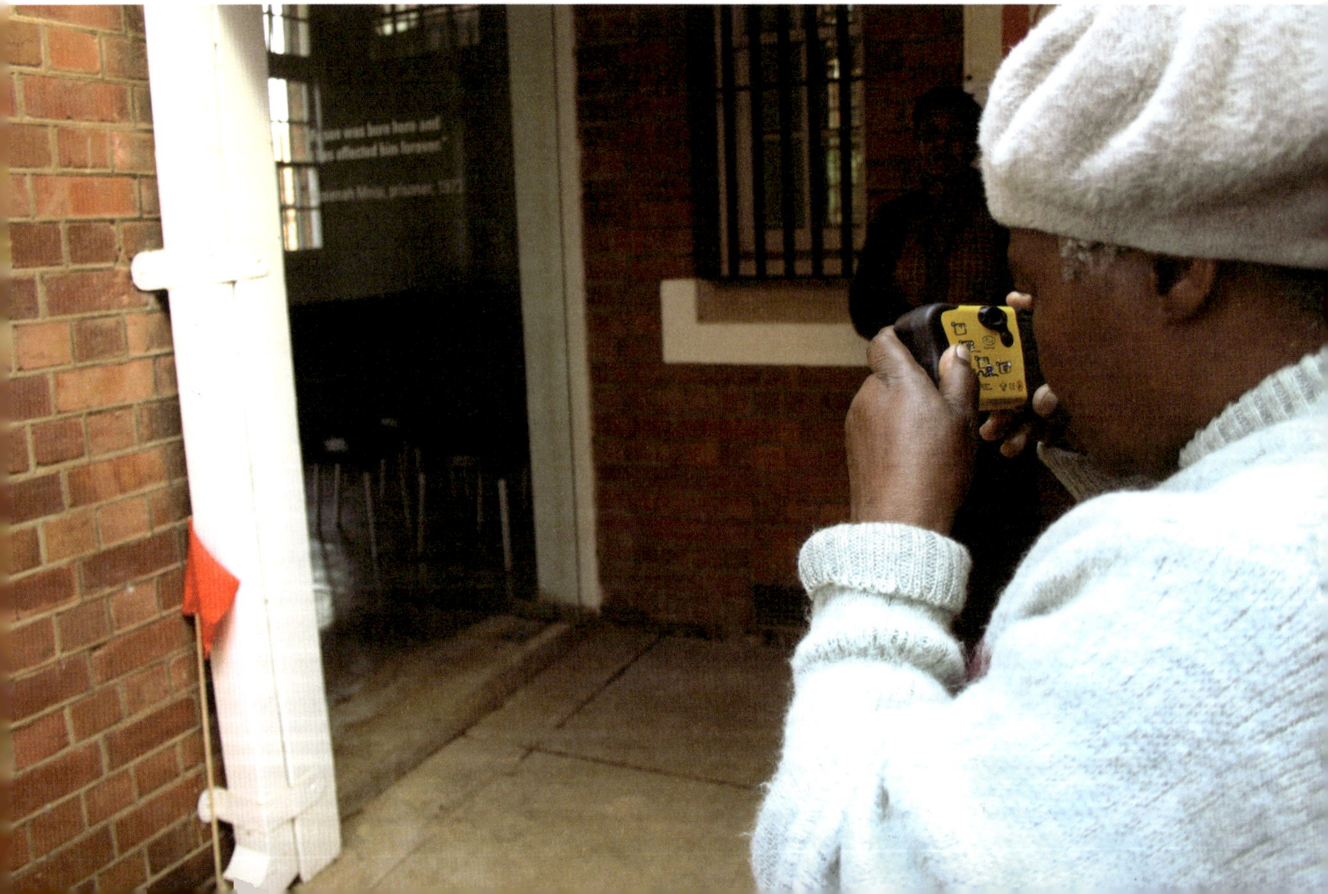

BELLA DLAMINI

Best Memory

I put my happiest flag at the front door because this is where I was going home. I had been in jail for two years. It was terrible to have been in this place.

Worst Memory

My other flag was in the atrium because they hit me there when I didn't know that I was not allowed to walk through the atrium. I walked through there when I first arrived and the wardresses hit me and kicked me. I was also punished and they threw me into the isolation cells and I had to go one day without food. So I was very upset.

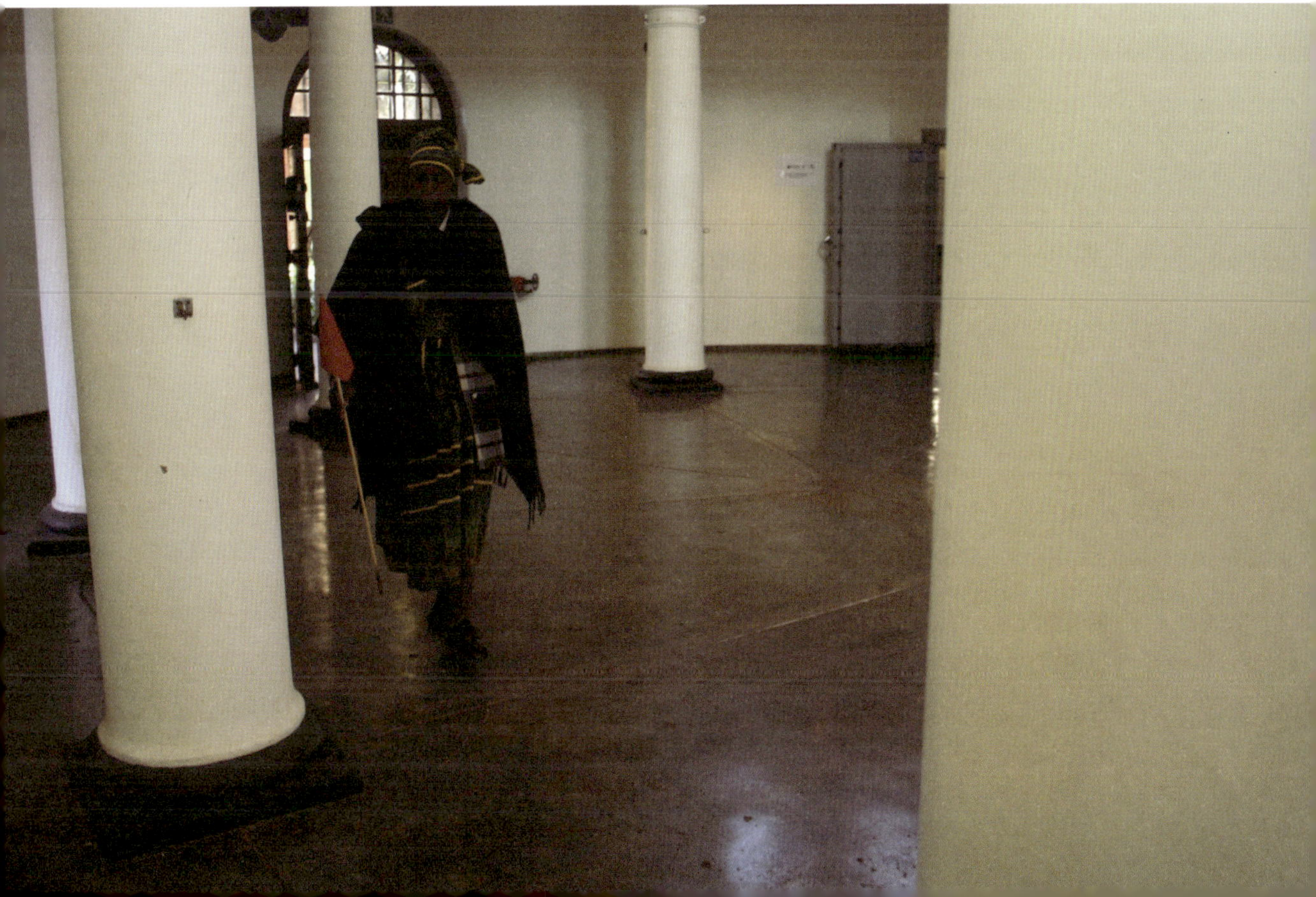

LILIAN KEAGILE

Best Memory

My happiest memories were when I was told that I had a visitor or when my lawyer came to visit. I looked forward to leaving the area where my cell was, that is, the area for black prisoners. I would pass the whites-only female prisoners' section on my way to the visit. Whenever I went into that section I had a smile because I knew that I was going to see Barbara Hogan who acknowledged me as Lilian, her comrade. She would give me that loving warm smile and I would wave at her. To me, that was everything that a prisoner in the Fort could want. It brought me joy. We never used to talk, but just that was enough.

Worst Memory

My saddest moment was when I was in my cell and I was called because my father had come to visit me. He informed me that my cousin Moabi Dipale had died at John Vorster Square. He had been detained shortly before me. He was released just before I was charged and I had felt very relieved that we hadn't implicated each other. (We had worked together with comrades from Botswana in the underground.) But then he was detained again and on the third day he died from torture. His clothes and body were apparently covered in blood. But they said that he hanged himself. I went back to my cell and I was all alone. I had no one to talk to. I had so many questions about how and why he had died. There was no one to counsel me. Days and nights became long and lonely and I became angrier and angrier.

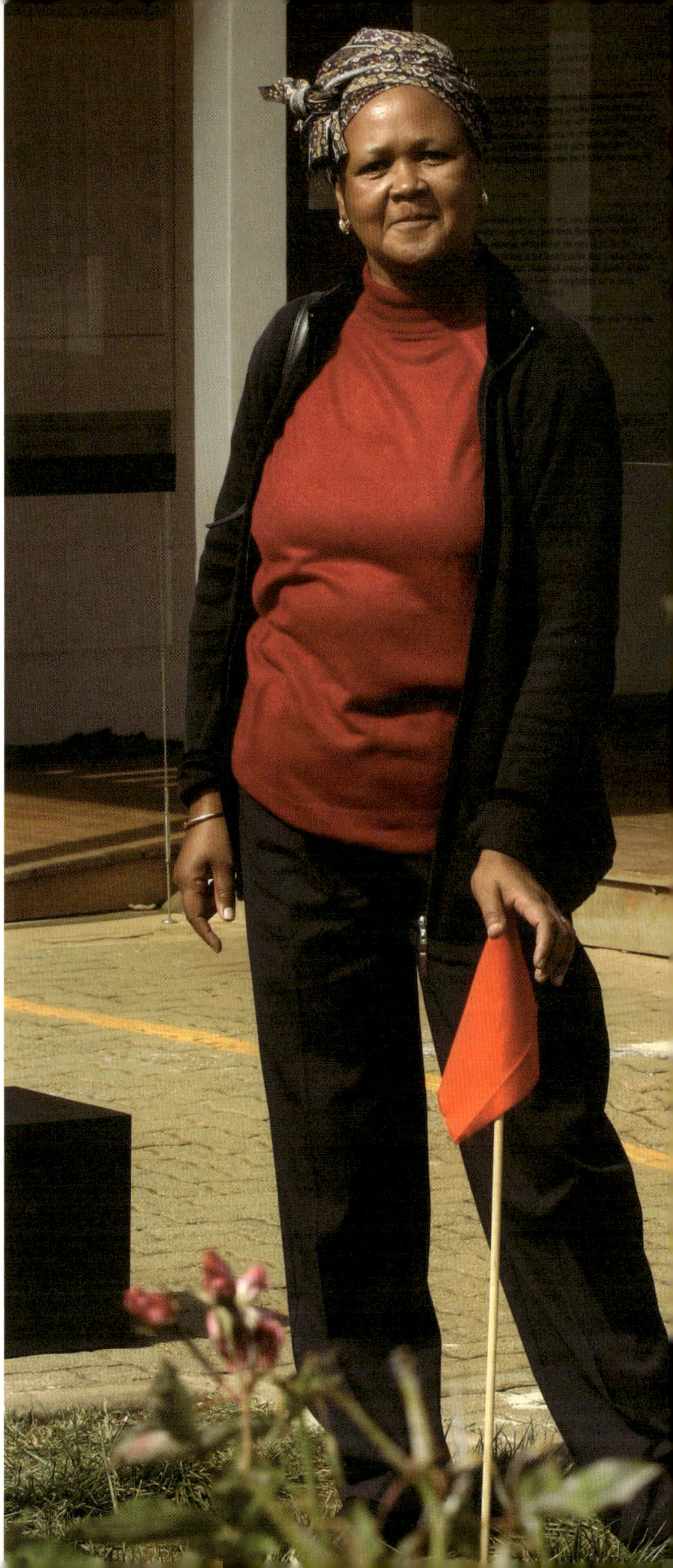

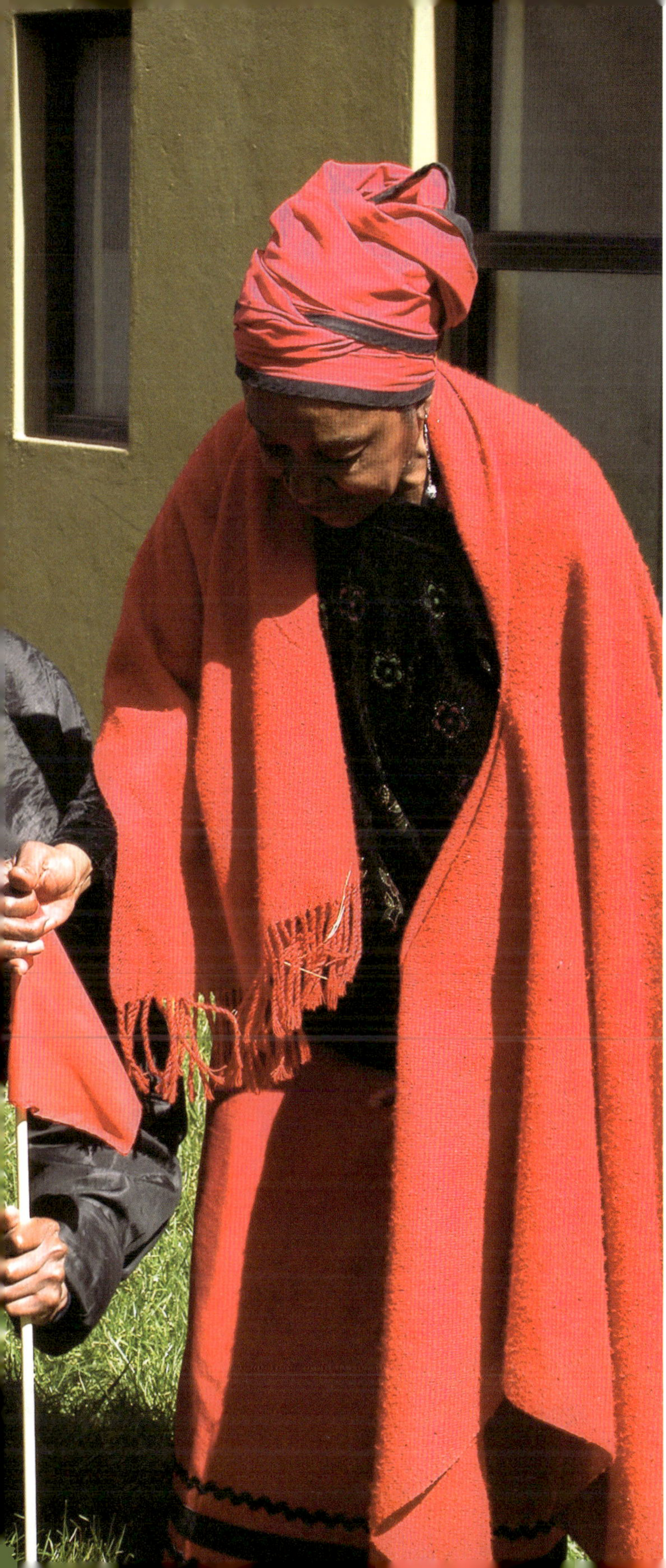

NIKIWE DEBORAH MATSHOBA

Best Memory

My best memory is when I discovered the other inmates that had been detained at the same time as me. There was much relief within me when I finally got a response from my knocks on the wall. This is how the conversation went:

"Ungubani?" (Who are you?) "Nomzamo Mandela (Winnie Mandela)," came the reply. "Lolo Tabane and Oshadi are also here but Oshadi is unable to speak. She has just come back from the torture chambers at John Vorster Square. She has been there for the whole night."

Further communication through the neighbouring corrugated iron shacks erupted. Fatima Meer, Sibongile Kubheka, Jeanne Noel (the Durban girl), Khanyo Mafuna were all here. Then Vesta Smith, Joyce Seroke, Sally Motlana and Cecilie Palmer arrived. We were finally allowed to interact.

Lolo, Oshadi, Nomzamo, Sibongile, Vesta, Khanyo and I spent our time singing and communicating.

Worst Memory

My worst memory was when I discovered that there were children held somewhere in the other cells. We heard their crying one night. We were so angry to think that children as young as 12 had been thrown into this jail. We mounted a protest to have them released. The warder told us that they were released. We later found out that they had just been moved to another section.

JOYCE DIPALE

Best Memory

My best memory is when I woke up the following day after being brought here and I saw I was with my comrades. I was with the youngsters, Baby Tjawa, Nomsa Maseku. We communicated with the prisoners on the other side of the wall using the 'aeroplane' method. We used to throw fruit, pads and messages in packets over the wall that separated us from our other comrades. I remember the fruit. For months I had been eating only pap. Now at least there was fruit. We could also shout to each other over the wall and find out how we were doing.

Worst Memory

I had already been in jail for almost one and half years. I had been in John Vorster and Bloemfontein. I thought that they were releasing me from Bloemfontien. But no, it was to be the same story all over. Jail again. Back to square one. I was in the *kwela-kwela* (police) van again being brought through the gates of Number Four. I was alone in the van and it was a big van. I didn't know where I was when we came into Number Four. I didn't see any other prisoners. They put me straight into the isolation cells. The light was on the whole time. This drove me mad. There was no bible, no church on Sundays. Nothing. "Why?" I ask myself. "I don't understand why?"

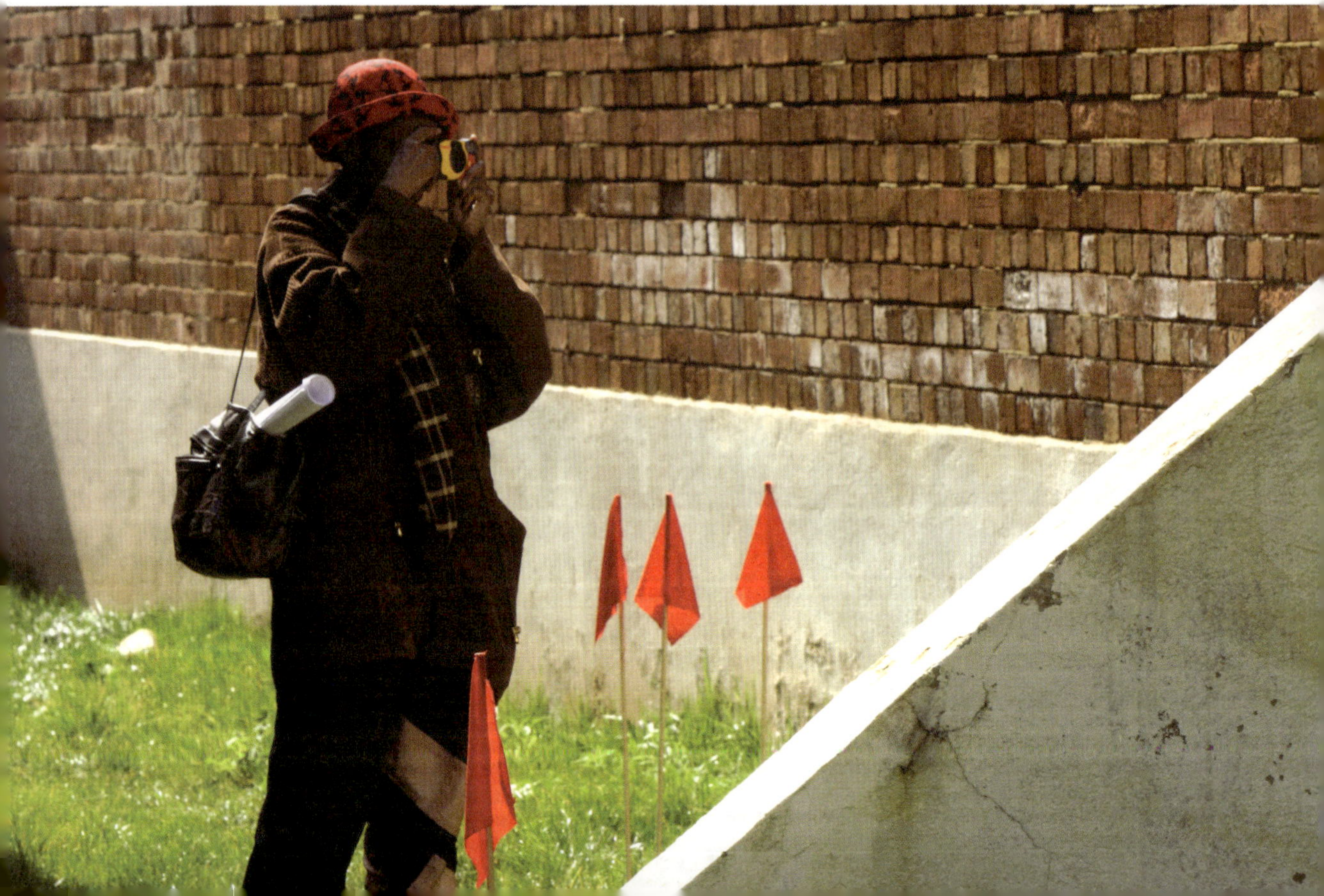

SIBONGILE TSHABALALA

Best Memory

My best memory was when my mother, who was also an inmate with me, gave me her Christmas ration, which included a candy and a bun roll. It was the best Christmas gift I had ever received from my mother. I will never forget it.

Worst Memory

My worst memory was when I was slapped across my face for not putting my hands behind me as I was entering the prison gate for the first time. I was a young 14-year old girl and I did not understand the prison rules. I was very shocked.

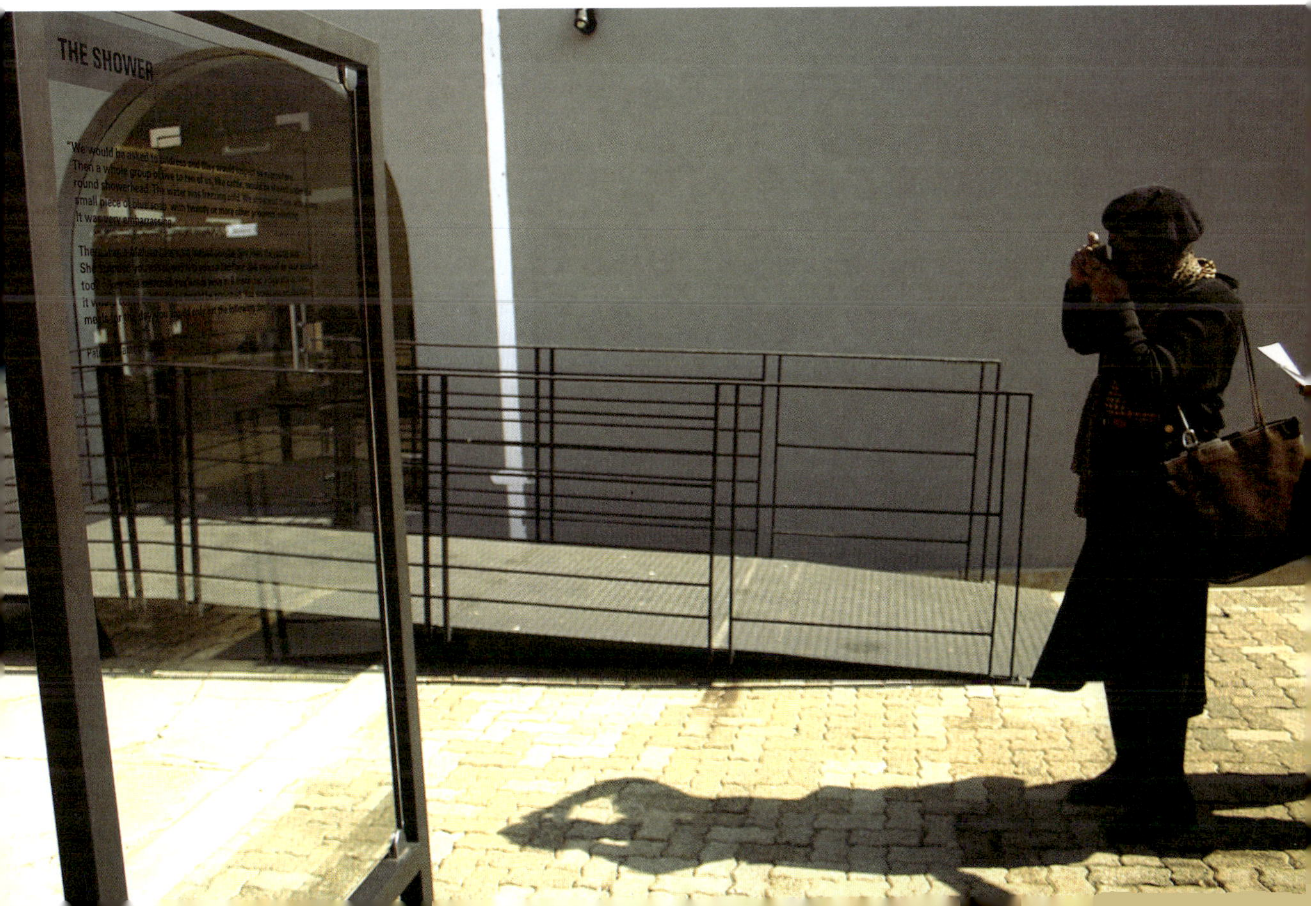

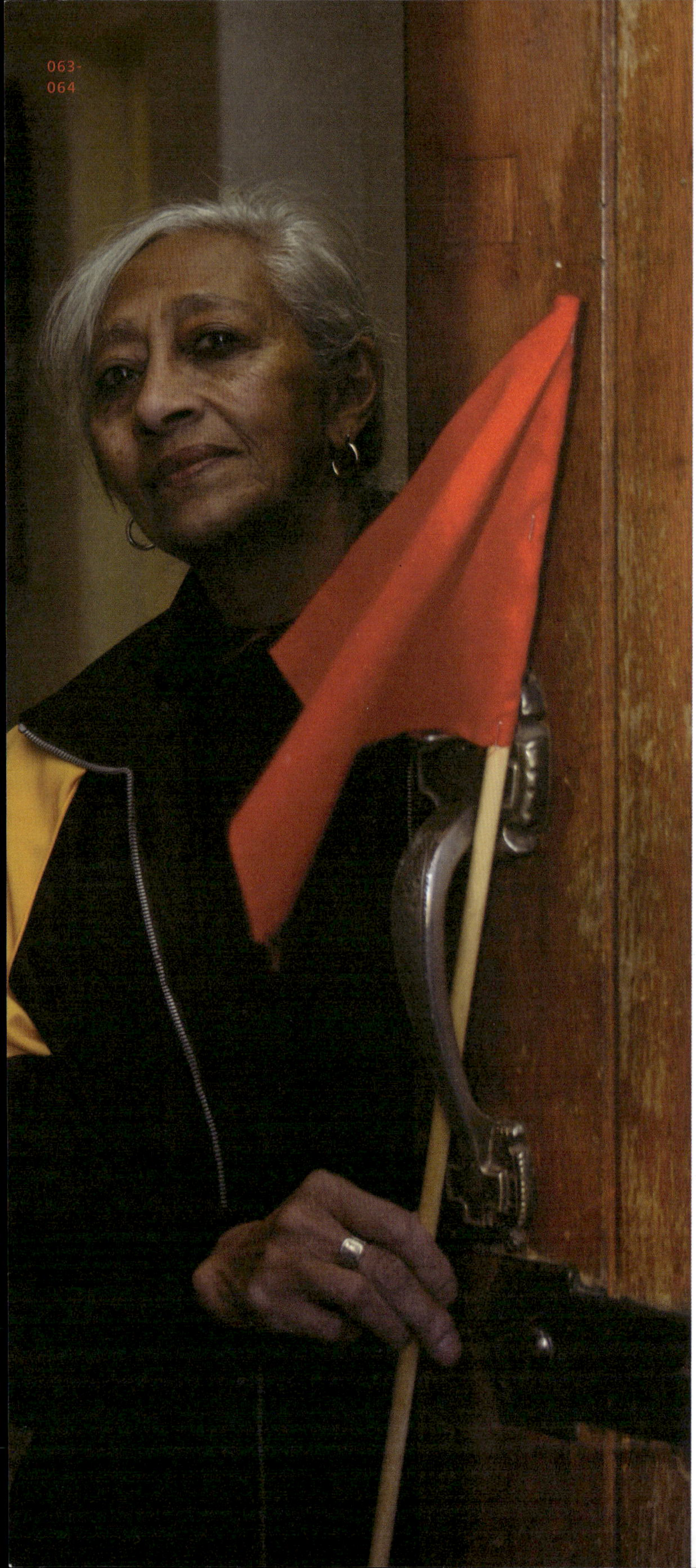

JUBY MAYET

Best Memory and Worst Memory

I put my flag at the big brown doors in the front of the Women's Jail. This is where both my worst and my best memories of my 'visit' to Number Four lie. Coming in and going out! When the doors opened on my release, I remember virtually leaping out and tearing down the steps with my hair flying out behind me as I headed for freedom.

YVONNE NTONTO MHLAULI

Best Memory

My best memory was when we were moved to Sun City – Diepkloof Prison – because we were told that we were going to sleep in beds and be able to watch TV. We were also told that we were going to eat better food compared to that junk at the Women's Jail in Number Four. The day we were moving to Diepkloof Prison I was dancing and jumping all the way to the *gumba gumba*. I was so happy for a while I even forgot that I was still a prisoner.

Saddest Moment

On my way to the visitor's room I was stopped by the wardress, Swanepoel. She said that I could not go and see my visitor because my hands were not at the back of me. I was punished immediately and instead of going to see my friends I was sent to isolation – *drie maaltye* (three meals) for ten days.

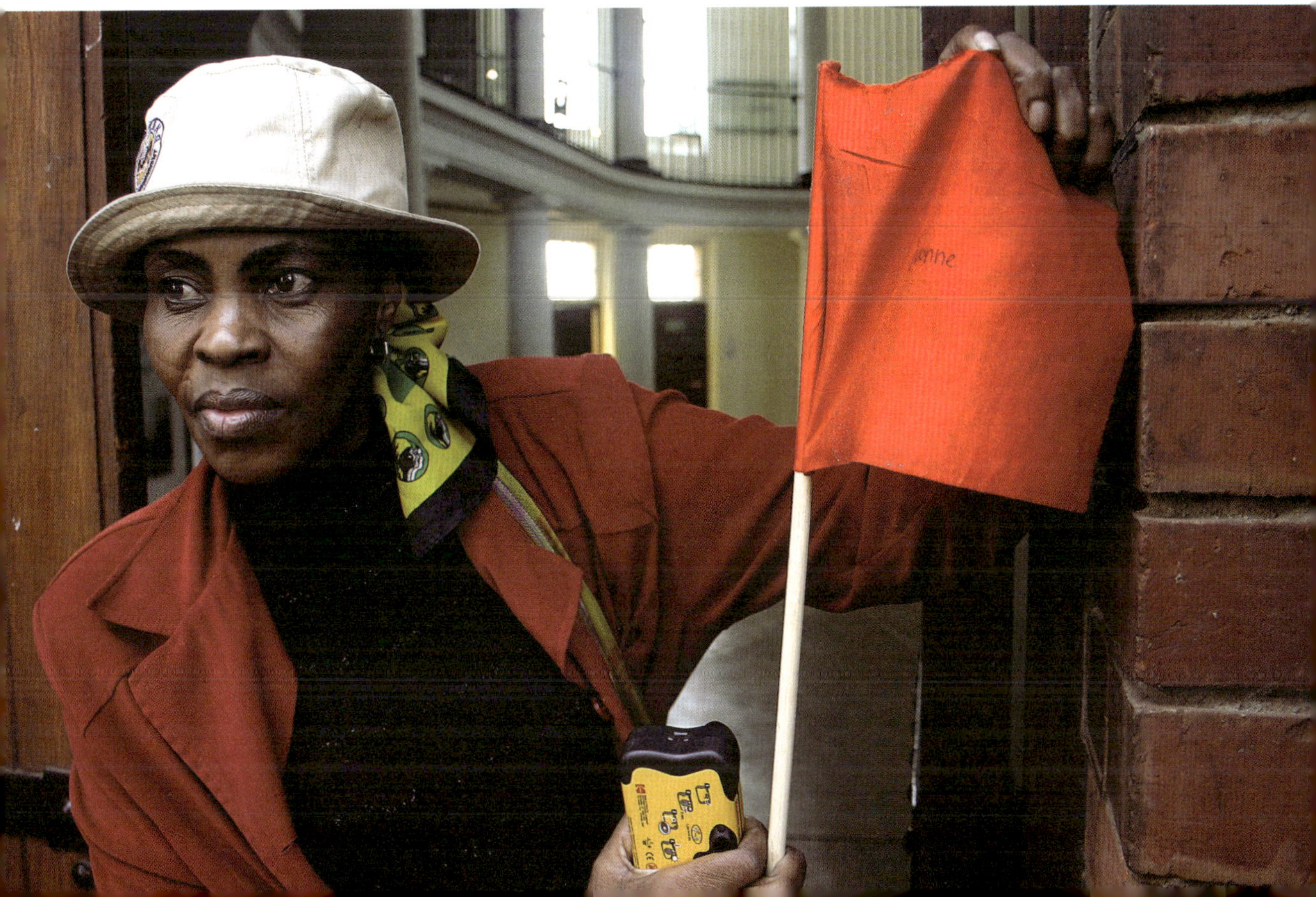

Best Memory

My best memory was when the board from Pretoria came to check the records and the behaviour of the prisoners. They visited us usually in April and May. They told me that after a month I would be given a date to go home and then after two months I will be seeing my family again. I was dancing and singing and I felt on top of the world. I was singing the song *"Umama uyajabula bangibuya ejele."* (My mother will be happy when I return from jail.) I was going home and that was the happiest day I ever had in jail.

Worst Memory

There was a time in 1976 when I was serving nine to 15 years and I was working at the record office in the reception of the jail, that I was most sad.

I used to get visiting hours on a particular afternoon in the week but that afternoon, I did not get any visitor. Then on Sunday I was called for a visit and was surprised to see my friends. We used to call ourselves the 'Big 18' shoplifters. My friends were dressed to kill and one of my friends by the name of Mahody said, "Be brave Tikie." And I said, "Why?" And she said, "I have just buried your father, Tate". I collapsed and I was taken to the General Hospital where I only recovered after two days. I was under the guard of wardresses. They were there until I was discharged back to prison. That was a very sad memory of my prison life.

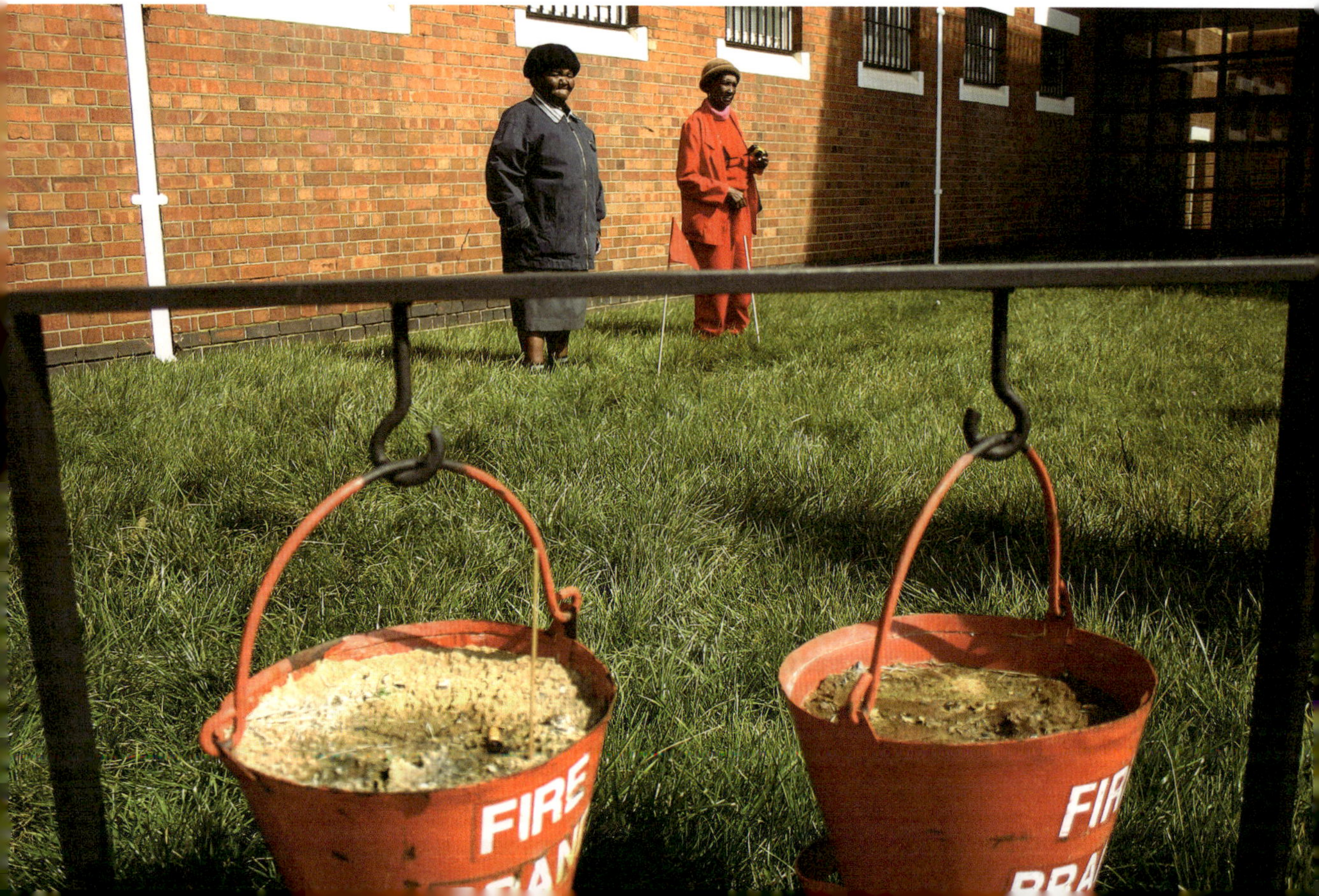

PATRICIA ALARM

Best Memory

My best memory is when I walked into the office of the lieutenant warder to be told that I will be released from prison the next day. I cried and hugged her and said, "God does exist!" I also put my red flag in the storeroom because I enjoyed working in there. We were not guarded when we were there and it was a relief.

Worst Memory

My worst memory was when I was beaten up on the stairs going into section three. I have made my exhibition about this. I was beaten up because I stood up for a new inmate who stepped into the *mbendeni* (the haunted area) where we prisoners were not allowed. They broke my arm. I will never forget that.

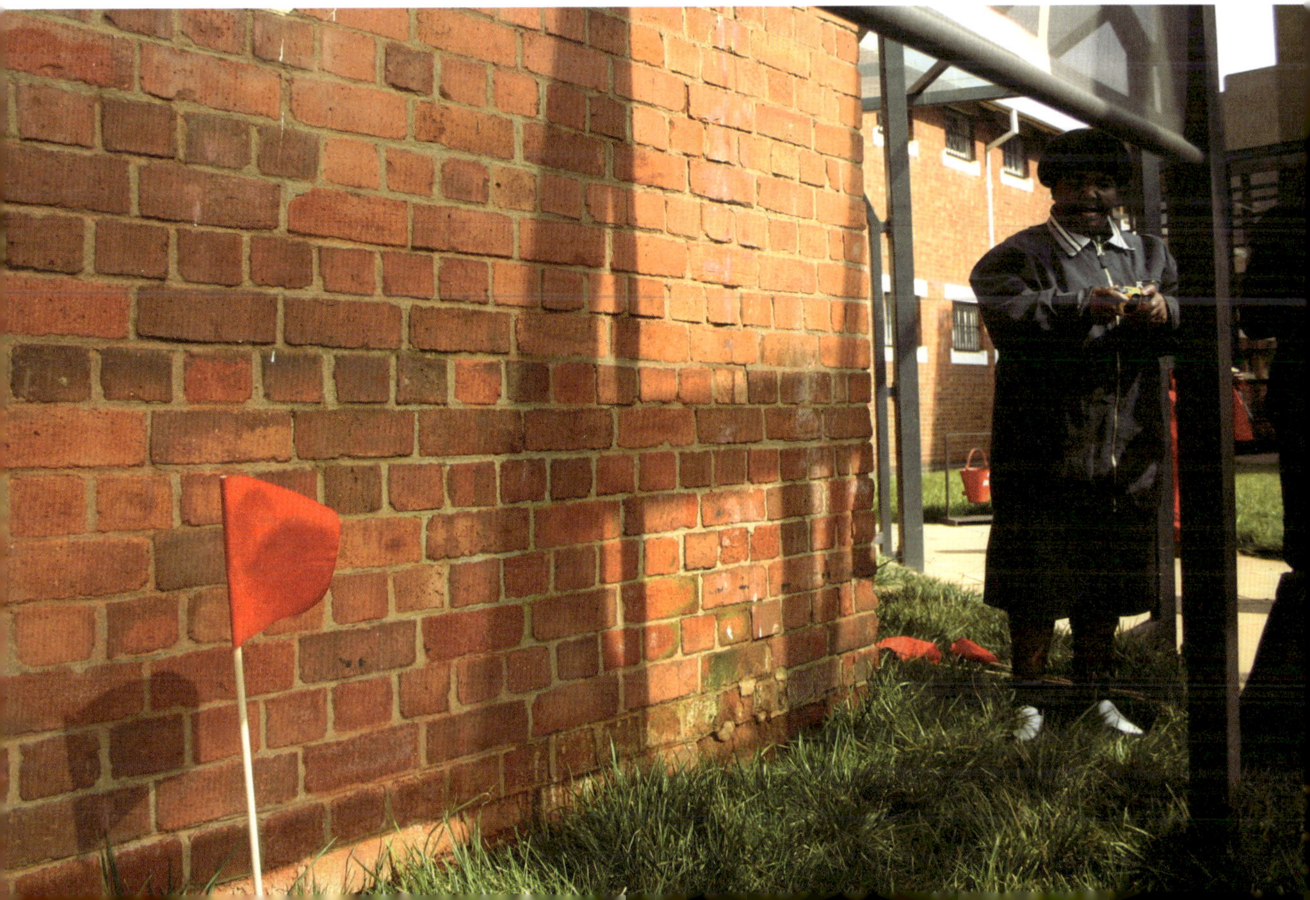

Worst Memory

My stay in Number Four was horrible! The filth, the debauchery and the squalor! To eat from rusted containers was terrible; not to speak of the treatment from the warders. Every morning we would stand in the shade feeling cold not even seeing the sunshine. In the court we will be stripped naked and subjected to utter humiliation of the worst order. The sleeping area was very cold with one mat and one blanket and also one filthy toilet. Cleaning oneself was impossible. This whole thing was my worst experience in the 1960s in this horrible Number Four.

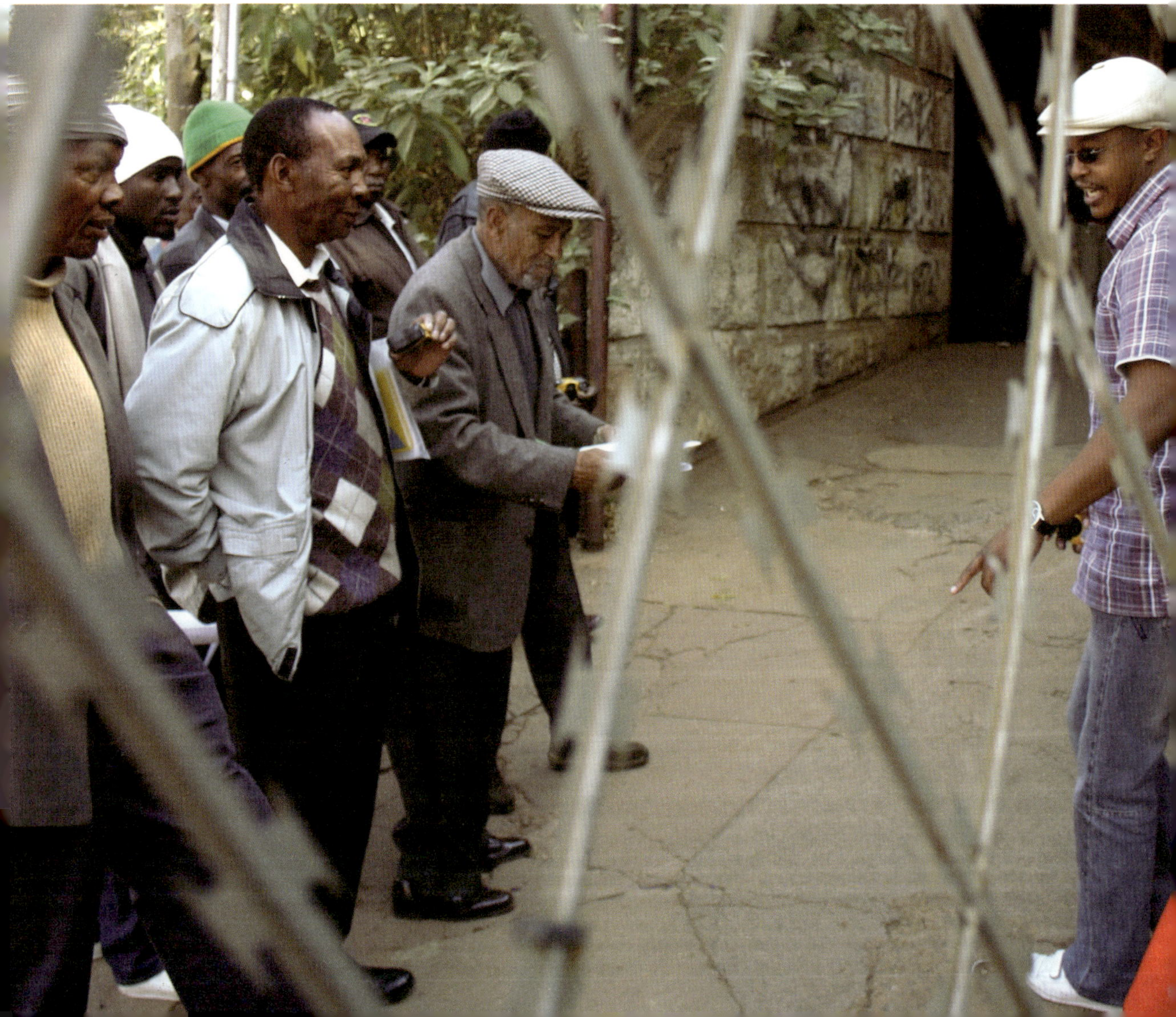

EDWARD SONNYBOY BHENGU

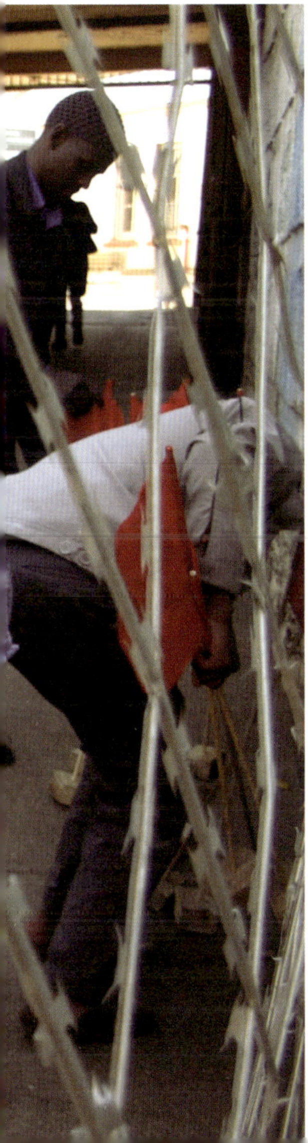

Best Memory

This was when I was detained in 1963 under the Detention Without Trial Act. It was after the passing of the Sobukwe clause in Parliament. We were arrested for belonging to the terrorist organisation *uPoqo*, which was the military wing of the PAC. We were detained at Number Four under the 90 days Detention Act and later the 180 days Detention Act. Our defence attorney was a young man now known as Justice Arthur Chaskalson. Most of the comrades who were in with us were sad and gloomy because they did not know whether they would be convicted or not. I was named minister of entertainment because I used to dance and do some acting. I was entertaining. I used to crack jokes and I was also the instructor of physical training and kept my inmates very happy. I used to sing and organise others to come up on stage and showcase their talents. We did not feel pain, those were our full moments. I used to read the newspaper to keep abreast with events internationally. We used to call the name of Mr Hammarskjold, he was an important person. He was the international figure in the United Nations. We would all call his name saying "*Woza* (come) Hammarskjold, come and liberate us from the *Boer* regime."

Worst Memory

It was on the Thursday before Good Friday in the early 1960s. The magistrate at the Bantu Affairs Court found us guilty of contravening the Communist Act of 1955. We were a group of 144 members of the PAC of Azania. We had two members of our group as spokesmen, namely Joe Thloloe who was 16 years old and a schoolboy, and Mathew Nkoane, a journalist who was with the *Golden City Post*. The magistrate asked us to plead in mitigation before passing sentence. Joe Thloloe was the first to speak. He said we are not going to plead for mercy or mitigation because we are under no more obligations whatsoever to obey the rules of the white man in this country of ours because we do not take part in the making of the laws of the country. The second spokesman, Mathew Nkoane, said, "Mr Magistrate, 2000 years ago on this day, Jesus Christ stood trial before his oppressors. He said that he was not going to plead for mercy because his cause was a just one. So Mr Magistrate you can also pass the sentence of crucifixion because our cause is a just one."

In unison we all sang our national anthem, *Nkosi Sikilel' iAfrika* followed by *Izwe lethu* (Forward to independence, forward to independence now. Tomorrow, the united states of Africa.)

The sentence was passed by the magistrate who found us guilty of contravening the Suppression of Communism Act of 1955. He sentenced us to three years imprisonment with hard labour.

NAPOLEON MAZABANE LETSOKO

Best Memory

When I was taking photographs of the places I was instructed to bomb as part of the workshop process, memories that Number Four was a hell place, came into my mind. This is a place that is meant to break one's soul, to regret why one became a member of a political organisation. In the same breadth, it made me laugh. This is the place that was made to crush us – morally, physically and otherwise. Even when a person is going down into the ground, there is time to laugh. As I was taking the photographs, it made me realise I am a free man now and it makes me to laugh. It made me realise that we have reconciled with the oppressors and we are subjects of the same country, regardless of if we are white, black, members of the PAC or not.

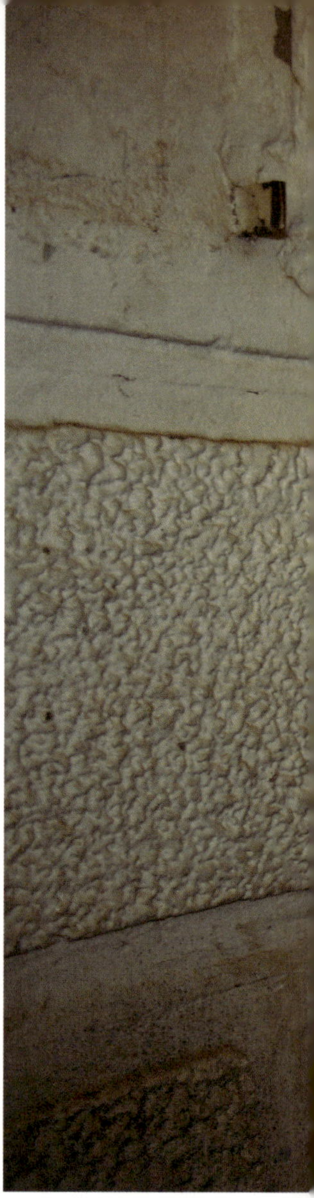

Worst Memory

Coming out of the reception area, on the right, was a huge wall built vertically inside the prison. You only come to see it as you come out of the exit door of the reception area. Having noticed these huge walls built out of rocks, I saw that we had no chance of escape and my soul was at the lowest ebb. We the prisoners at this point were on the way to our cells.

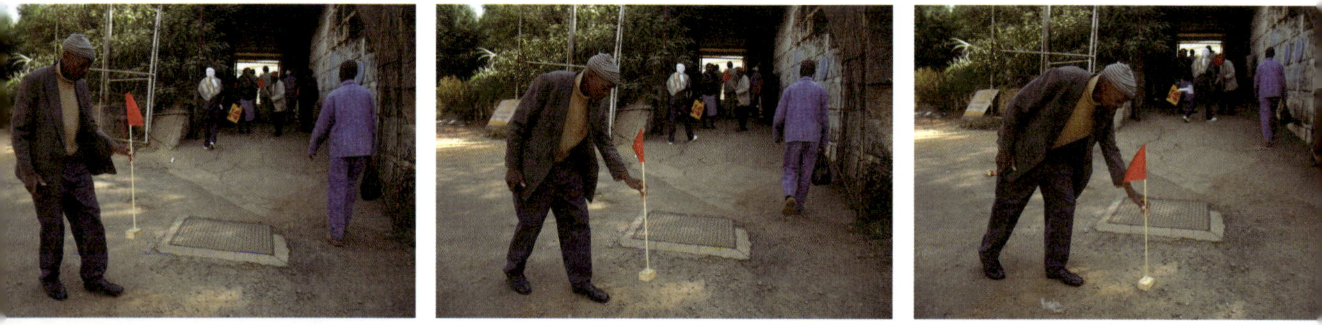

NAPOLEON PLANTING HIS FLAG OUTSIDE THE FORT ENTRANCE

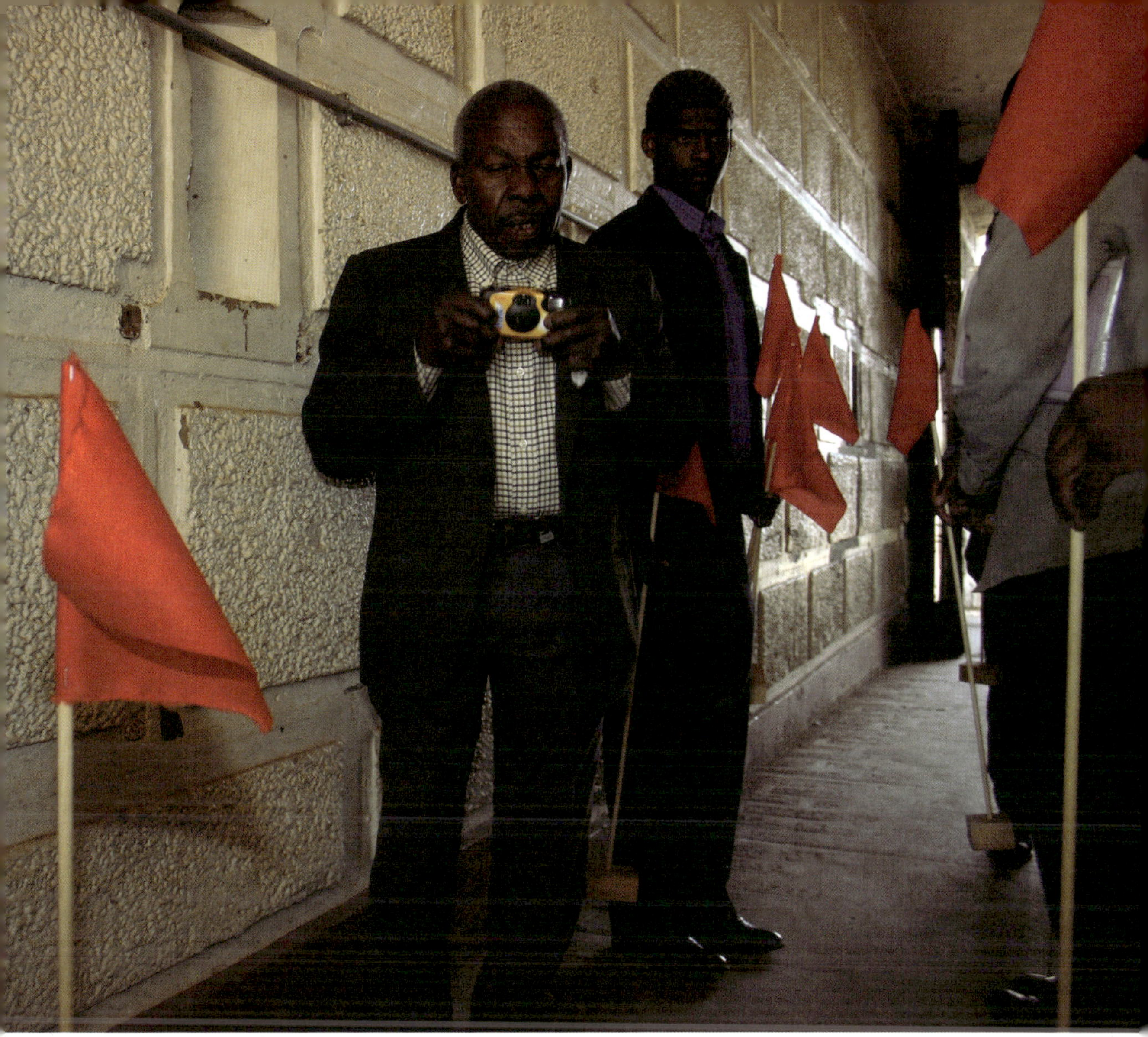

MEHLOKAZULU LUKHELE

MEHLOKAZULU LUKHELE

Best Memory

I remember my comrades and how we used to sing the song *Mabawuyeke umhlaba wethu* and *of course Nkosi Sikelel' iAfrika.* One of our comrades, Madingoane, had a beautiful voice. We were moved whenever we sang these songs.

Worst Memory

I remember getting a letter while I was in Number Four telling me my mother was no more. I cried so much but the others comforted me.

MABANA RAYMOND NENE

My memory of prison is hell. The Fort itself was just not a good experience, from the reception to the cells. I did not have any personal bad encounter in prison except when one guy was pulling me into his cell and I was resisting and helped by my cellmates. And that is where I placed my flag. While in Number Four, the most things that I missed were my father and my girl friend.

My only good memories or moments were when I received a visitor. They used to bring me food and tobacco and money.

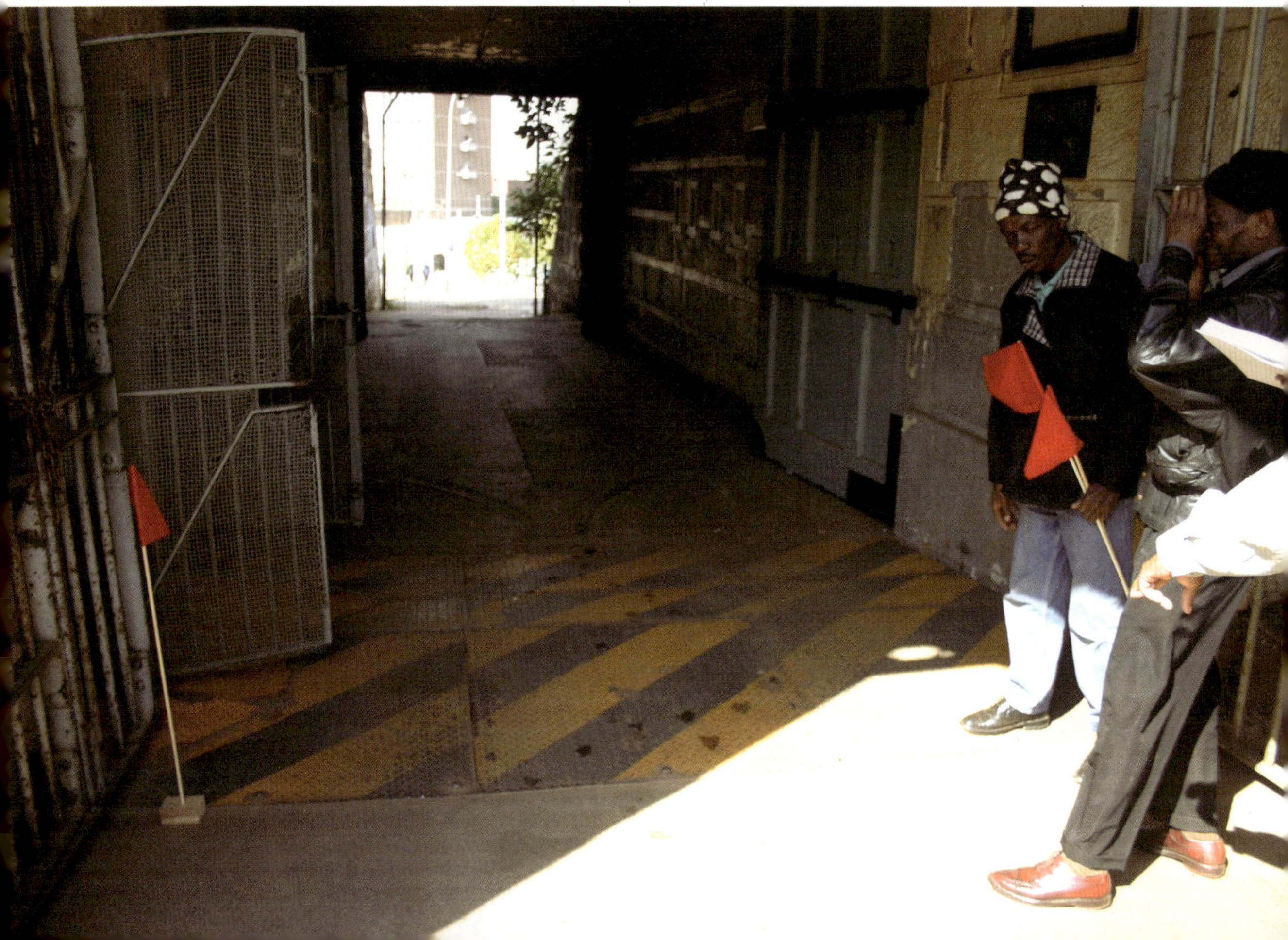

SIPHO VICTOR NKABINDE

The good thing that I learnt is that as a group we would deal with anything that came our way and fight it together without any fear. It was also a good experience to see when someone has nothing that we can be taken care of by those who had something. That is when life became worth living.

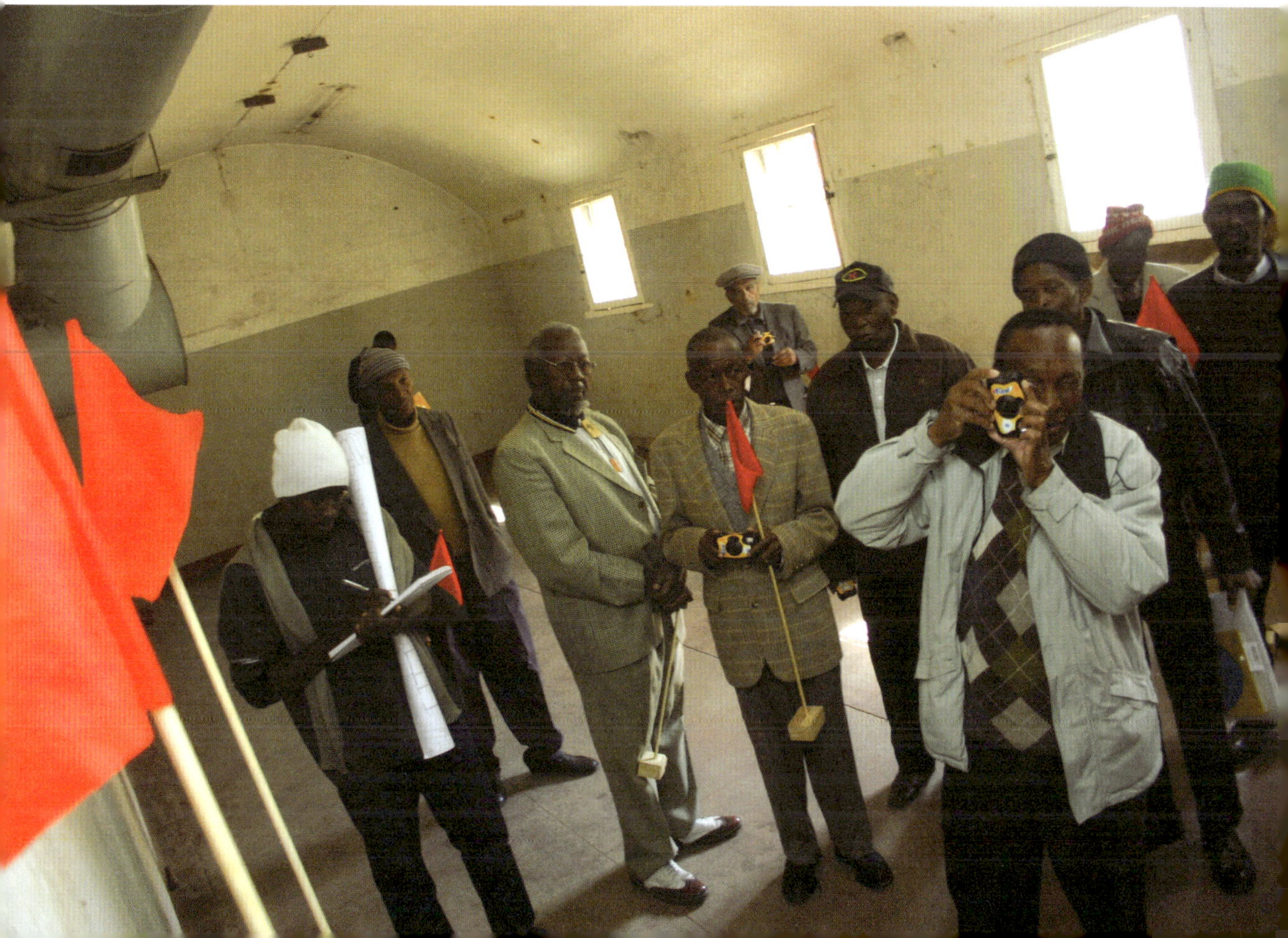

KHAYA ISAAC MAGI

When coming to these workshops we were asked to place flags on places that had the most impact and memories of our time here. I placed the first flag at the reception area because for me this was a very outrageous place when I first saw it. There were so many people in one place either waiting to be booked in or waiting to be taken to court. What I found really appalling was that there were open toilets in the same room where we were expected to relieve ourselves in front of everyone.

There was a second room that you were taken to after reception where your fingerprints were taken and your belongings kept. Here we were grouped in fours while waiting for the *kwela-kwela* to take you to court. This is where I placed my second flag because I remember a particular incident when I was pushed by another prisoner using a needle-like object. This almost landed me in trouble because in this room you were not supposed to make any noise, so I stood up to report this to a nearby officer but he just ignored me.

I placed the third flag at the visitor's centre inside Number Four. This was a very painful experience for me because we were placed in a crowded room where you had about 20 prisoners at a time all waiting for their visitors. Prisoners were standing very close to each other and so as soon as the bell rang, you had to start shouting, communicating with your visitor who was about two to three metres away from you and was separated from you by a partition. This was very hard for me because my mother had a hearing problem and she did not have 20/20 vision. We were only allowed to spend about five minutes with our visitors and were limited to one visit per week. If your visitor brought you some goodies like food or cigarettes, it was common that you would not get everything because they would either be stolen or be taken by the bosses inside the cell. It was particularly difficult if you had no homeboys in your cell because you would end up getting nothing.

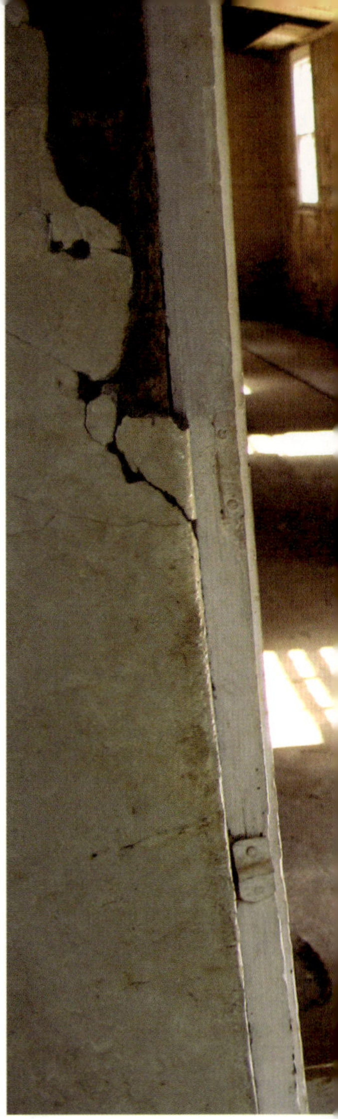

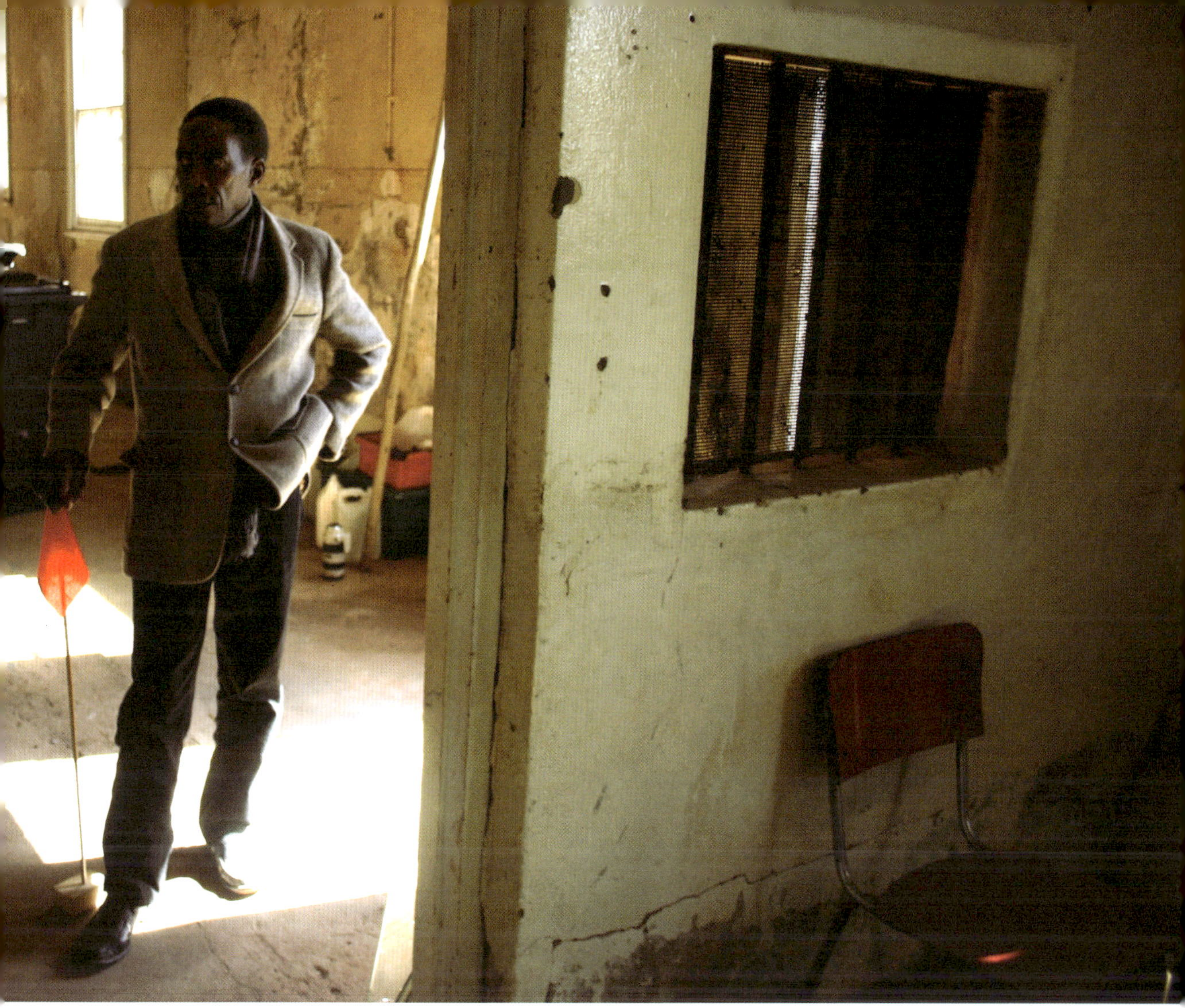

KHAYA ISAAC MAGI

WHITE SESINYI

Best Memory

The wealth and quality of political lectures that we received from Mr Zephania Mothopeng popularly known as the 'Lion of Azania', counts as the happiest recollection I have of Number Four. He was later elected President of the PAC.

Worst Memory

I witnessed for the first time in my life someone sentenced to death. I just wondered how he felt and how it affected him mentally.

JOHN MOEKETSI MAHAPA

Best Memory

One of my happiest memories is in the isolation cells where I was kept with Themba Selby Ngedane. I remember this area because it was this area where I enjoyed communicating messages with my colleagues who were in the communal cell down the stairs. Another positive memory is when every morning when the wake-up bell rang, we would all get out of our bed and sing the national anthem and this would spread to the other cells. The same would happen at night when the sleeping bell sounded. This was a great moment in the prison. The walls of the prison used to shake with our singing.

Worst Memory

I remember being loaded into the trucks that would take us to court, not knowing what the day had in store for us. We would ask ourselves if we would be convicted and for how long? It was nerve-wracking.

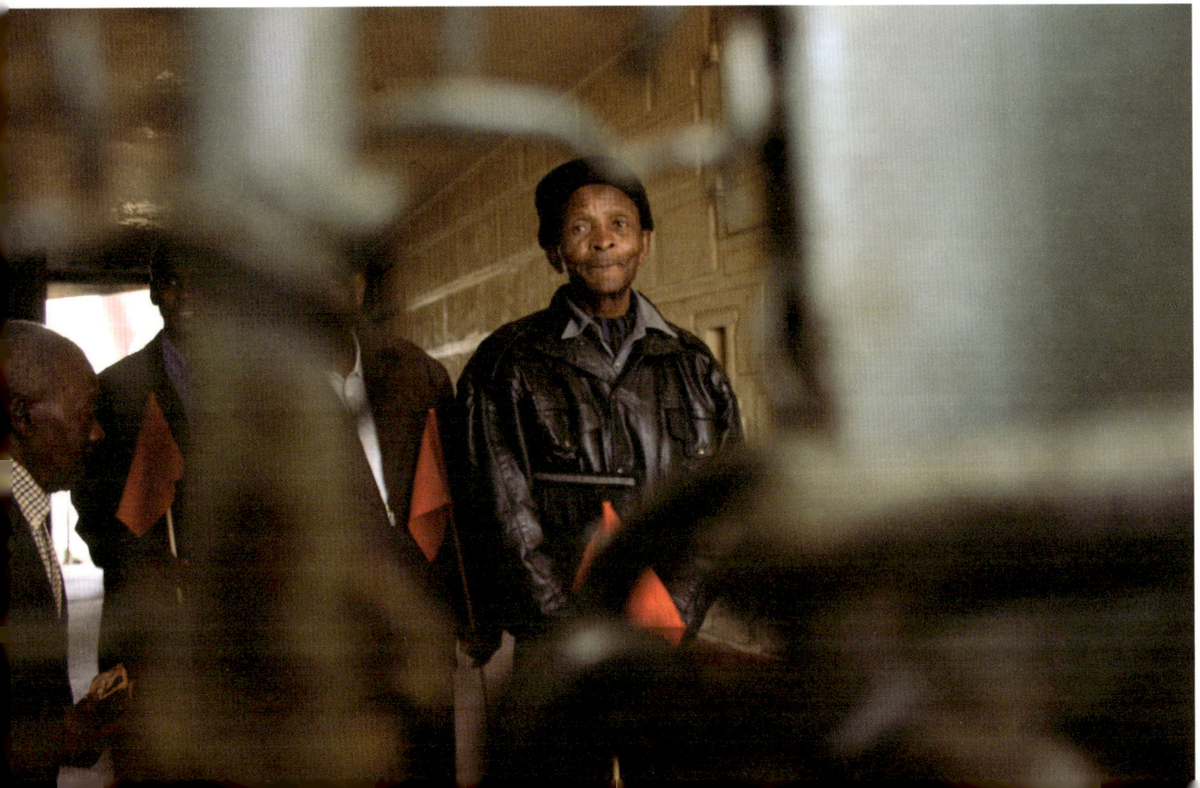

RASELEPE GIDEON NTHELEDI

Best Memory

My happiest memory was when we received visitors who brought food and we all shared the food as communists. It was a struggle to pass messages or to hear what the visitors were saying but at least we got food.

Worst Memory

I placed my other flag at the entrance because I was shocked to see such a big gate when the truck reversed into the Fort. The worst memory was when we were made to squat and stripped naked and then registered before we were led to the cells.

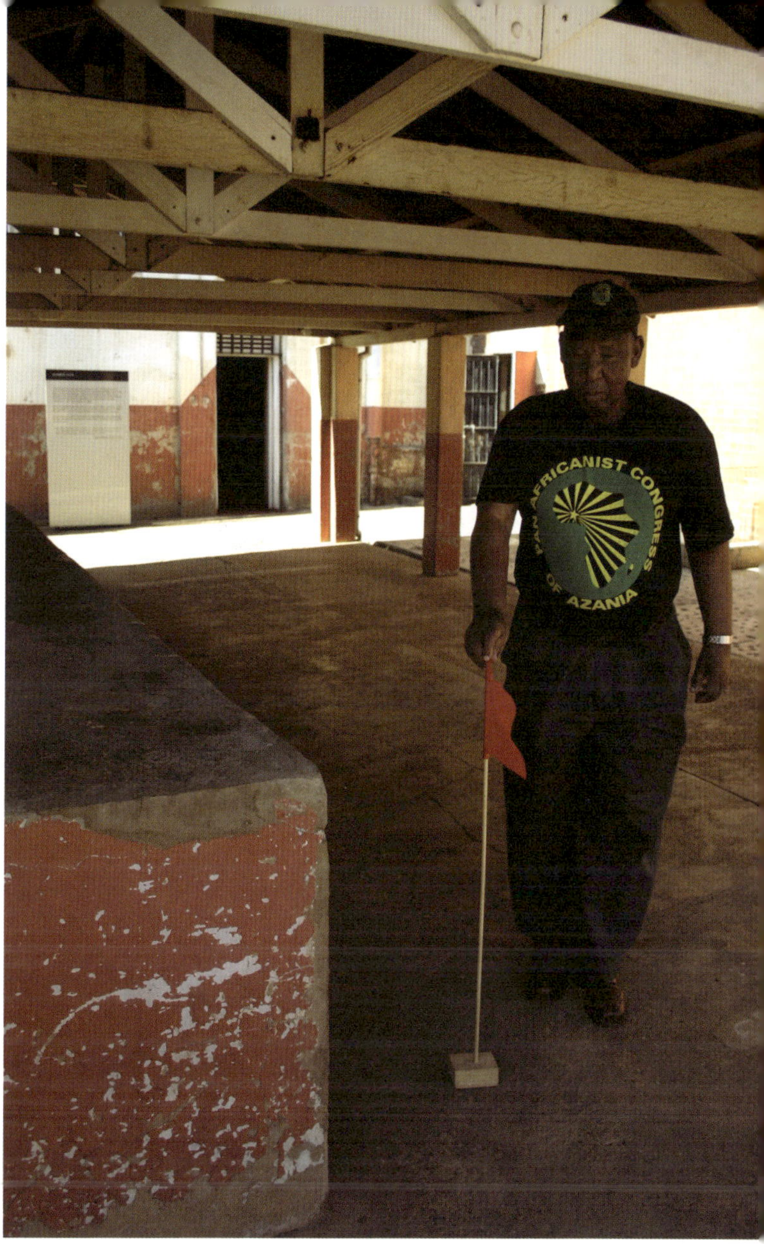

JOSEPH GOGO KHOZA

Best Memory

It was at the Fort when I met fellow Africans from different members of the PAC. I was also excited to meet the leadership, which of course included the 'Prof', Robert Sobukwe.

Worst Memory

My worst memory was when the detailed report of the aftermath of our campaign in Sharpeville came through. The thought of so many unarmed civilians being mowed down by the system made me even more committed to the struggle.

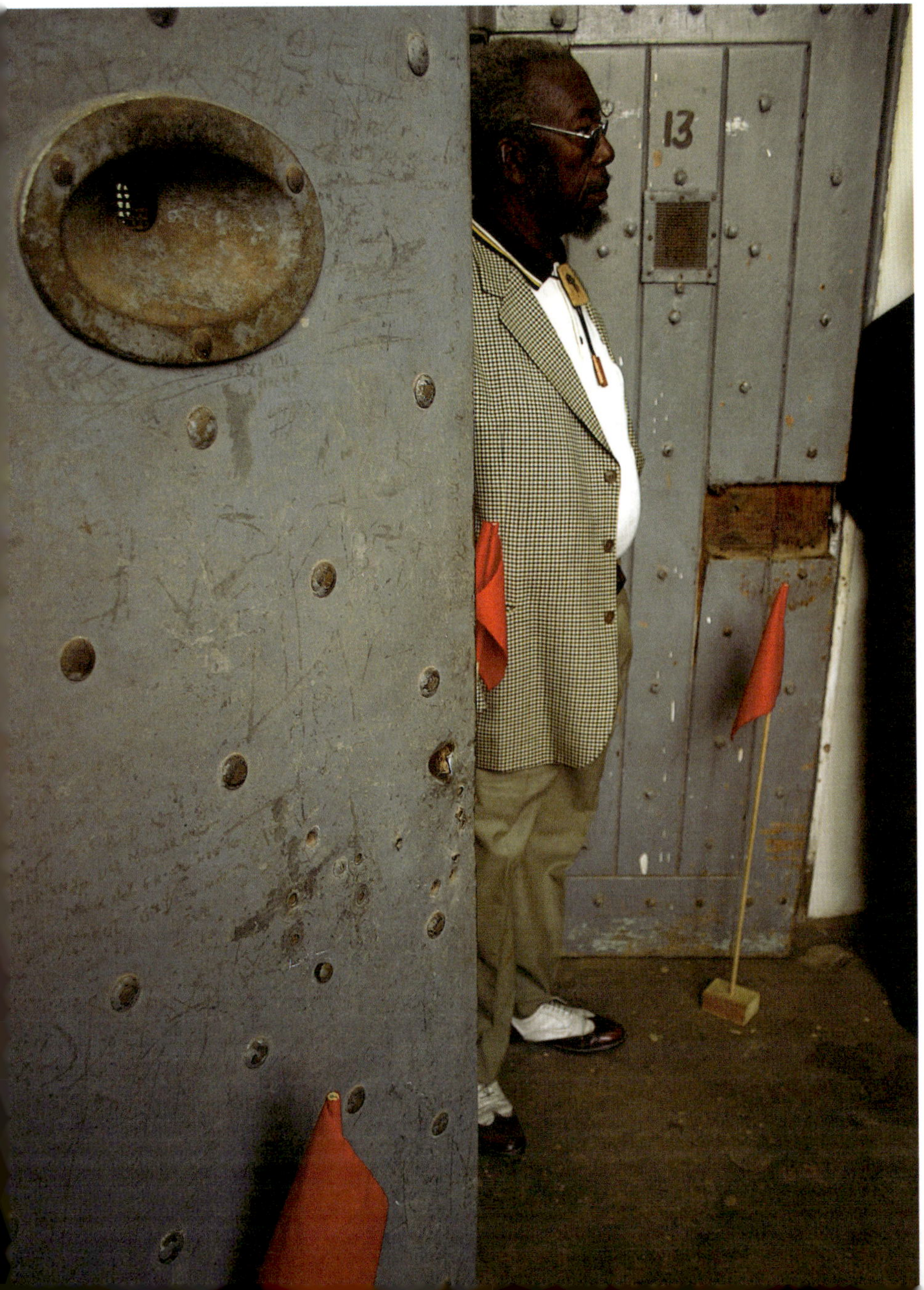

ZOLILE WILLIAM MGWEBA

Best Memory

My best memory was the day that they discovered me in the cell because the authorities thought I was dead. I was hidden by the cell bosses because they wanted to keep me in the cell and do things that the other prisoners could not do. One day a prisoner in the cell asked one of his visitors to report to my family that I was still in prison and not dead as they had been told. Then I went to court and got out of Number Four.

Worst Memory

My worst memory was the first time when I saw a dead person. It was Bheki my friend who was killed trying to save me. The other memory that I cannot forget was at night I was sodomised by the cell boss.

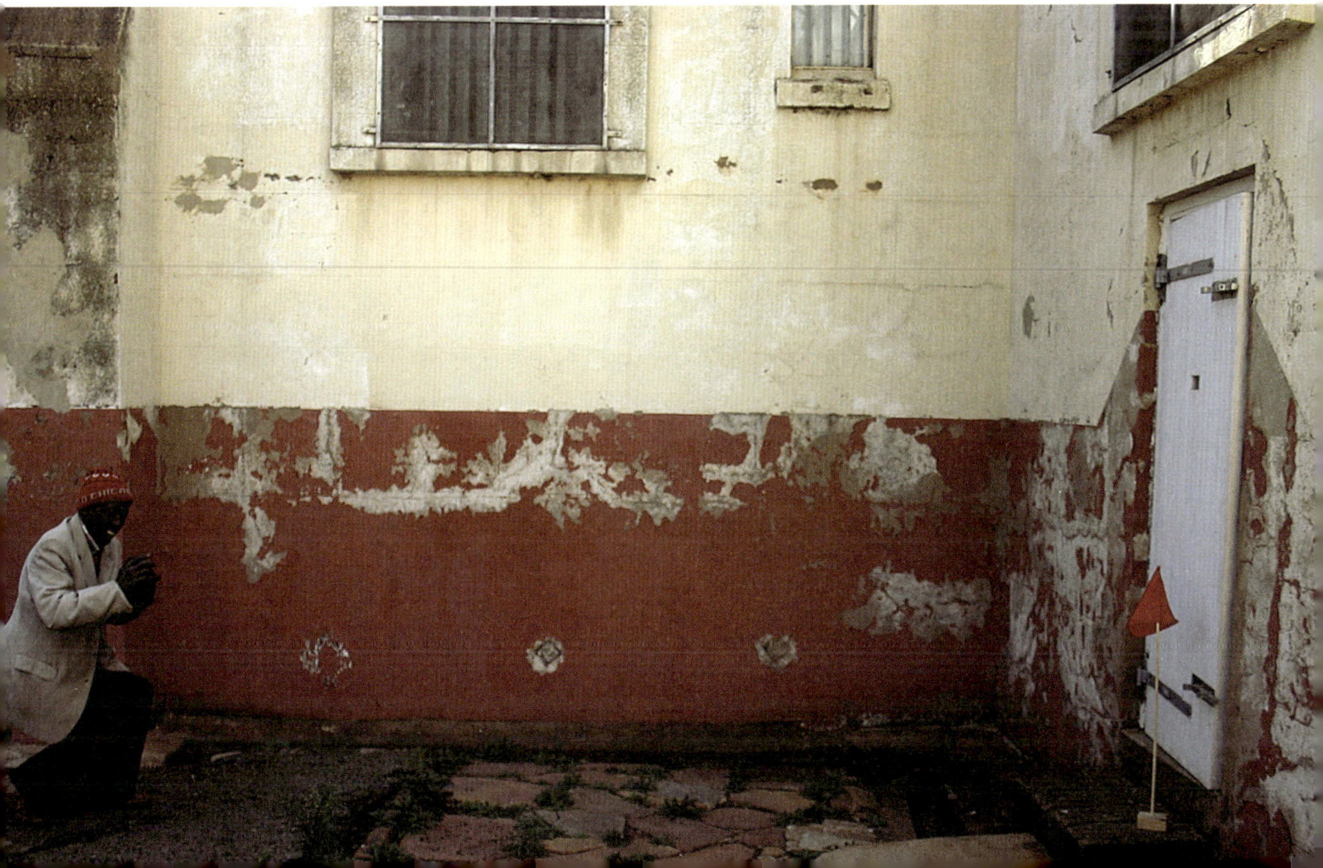

CELL DRAWINGS

Cell geography - the question of how the cells were organized - has been an ongoing area of interest for the curatorial team. The prisoners spent almost all of their time in the cells and the arrangement of these spaces had a massive impact on their experiences and their sense of dignity. Research to date has shown that the cell geography was shaped both by the prison authorities and the prisoners themselves. The authorities had to respond to the challenges of increasing numbers of prisoners and massive overcrowding in the jails, particularly in the 1950s and 1960s when apartheid was at its height. The authorities also had to respond to the challenge of dealing with political and 'common' prisoners in one space.

Once the cells were locked each night, the geography of the cells was determined by the gangs that operated in the prison, particularly in Number Four, where gang leaders took complete control.

In the workshops, we asked the former prisoners to draw the layout of their cells as a way of exploring the power relations in the prison and explaining how the spaces they were forced into affected their dignity. It is interesting that some of the prisoners also chose to draw other areas of the jail in response to this exercise. Some chose to draw the whole experience, from registration of prisoners until they entered the cells.

All of the drawings that resulted are a valuable archive of the intersection of personal and official records of prison life.

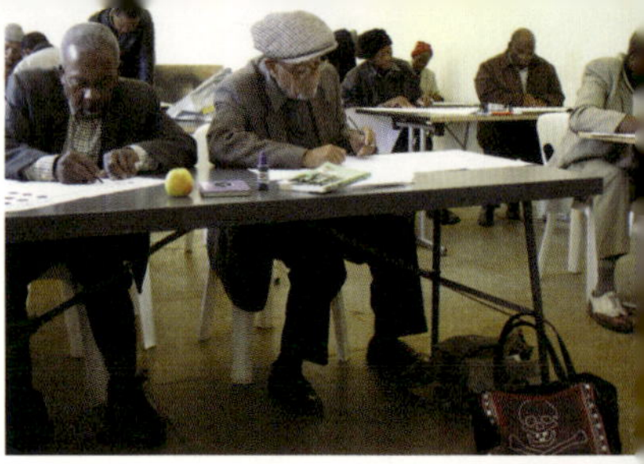

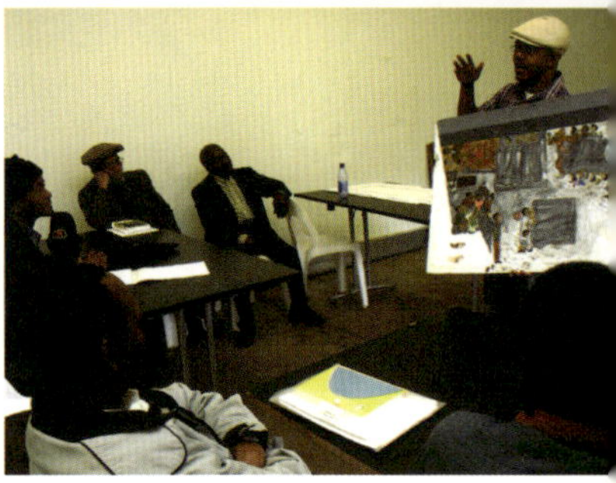

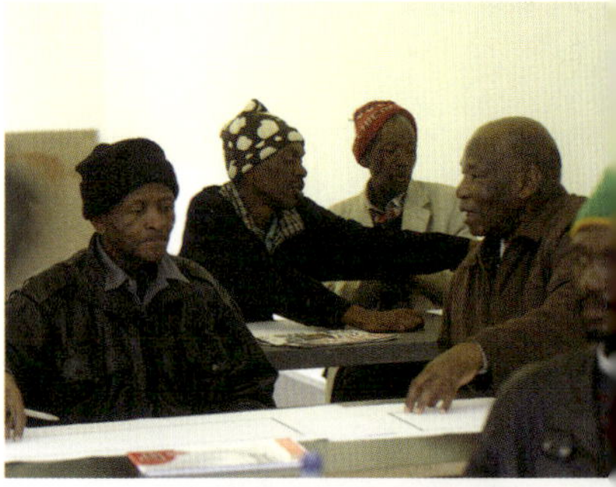

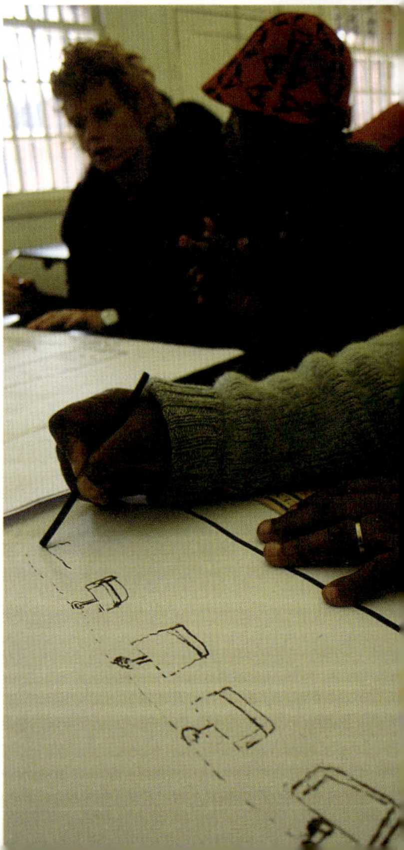

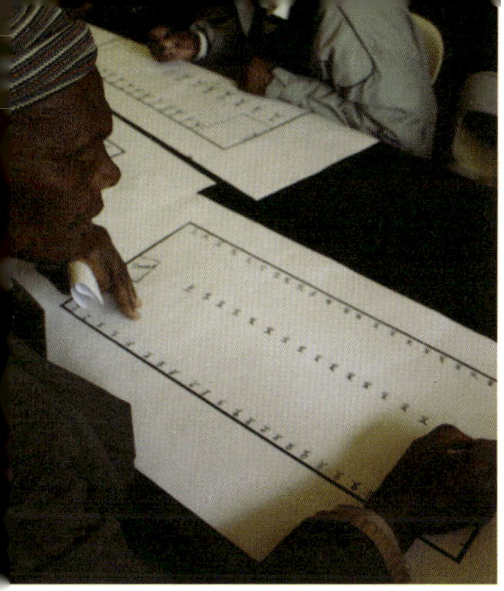

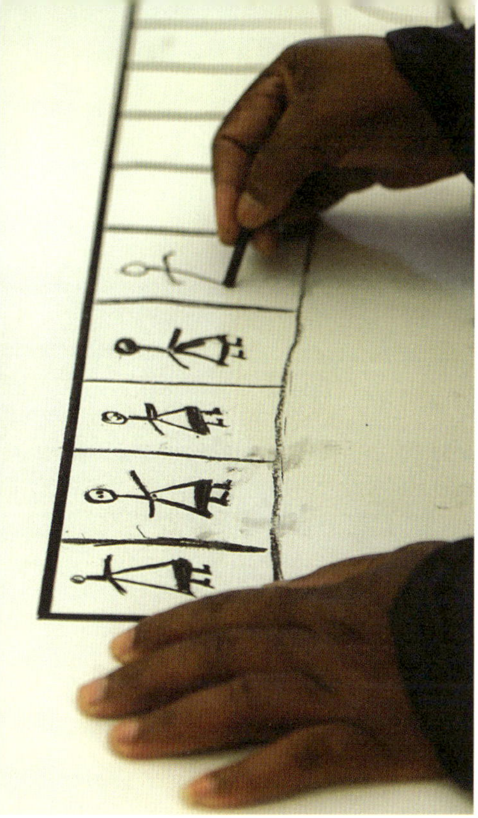

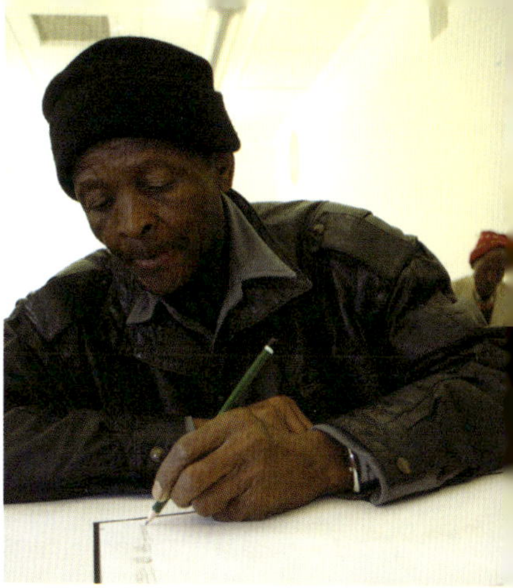

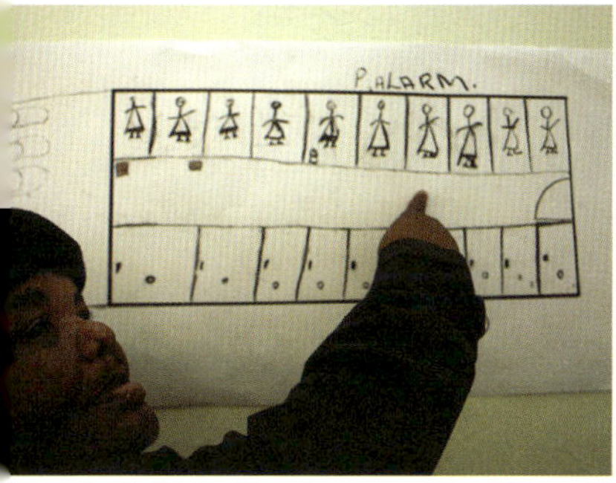
P.ALARM.

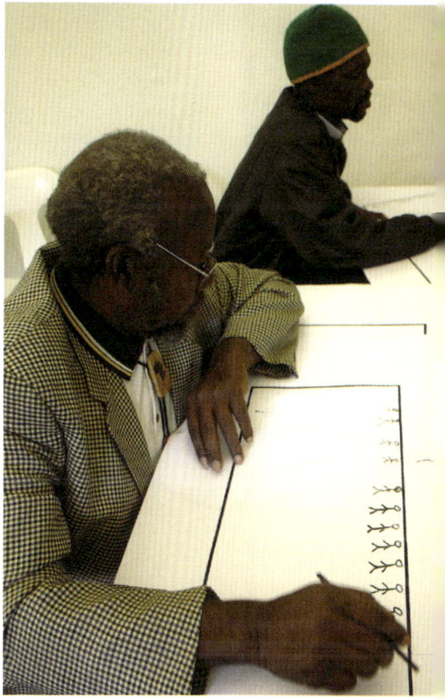

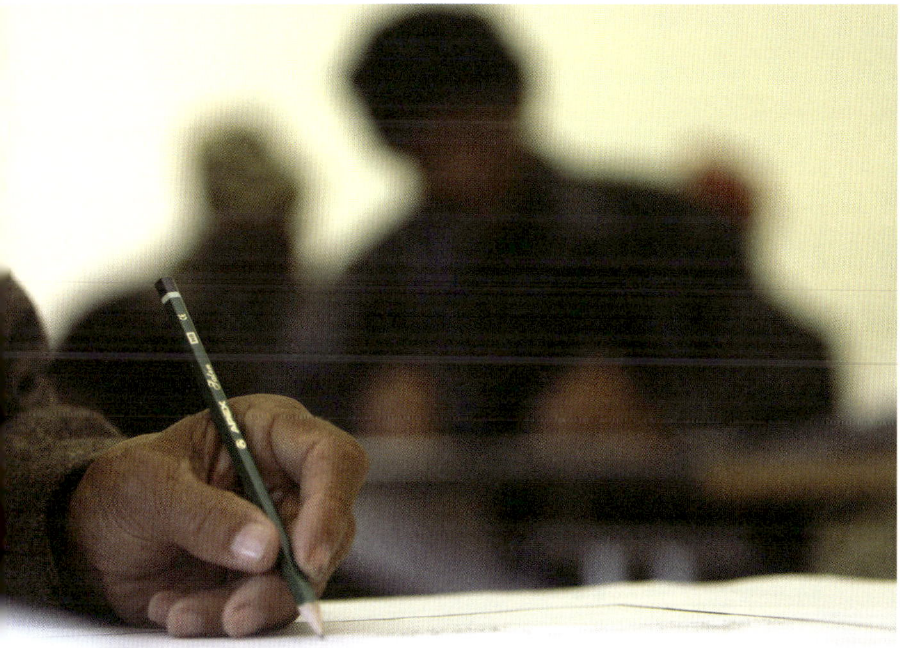

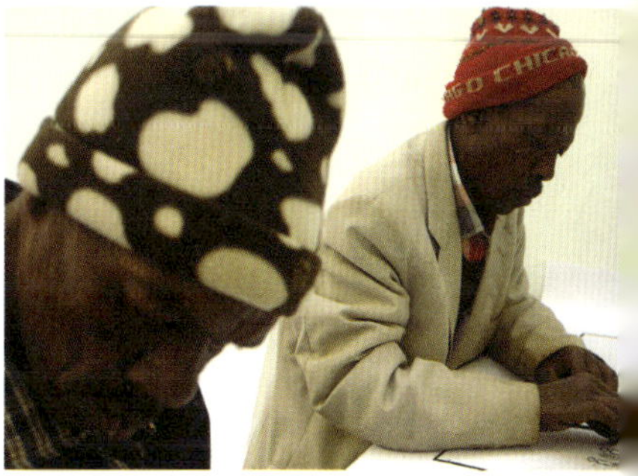

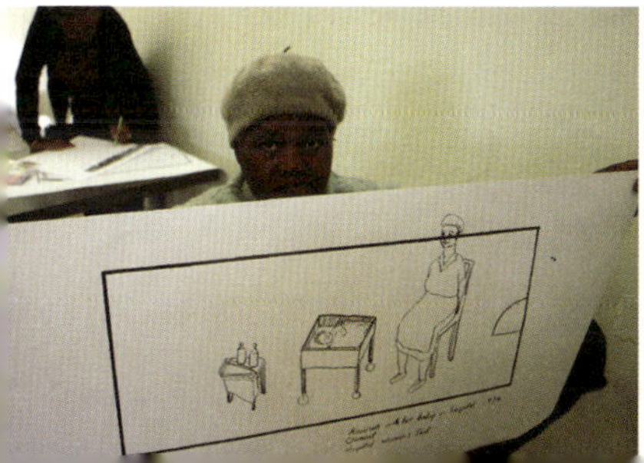

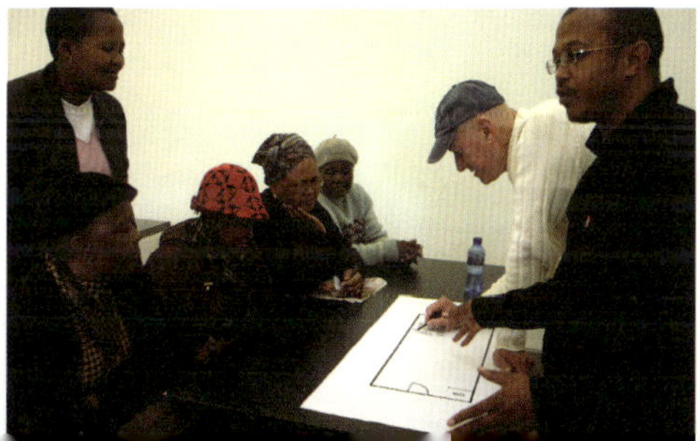

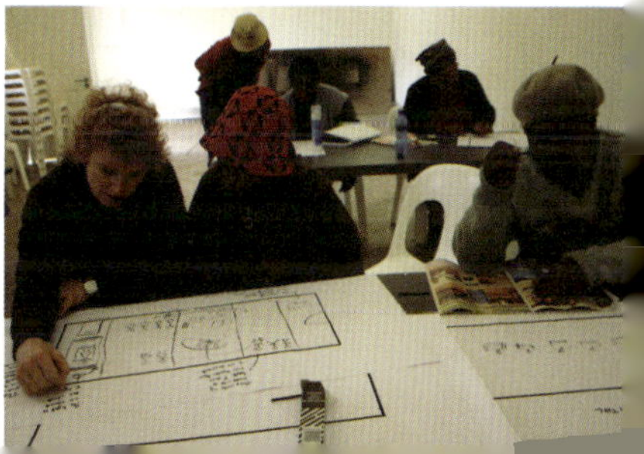

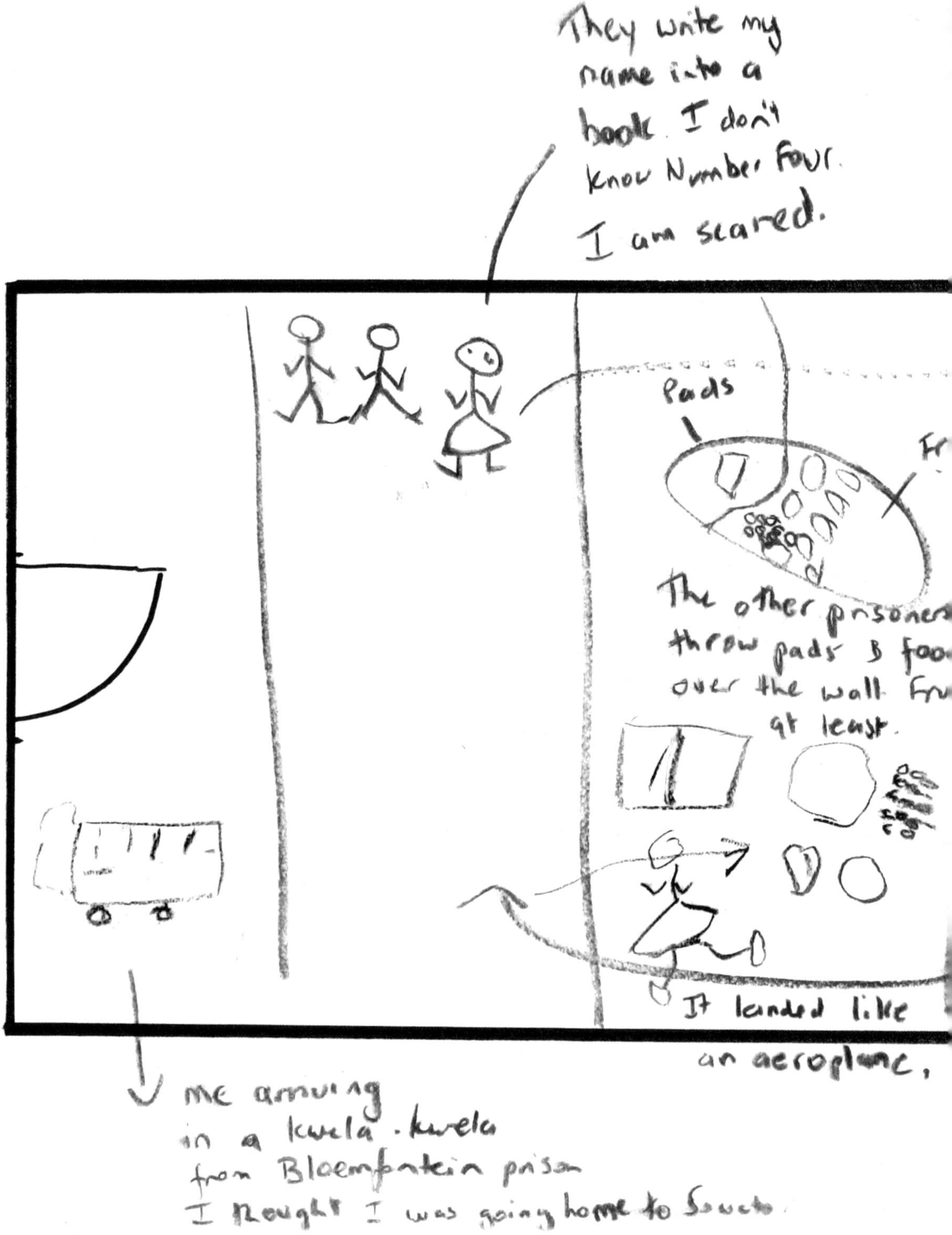
They write my name into a book. I don't know Number Four. I am scared.
Pads
The other prisoner
throw pads & foo
over the wall. Fr
at least.
It landed like an aeroplane,
me arriving in a kwela-kwela from Bloemfontein prison
I thought I was going home to Soweto.

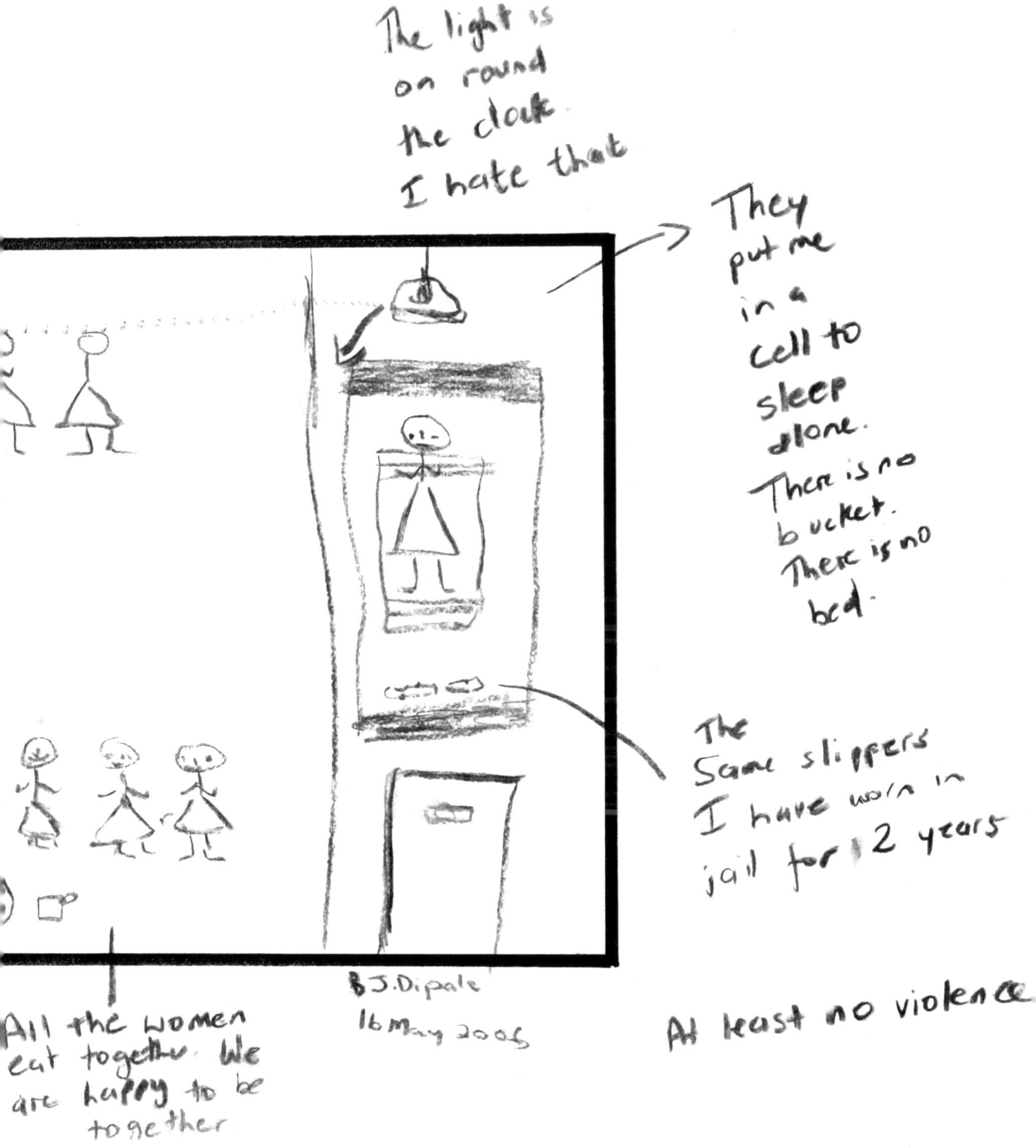

JOYCE DIPHALE'S CELL DRAWING

083-084

TIKIE MTHIMUNYE

This drawing illustrates the cells in which we were kept. In the front, there was a wardress and I was kept in a section one. My cell had a mat and a blanket and we would sleep on the floor on the mat provided. They would count us in the morning. Each person would stand in front of her cell door. From the entrance, there was a passage and at the end of the passage there were two showers and three toilets.

Each cell block had 22 or 24 people. It wasn't cramped because we each had our own cell.

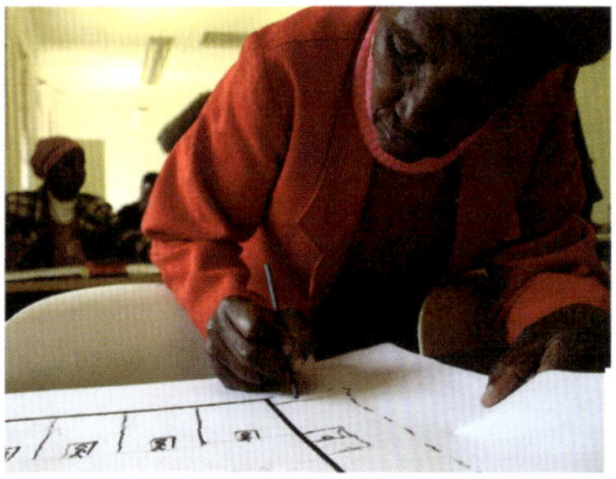

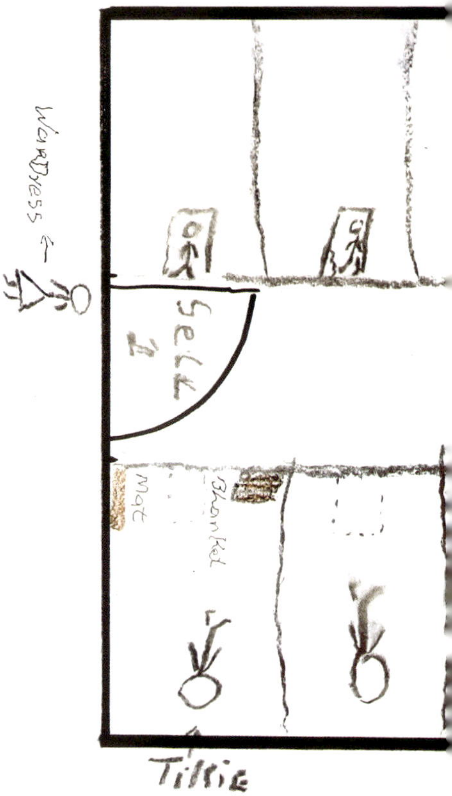

PATRICIA ALARM

This is a drawing of the section one cell. It had two showers and three toilets at the end of it. Each cell was a separate cage where a prisoner slept. The cage was made of metal netting. We had a bucket to use at night. We were given four blankets and three mats to sleep on.

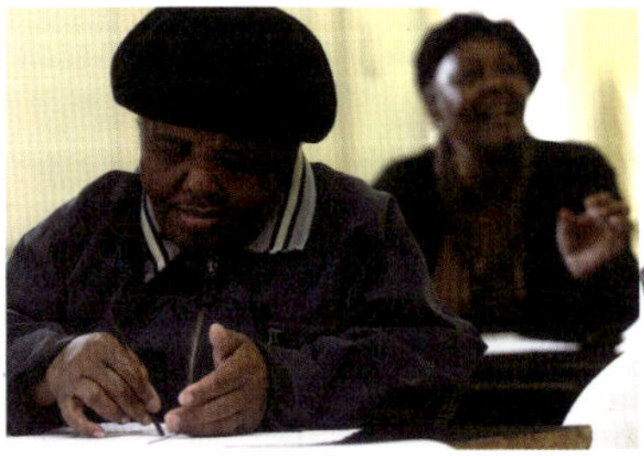

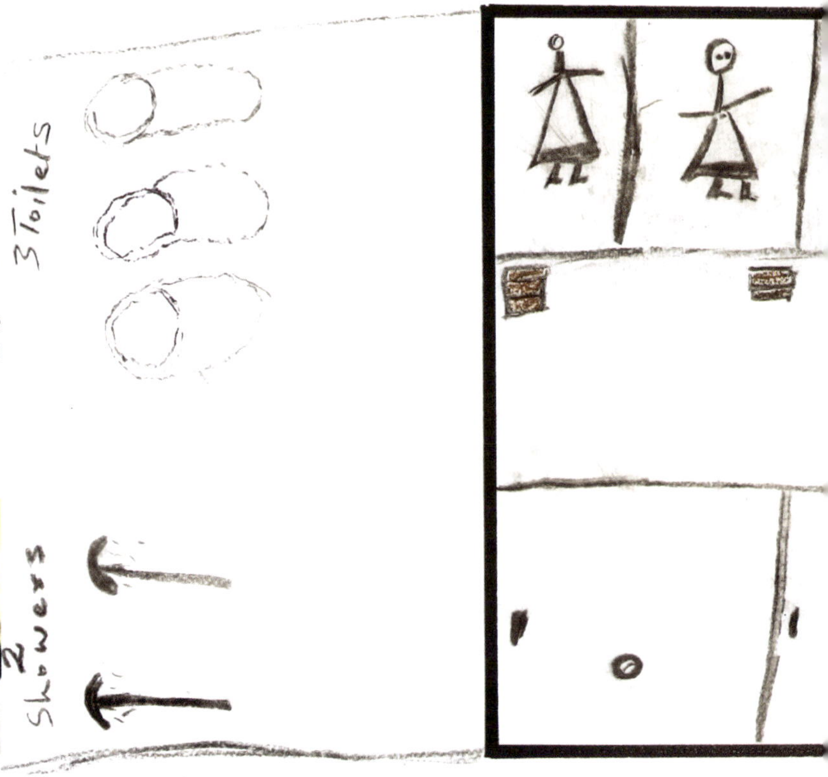

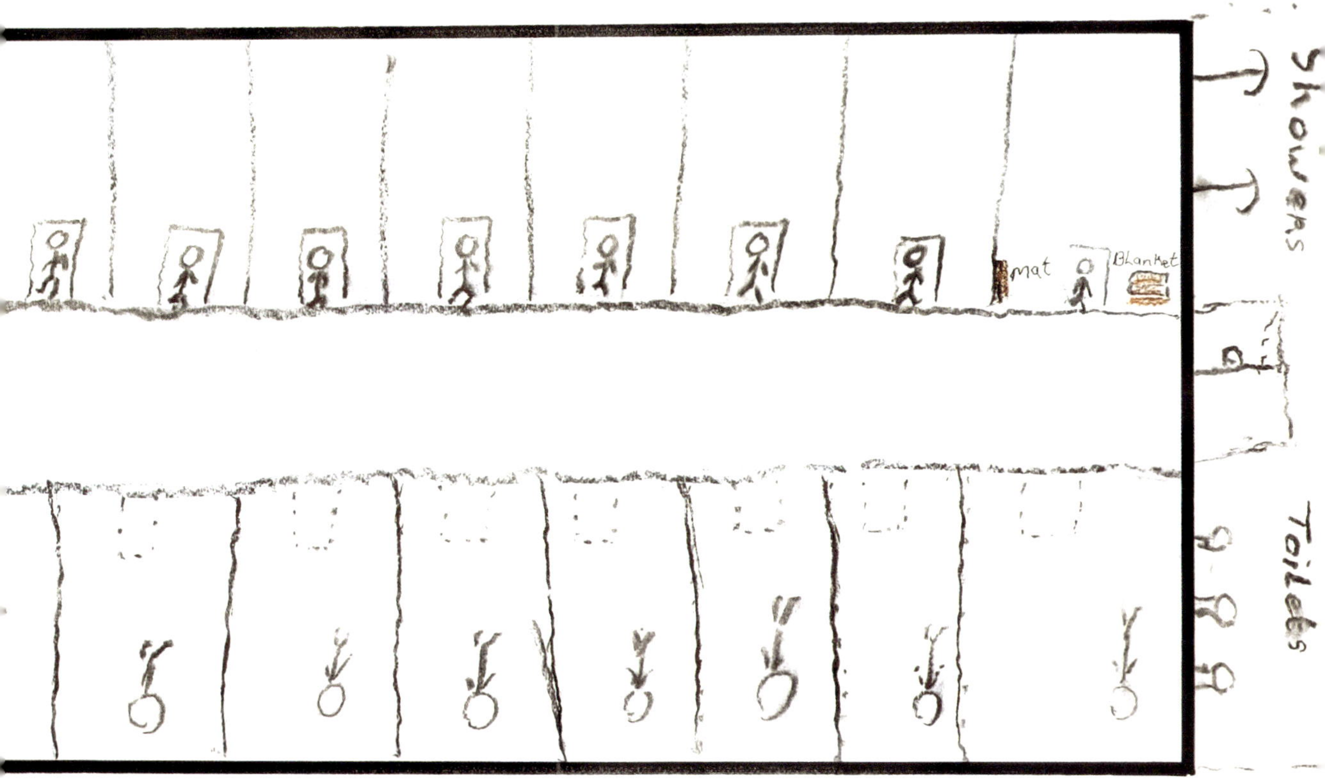

P ALARM.

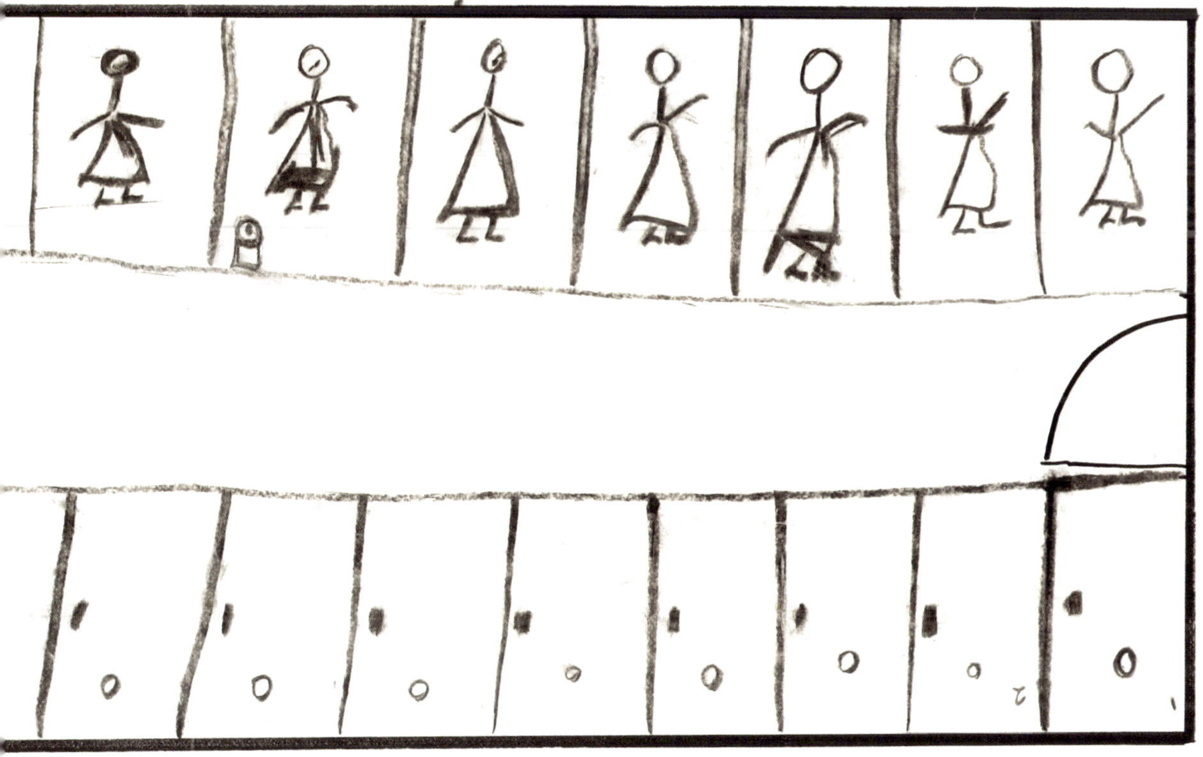

085-
086

ASSIENAH MNISI

This is a drawing of me watching over my sleeping child. His bottle and nappies are on the side table.

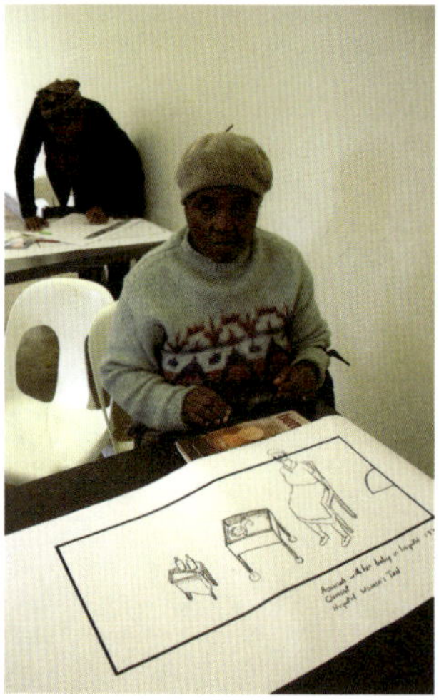

SIBONGILE TSHABALALA

These were the different cells in the 80 section. We would sleep in fours or eights. In the bigger cells there would be 120 prisoners. We had a storeroom where we kept our blankets after nicely folding them.

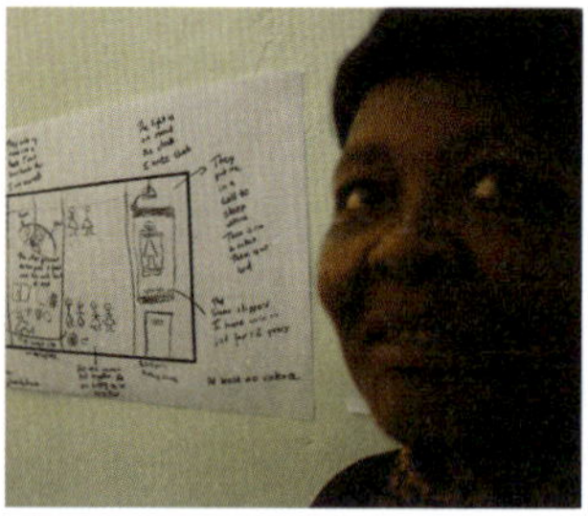

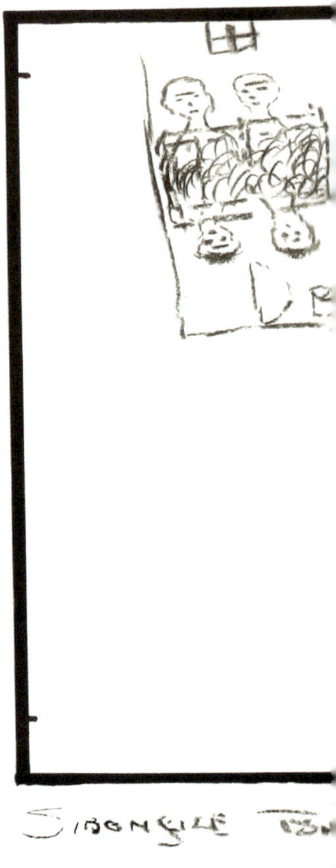

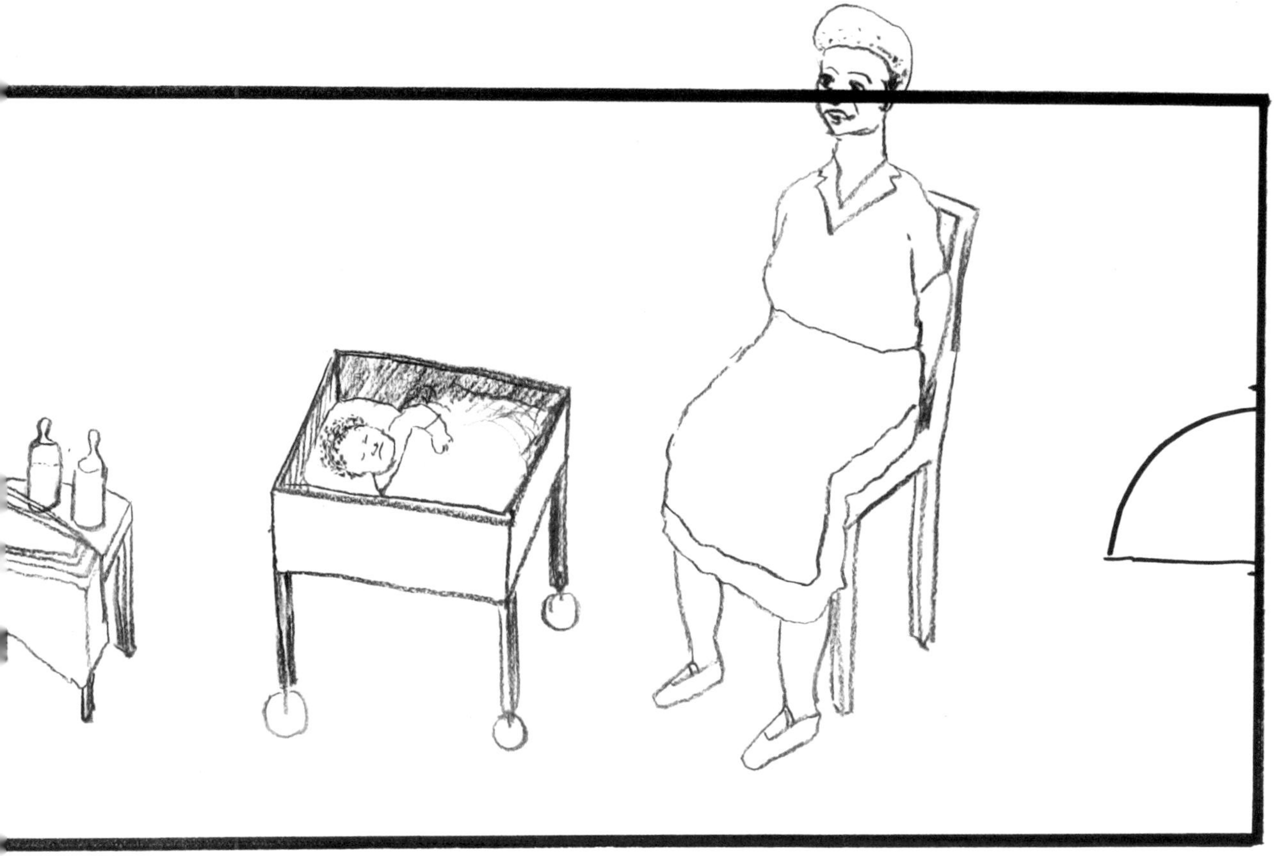

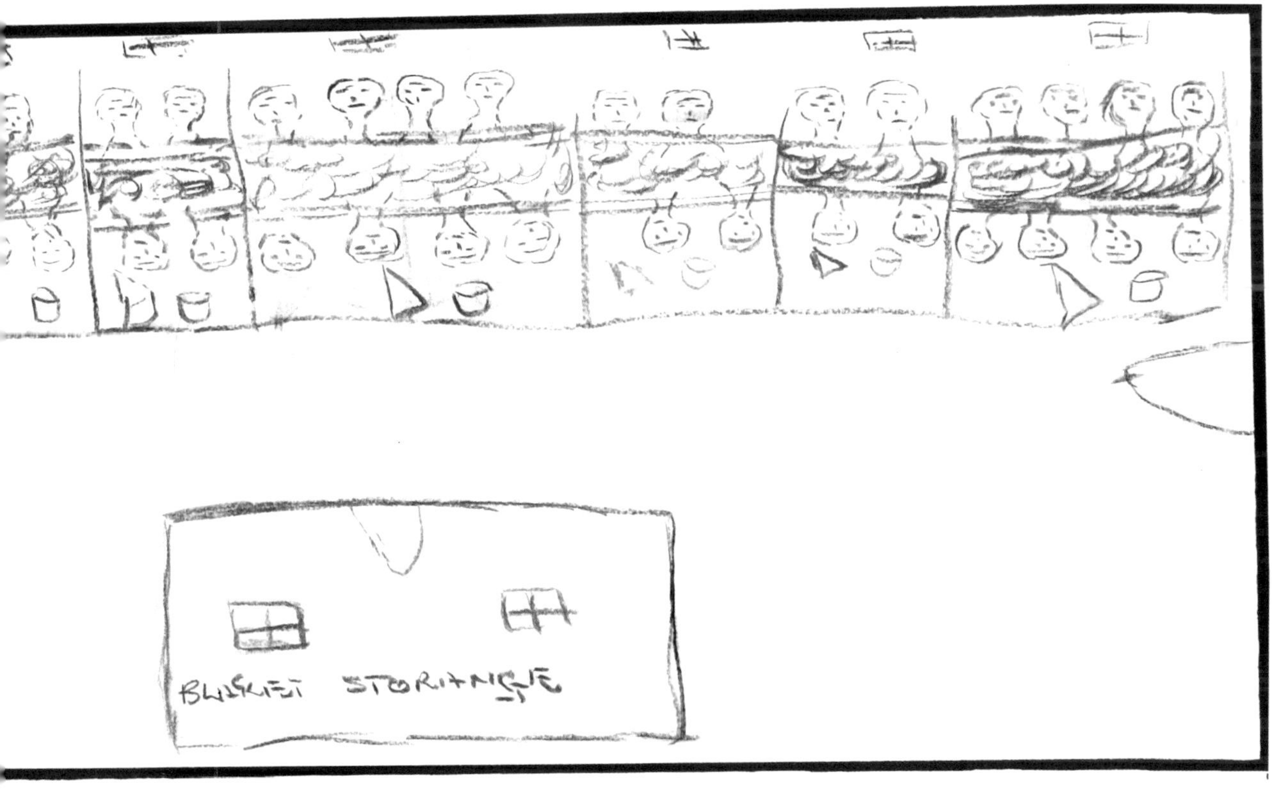
BLANKET STORAGE

087-
088

LILIAN KEAGILE

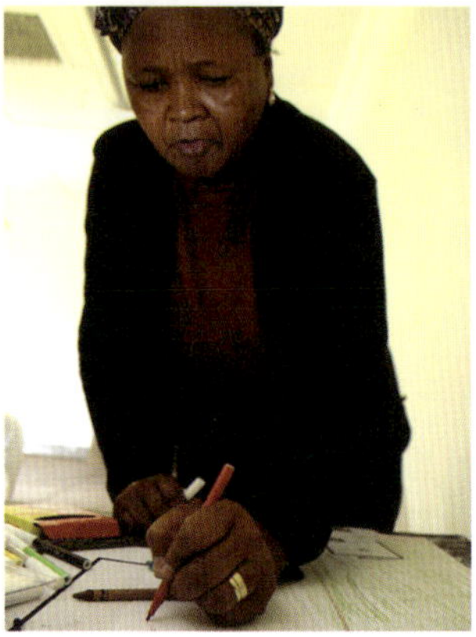

My cell was made of corrugated iron. We call it *mazenke*, which means zinc or steel sheets. It was painted green both inside and outside with a step by the door that was red. Inside I could stretch my arms and touch both sides. In the one corner, there were blankets and a mat. In the other corner there was a nail to hang a plastic bag with food from home. On the other side, I would hang my clothes. Bags were not allowed. Towards the door, there was a bucket with fresh water. Parallel to that in the other corner was a 'piss pot' to be used as a toilet.

If there was a storm thunder and lightning would strike. It felt like the lightning was striking the cell itself. It felt like I would die at any time. For those 15 minutes, I was filled with fear and trauma. Then in the heat of summer time I would bake inside that cell. I would be sweating because there was no window. I would literally bake. One day, I requested that I should be allowed to sit outside or leave the door open. It was like I was asking for God himself to come. It was never allowed. In winter, the cell was like being in a fridge. It was extremely cold. Those were conditions I lived under.

YVONNE NTONTO MHLAULI

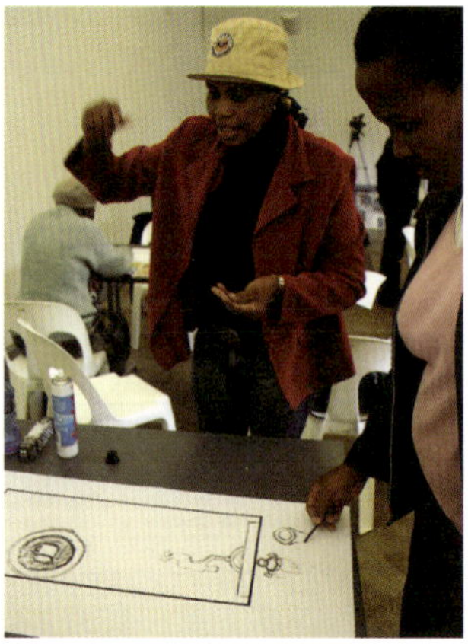

In my drawing you will see how I used to sit on top of the mat and the rolled blankets when the doors were closed in the late afternoons when I was in isolation. I have also drawn how I used to get my food in the isolation cell. The warders escorted the prisoner who brought food to my cell. Inside you will also see that I have drawn a plate and mug that I was using. You also see a bucket that I used to ease myself. 6411 – the number of the isolation cell where I was held - is very narrow and long and it felt as if I was in a tunnel.

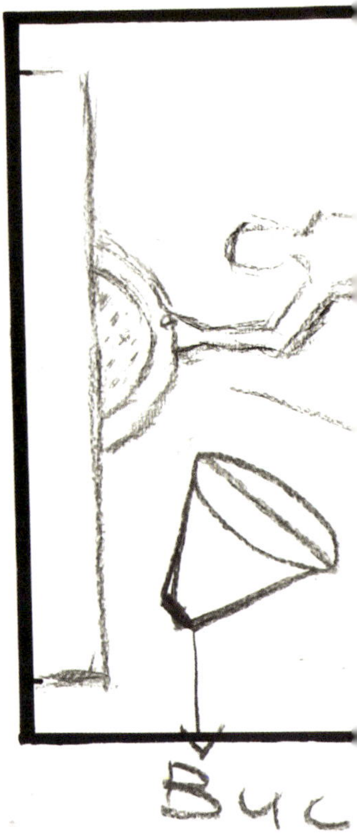

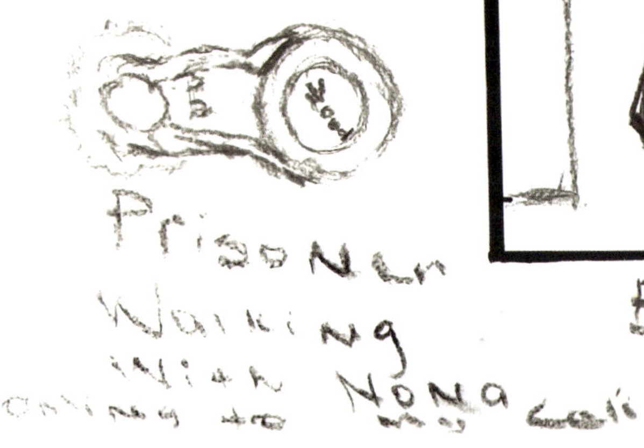

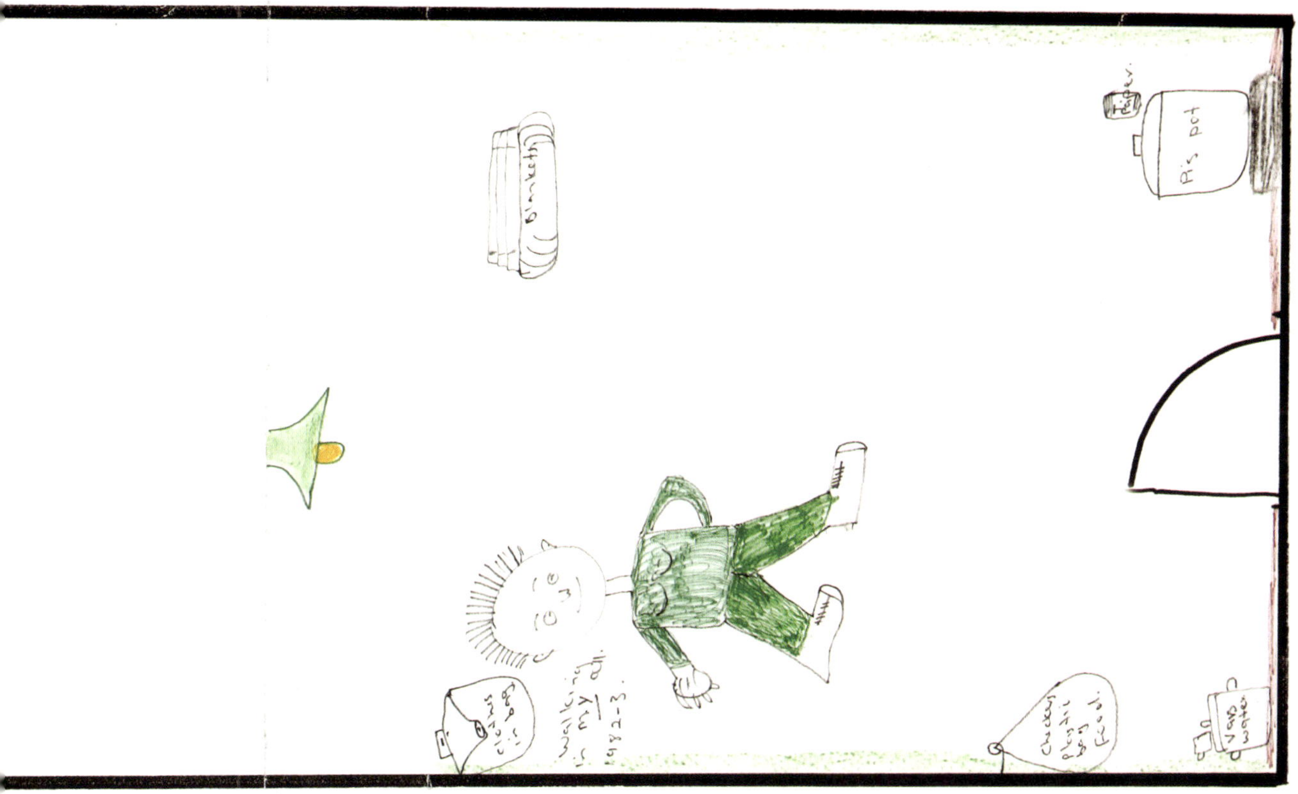
Blankets
Pis pot
clothes in bag
Walking in my cell. 1982-3.
Chicken plastic bag food.

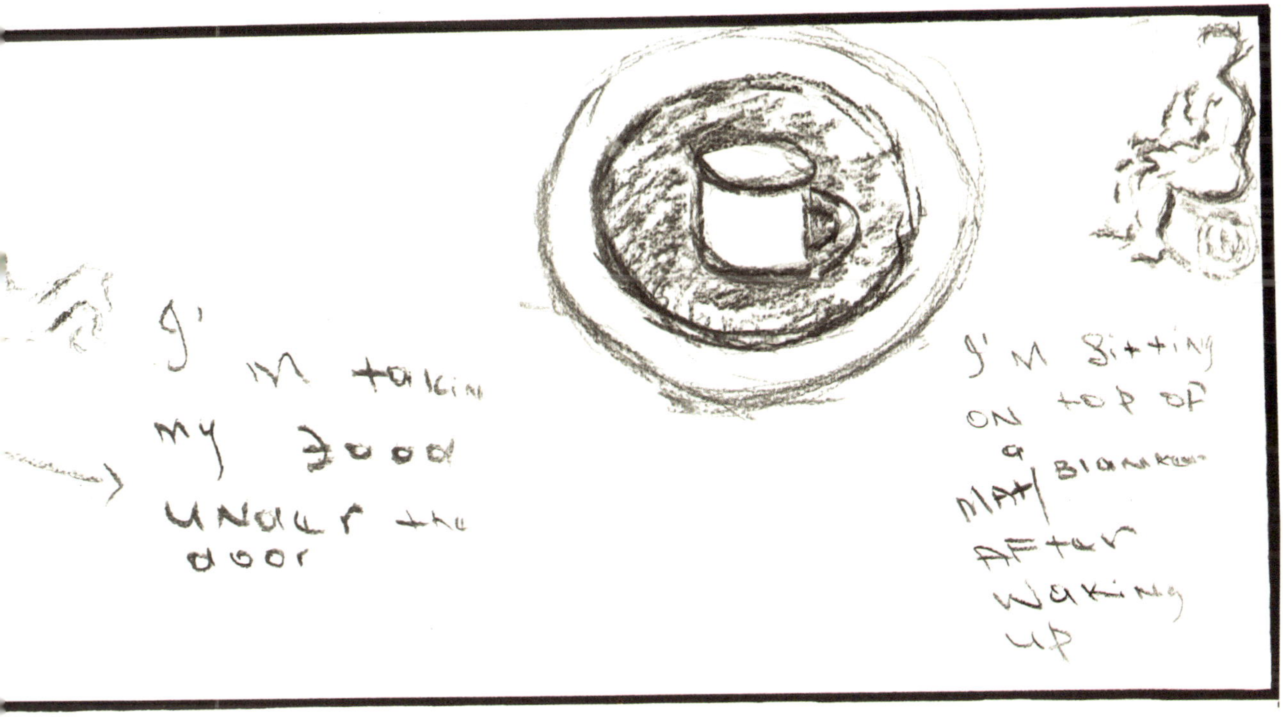
I'M takin my food under the door
I'M sitting on top of a MAT/Blanket After waking up

Yvonne

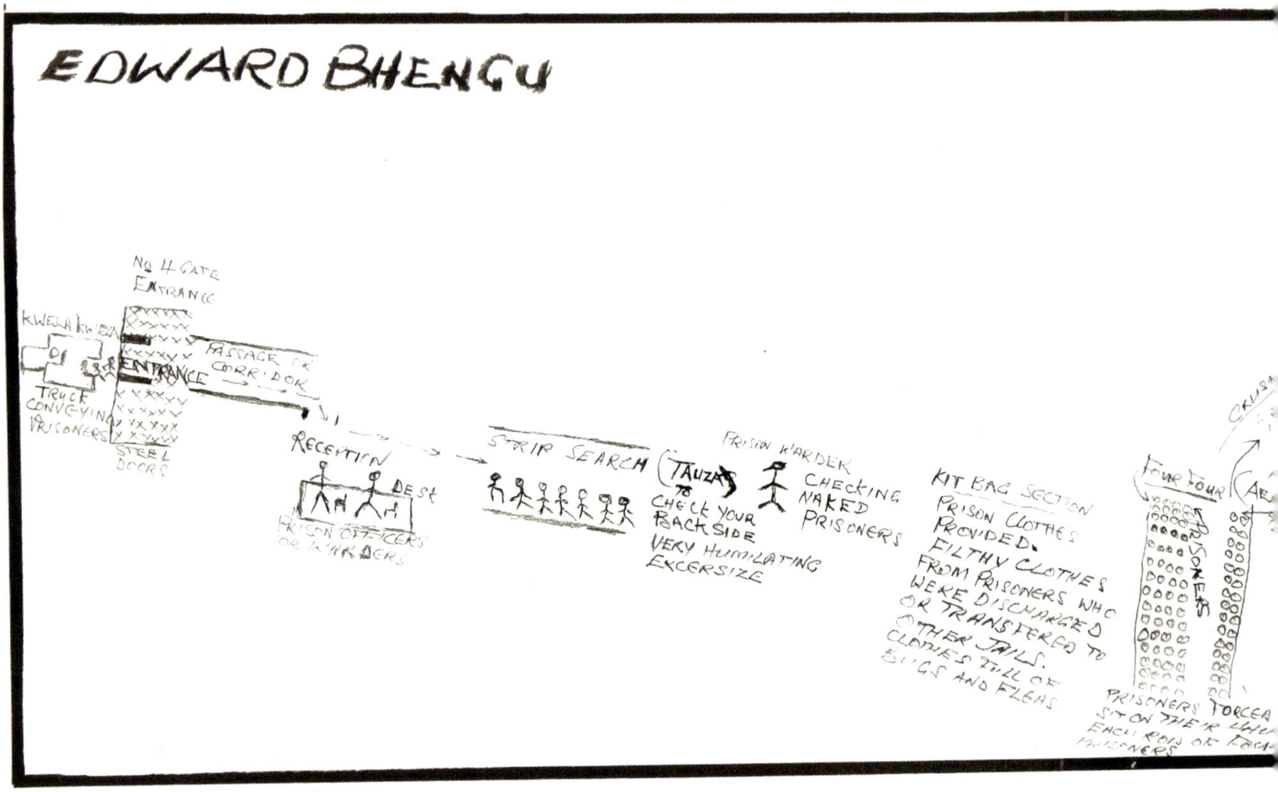

MEHLOKAZULU LUKHELE

The cell is the reception room, which is where I went to when I first arrived in this prison. This is where prisoners were fingerprinted, handed in their personal possessions and made to strip. The warders never succeeded in making us do this. I am so proud of what we Africans achieved, we were united and respected each other.

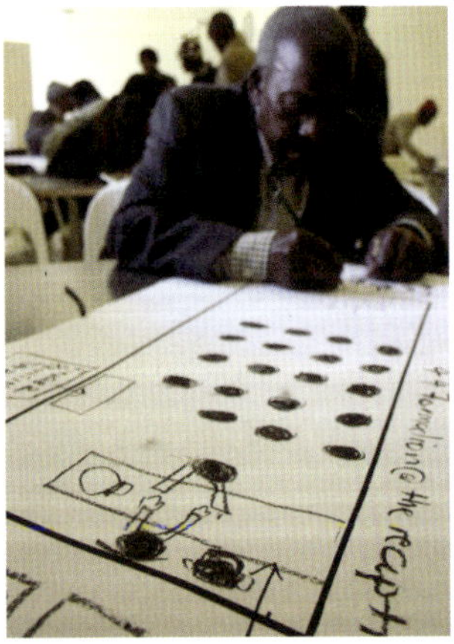

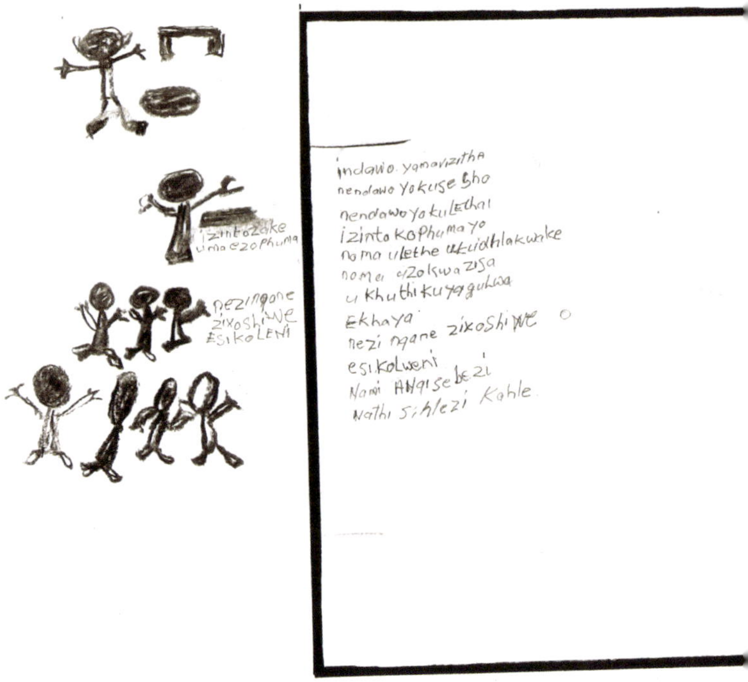

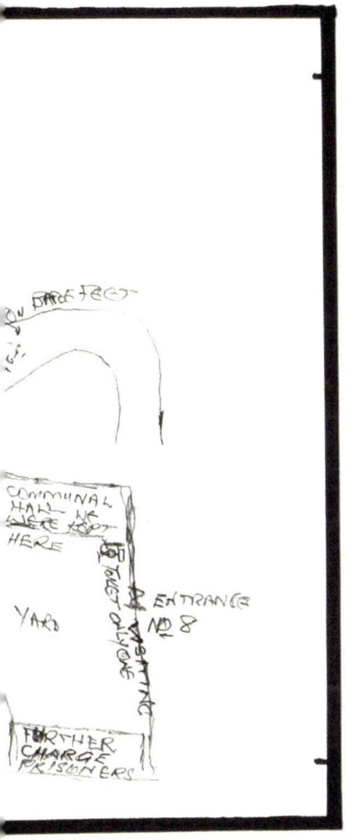

EDWARD SONNYBOY BHENGU

In my cell drawing I have shown the whole process of entering the prison because is was so traumatic. We were driven to Number Four in a *kwela- kwela* (pollice van). We arrived at the reception and were given kit bags to put our clothes and we were given prison clothes to wear. They were filthy and dirty and had bugs and fleas. Others had bloodstains from prisoners who had got lashed and were being transferred to other jails or were being discharged. We were given razor blades to shave off our hair and beards. Six of us had to share one blade so we had to break it into two pieces so that three of us could use the one piece of the blade and the others could use the other piece.

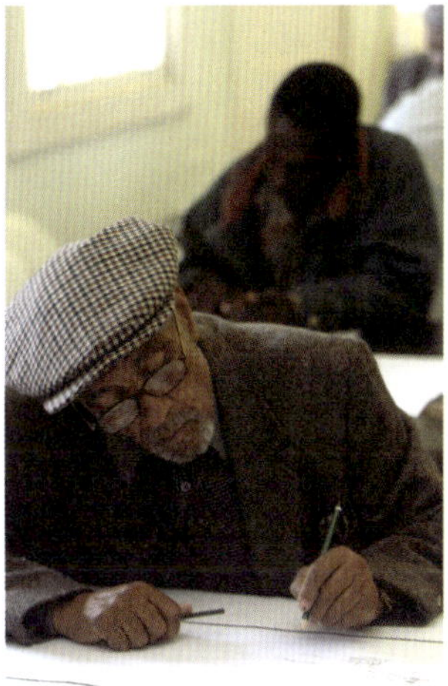

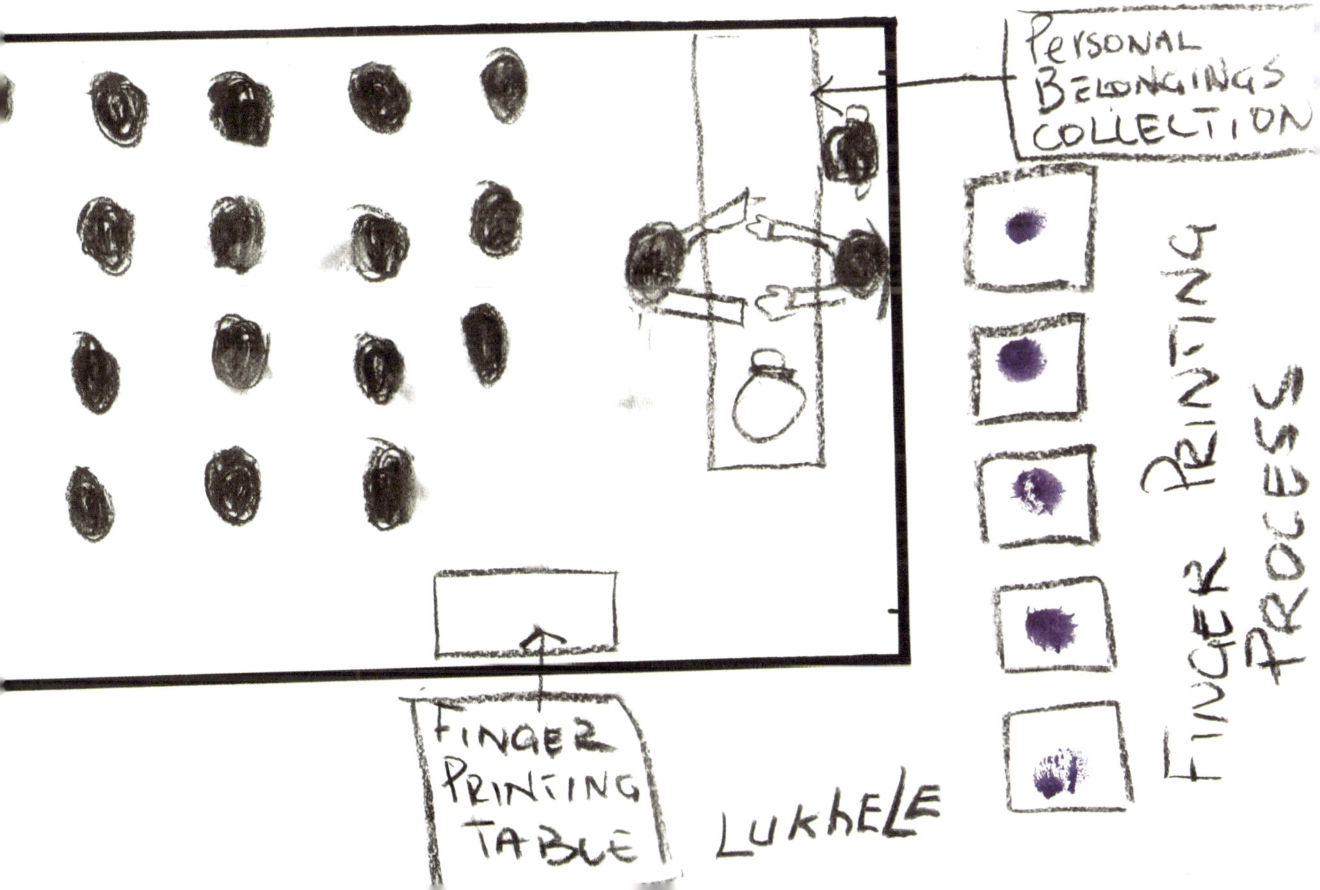

091-092

CORNELIUS MPSHE MANOTO

In this cell we had divided ourselves; our elders were in the one section and the boys in the other section. We were about 126 in a cell, including elders and children. We were separated from the ordinary prisoners as we were the political prisoners. We acted as one and we spoke as one. In a cell we had one area to put food and everything was done communally. We would share everything brought by whoever's visitor. We used to sleep in the middle of the cell. In the mornings at around 5 a.m. they would wake us up. We would fold our blankets and empty our toilet buckets. The whole cell – all 126 of us – only had two buckets to relieve ourselves. From there we would wait for our breakfast and get ready to go to court because we were still awaiting trialists.

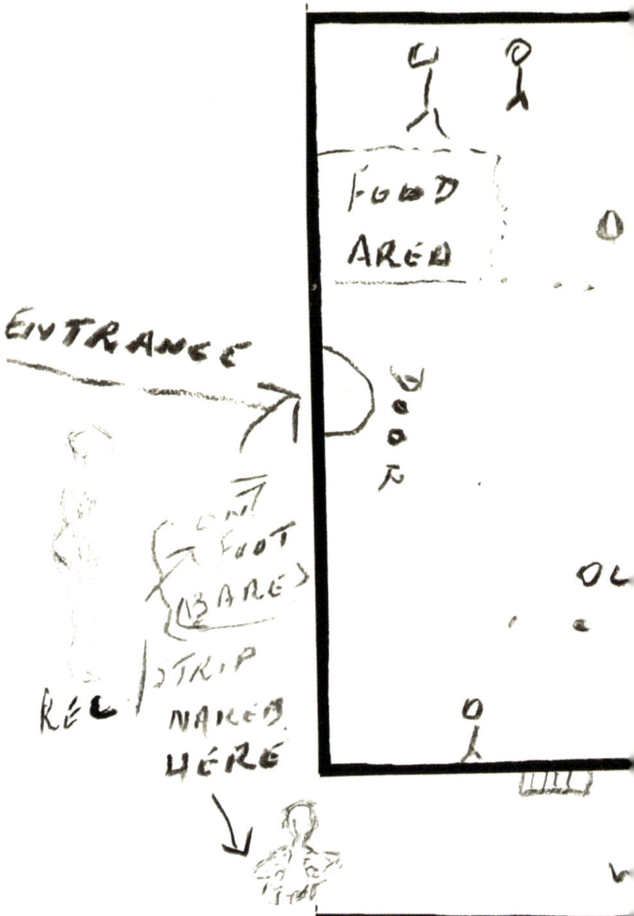

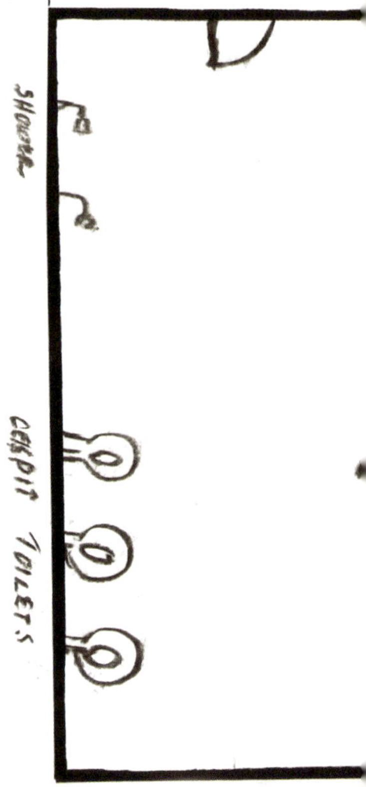

JOHN MOEKETSI MAHAPA

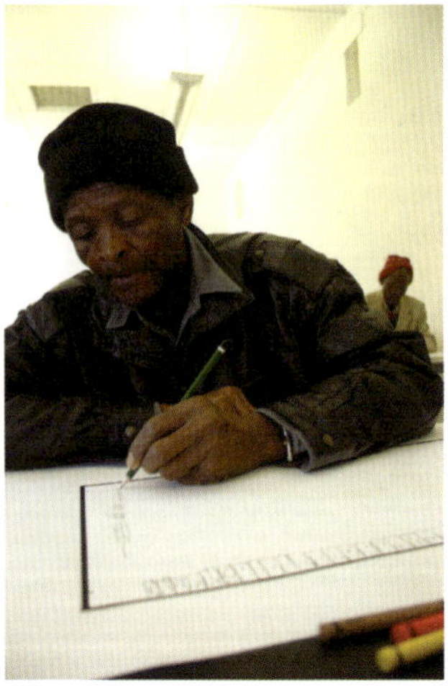

In my communal cell where I was held in 1960 there was Sonnyboy Bhengu entertaining us with music; Cyprian Sothondoshe entertaining us with jokes; Boy Shogwe, the storyteller.

Dr Aubrey Mokwapa, Phillip Makhale, Amos Dlamini, Wonder Ngwenya, Joseph Gogo Khoza, Joe Thloloe, Cornelius Manoto. They all became my friends in prison. We were the youngest, ranging from 17 to 20 years old and we were all from different areas in Soweto.

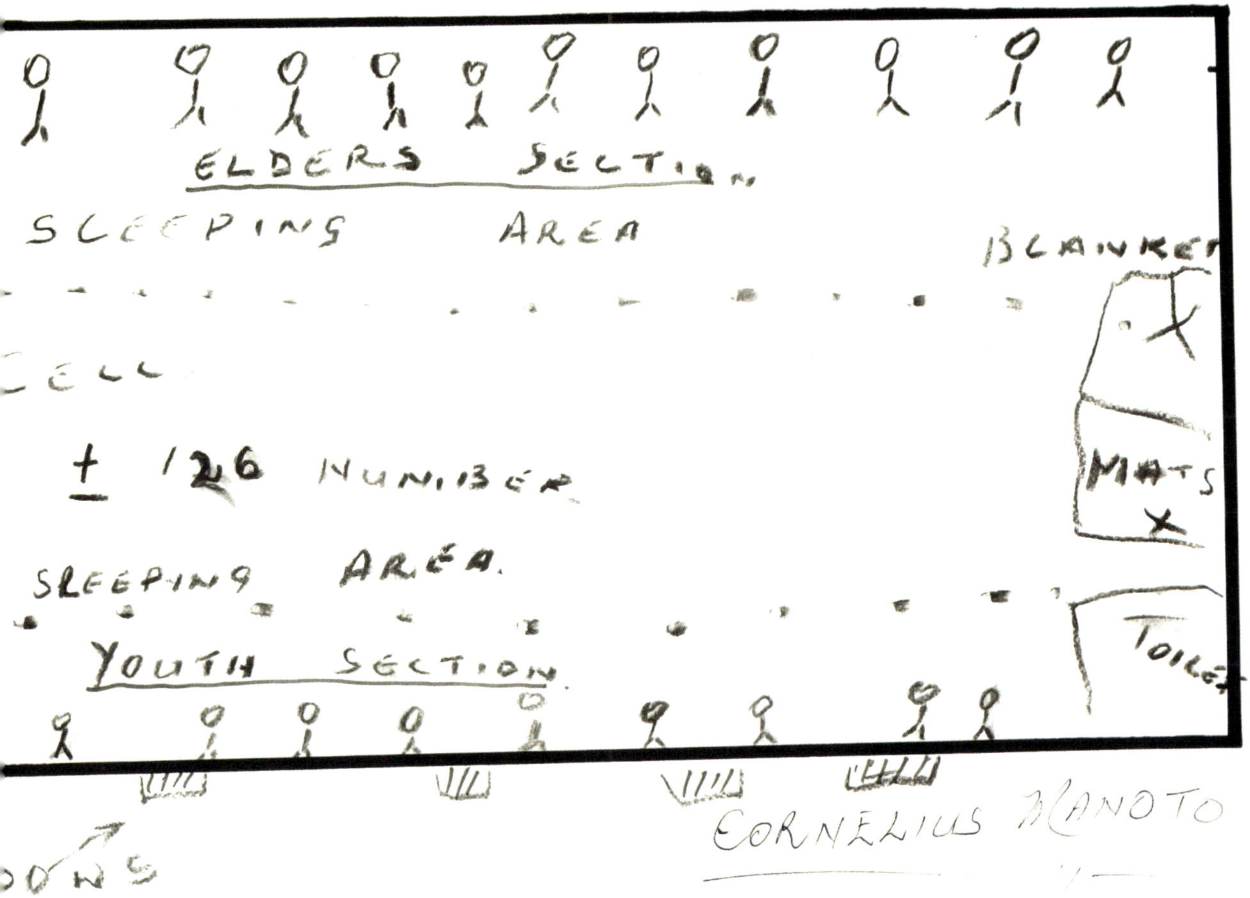

CORNELIUS MANOTO

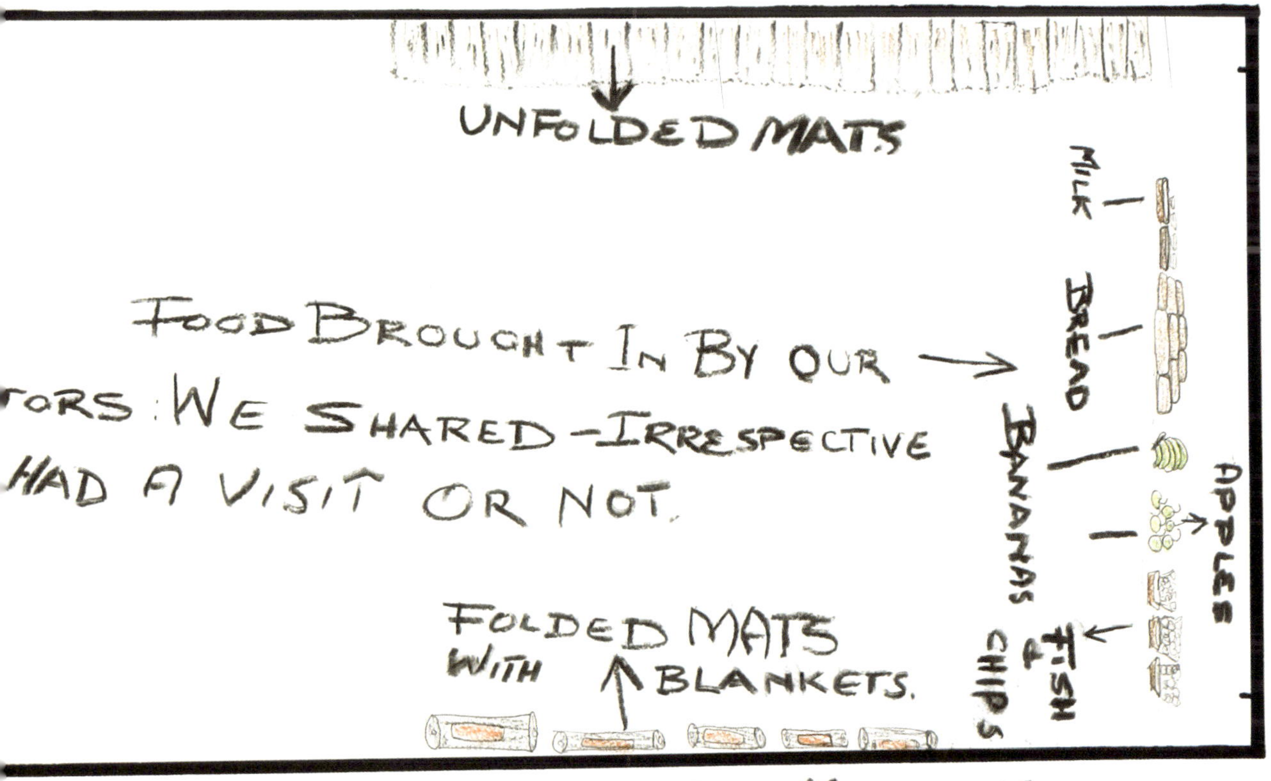

JOHN MOEKETSI MAHAPA

093-094

NAPOLEON MAZABANE LETSOKO

As we left the reception to go to the cells, I was not aware of what the future had in store for us. As we entered section eight, we were led to these stairs going downwards. To my surprise, we were pushed one by one into separate single or isolation cells in the basement. 'Two Boy', the warder in charge said, *"Julle will onse land oornneem. Nou is julle in julle land om te regeer."* (You want to take over our land. Now you have your own land to govern.)

It was about 5pm. It was like being pushed into a hole. They closed the door. There was a small window in the wall. Through it I could only see the stairs.

It was after 20 minutes or so after the warders left that the silence broke, when I managed to say to Victor, my co-accused, "*Kunjani*? How are you feeling?" And the response was, "Not positive." After we were locked separately, a cloud of hopelessness descended over me. I reflected on my mother, brothers and sisters because we had no father then. I was the only breadwinner to care for the whole family. On this reflection, on a second thought, I remembered what my mother taught us. "Pray in the morning and give thanks to God and give thanks to each meal you get and pray at night." It is at this point in time, I said, "My God you are the only one who will protect us. Safety and security rests in your hands." And I survived because of that. The mind must believe in something.

Later we were taken to a communal cell like the one in this drawing. All the PAC prisoners were held together.

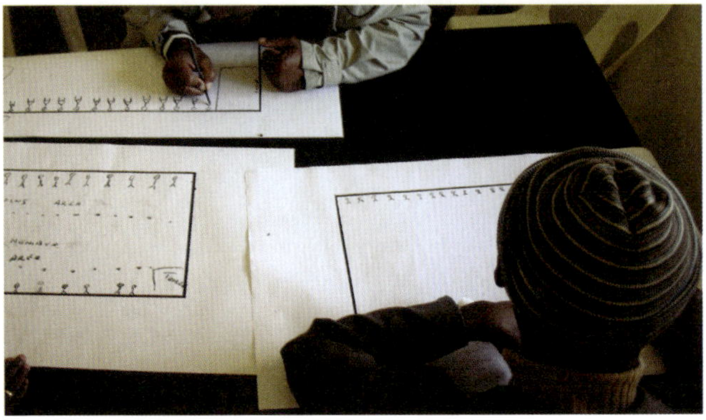

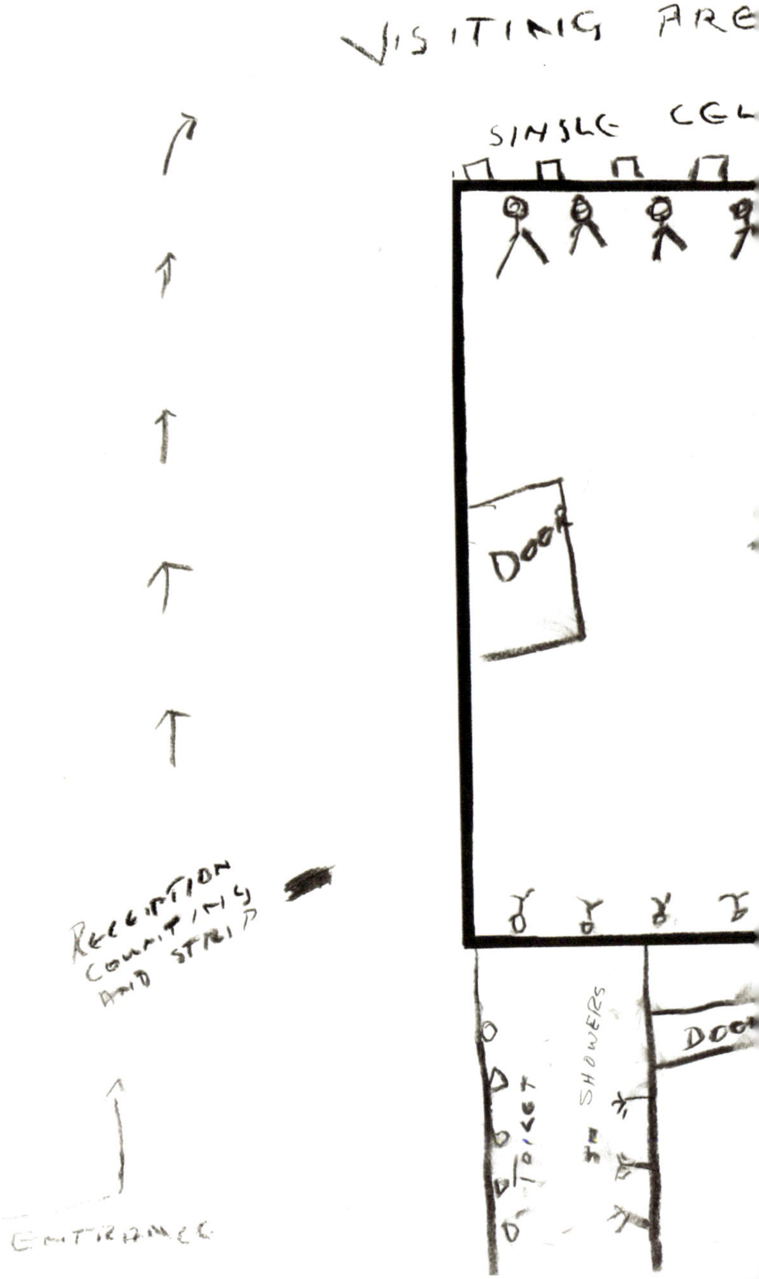

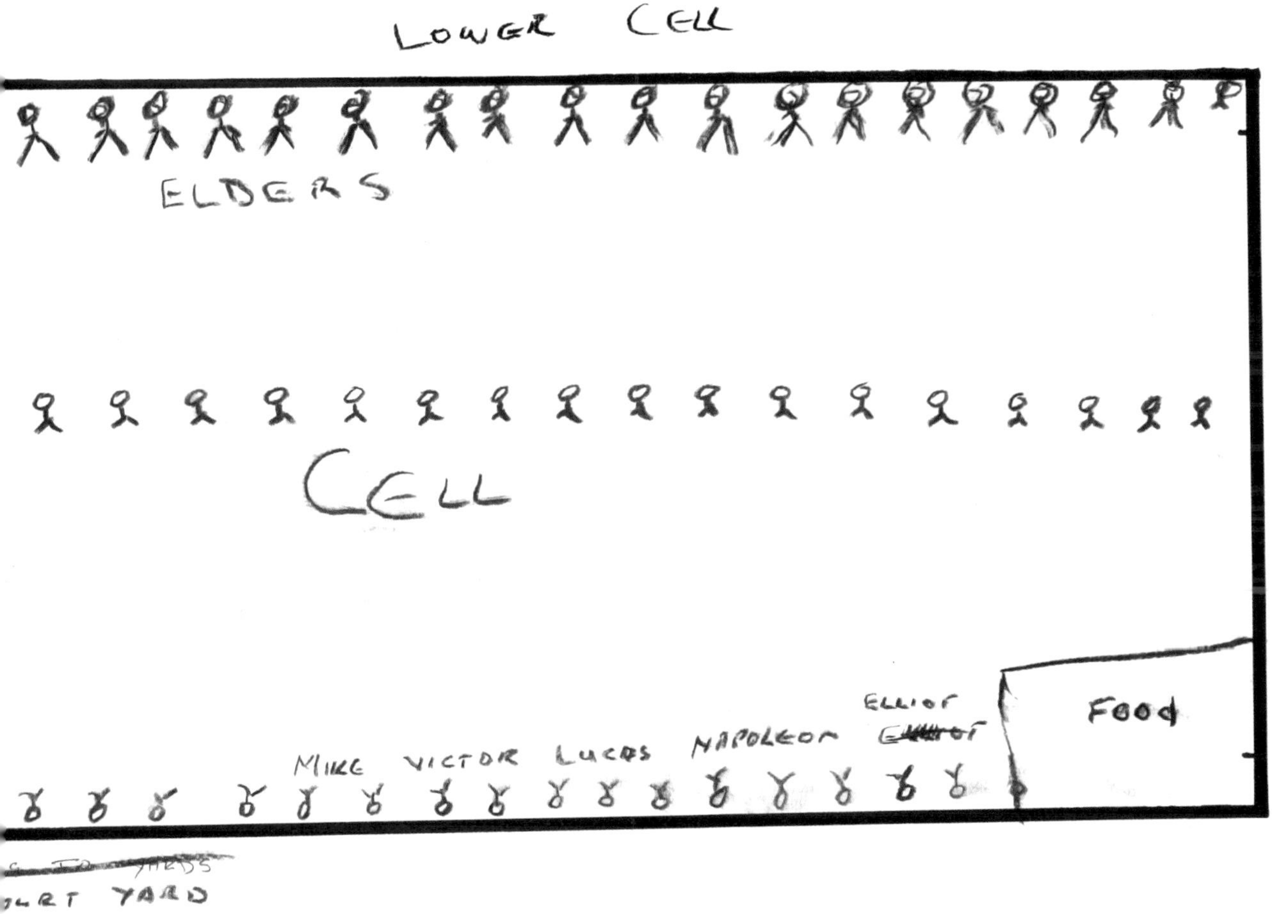

NAPOLEON M LETSOKU

SIPHO VICTOR NKABINDE

This was the cell where we were kept during our stay at Number Four. It was a big cell. We were plus or minus 180 in the cell. When sleeping time came, we had to divide ourselves into two groups. The youth were on the one side and the elders on the other side. The youth used to clean our cell, not as a form of punishment, but rather something that we would do for our elders and it would keep us busy and allow us not to think about being in prison.

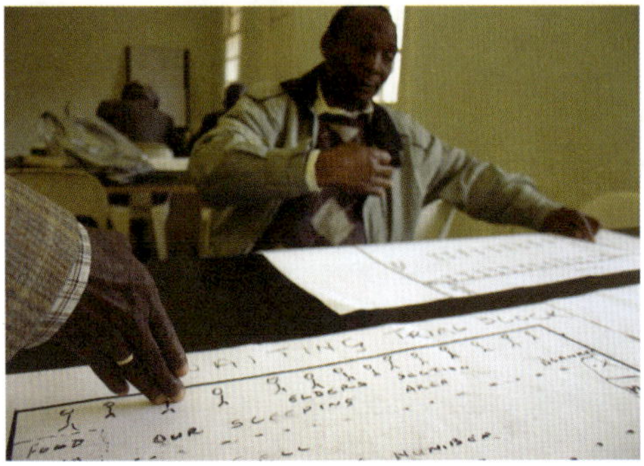

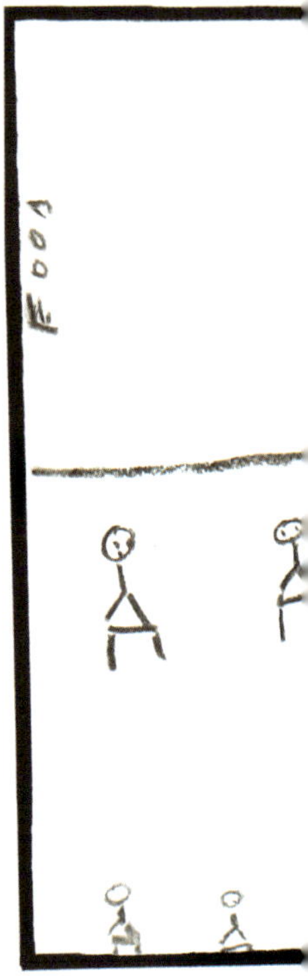

KHAYA ISAAC MAGI

Sunday – Cleaning day
On Sunday we had to clean our cells and neatly fold our blankets. You would then stand next to your bundle holding an identification card, waiting for inspection by the officer. This card stated your prison number and the crime you were held for, which could be very embarrassing.

Meal times
On days when meat was served you would find cell bosses standing by the door waiting to grab the very small ration of meat that you were served.

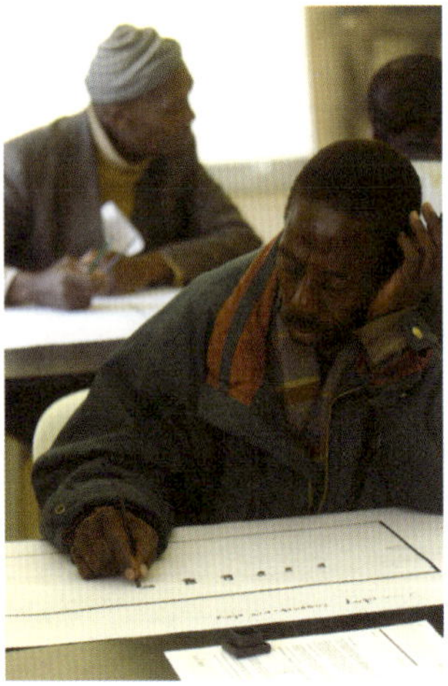

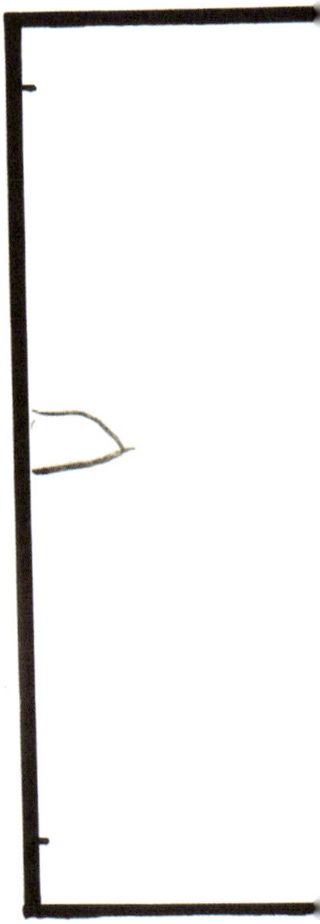

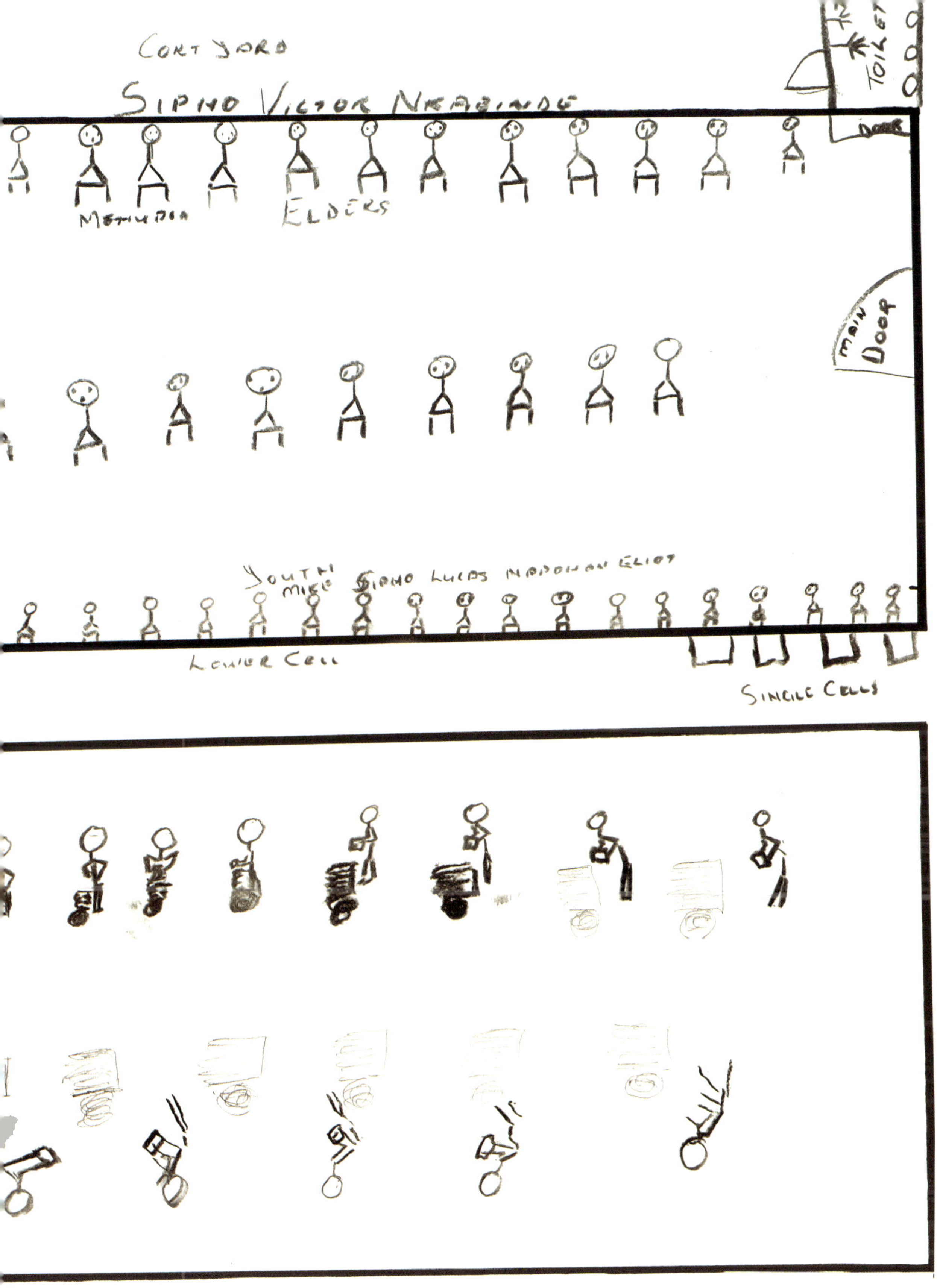

CORT YARD
SIPHO VICTOR NKABINDE
TOILET
DOOR
ELDERS
MAIN DOOR
YOUTH
MIKE
SIPHO LUCAS
ELIOT
LOWER CELL
SINGLE CELLS

097-098

MABANA RAYMOND NENE

While I was in prison, I never joined any prison gang. My first drawing is based on the life of the prisoner in a cell that is controlled by 28s.

The person sleeping with the others is the gang boss. And below him there is a person sleeping alone, the second in charge boss. The boxes that are above them are used to keep all the things they forcefully took from others.

Sakabams (lieutenants) – this guy served as the boss. He was also a gang member and his role was to search the *mgwaja's* when they arrived or when they came from the court.

Japan (the merchants who traded in jail) – all the guys in the *Japan* are members of a gang. They are given preference only because they have people who visit them and all the food and their belongings were controlled by the gang.

Mgwaja's (underlings/sardines) – these are the prisoners that also do not have a gang membership, don't have visitors and are not known by the gang bosses. They would sleep next to the toilet and be given blankets and are made to sing and clap. These guys receive the worst treatment in prison.

Toilets
These are an enclosed hole in the cell where inmates relieve themselves.

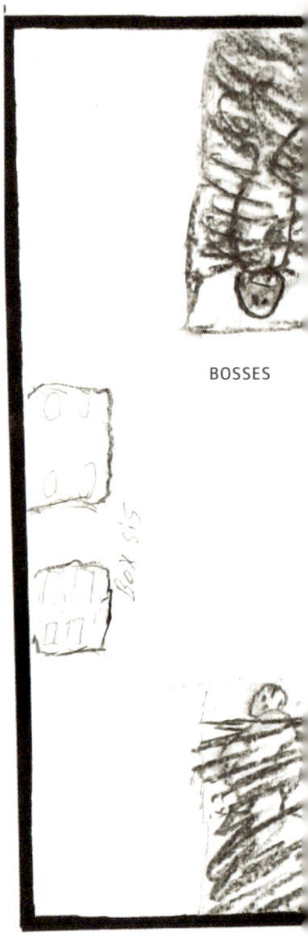

BOSSES

MUTHUPHEI PATRICK MUDAU

I was in a cell that had different 'grounds' (areas) or rather that was the way we prisoners classified ourselves. There was a section for the bosses and there was a section for the people called the *gwaja* (people who were scared of the bosses). There was also a section for prisoners who were guards for the bosses. They slept next to the toilet. If it happens that you get a visitor bringing you food, you will be required to give your food to the bosses of the cell and be left with nothing. This was a cell rule. In other cases you will find that if there are little boys in the *gwaja's* section, they will be taken by the bosses and be made their wives and they would enjoy their life during the day but at night there would be trouble and screams.

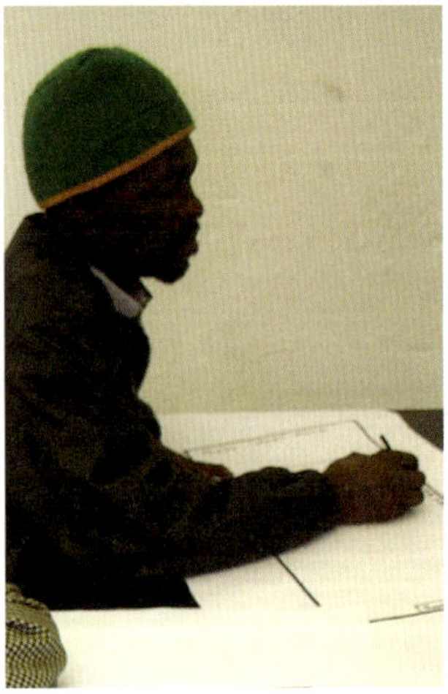

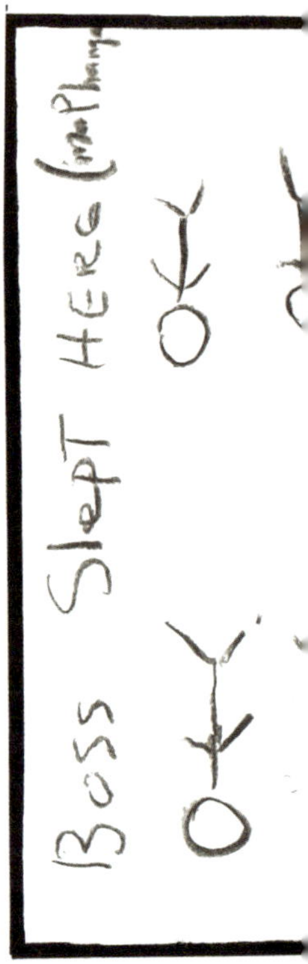

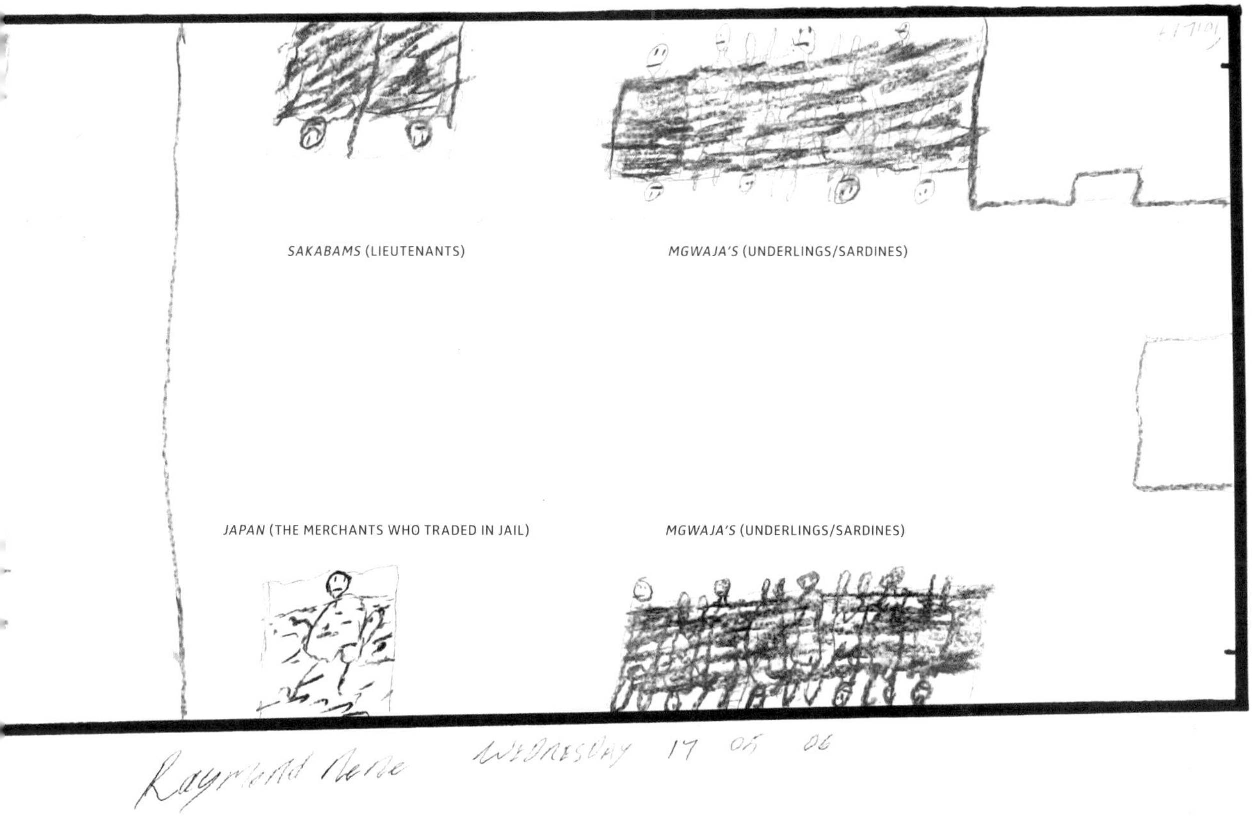
SAKABAMS (LIEUTENANTS)
MGWAJA'S (UNDERLINGS/SARDINES)
JAPAN (THE MERCHANTS WHO TRADED IN JAIL)
MGWAJA'S (UNDERLINGS/SARDINES)
WEDNESDAY 17 05 06

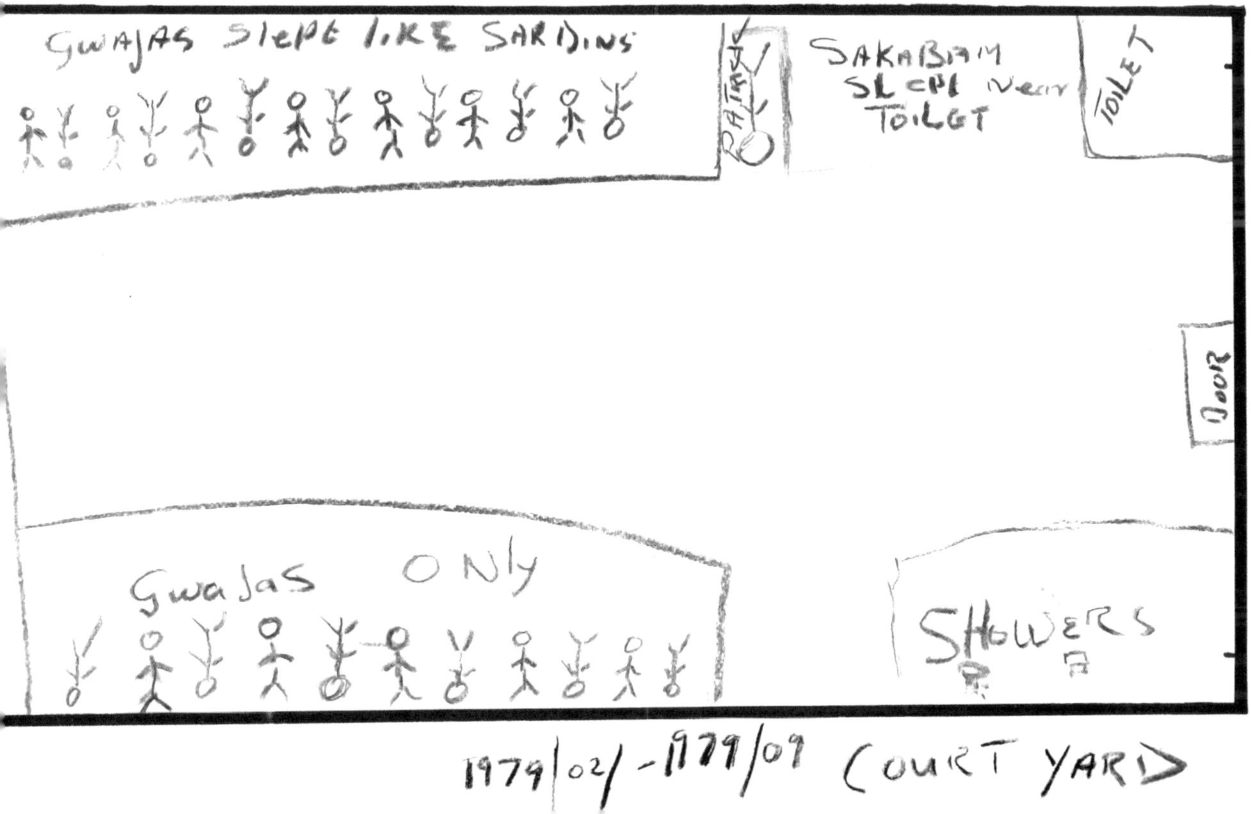
GWAJAS SLEPE LIKE SARDINS
SAKABAM SLEPT NEAR TOILET
TOILET
DOOR
GWAJAS ONLY
SHOWERS
1979/02/-1979/09 COURT YARD

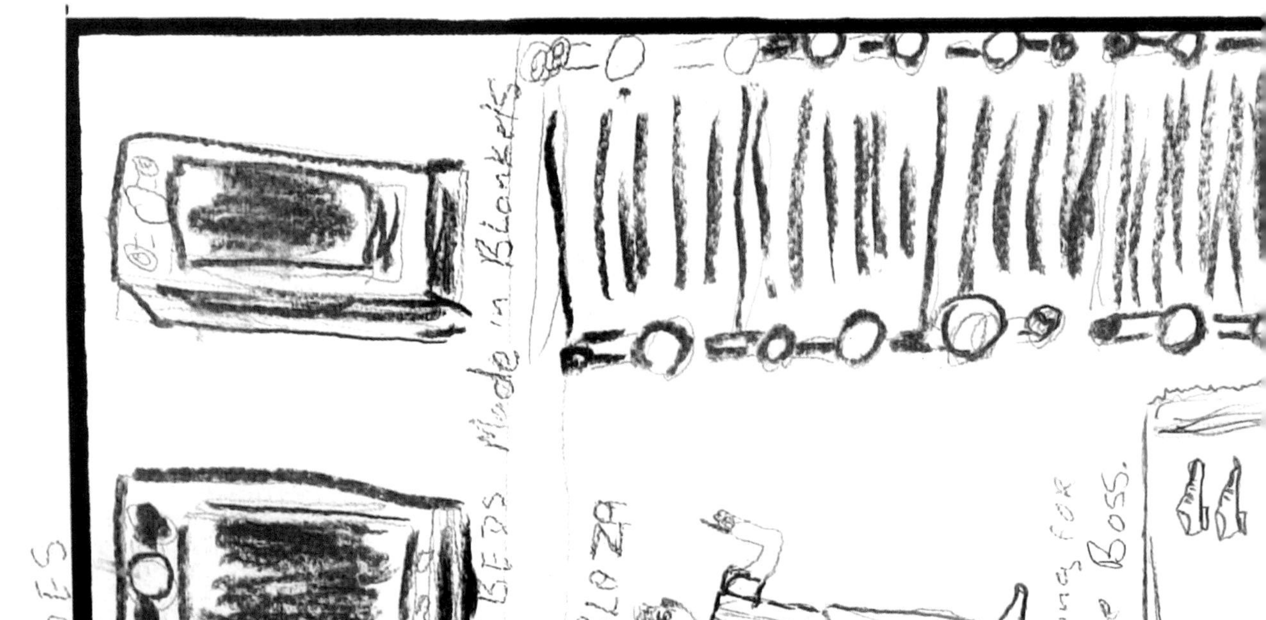
BOSSES
HIGH BEDS Made in Blankets
Me Blaza
Working for The Boss.
Rolled Blankets
Top

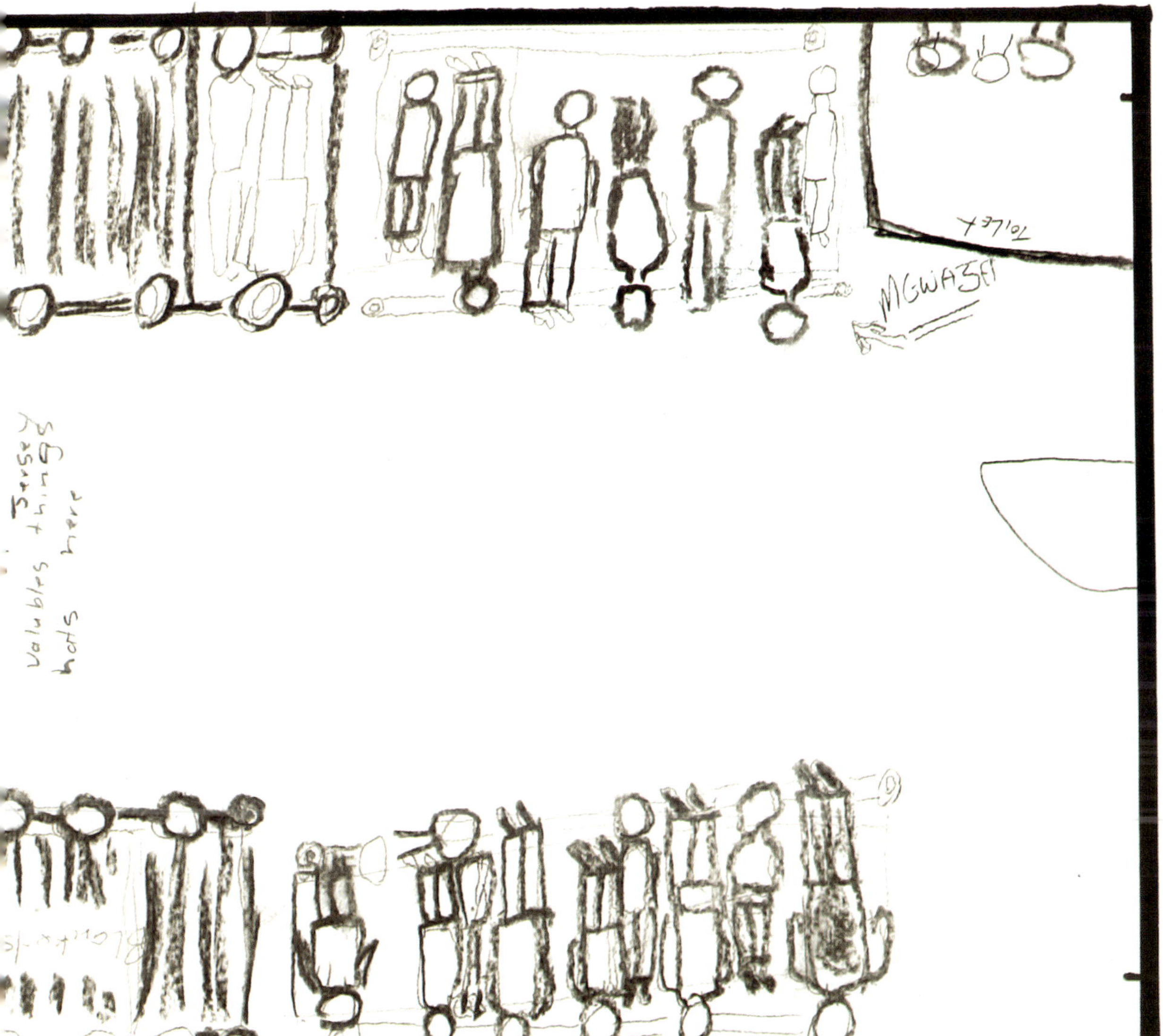

Zolile

FAMILY DRAWINGS & VISITS

Previous workshops with former prisoners have demonstrated to us that former prisoners are often reluctant to talk to their families about some of the memories associated with prison. We felt, therefore, that they need prompts to assist them in dredging up often traumatic memories. In the second workshop, we asked former prisoners to draw their family members and talk about how their families coped while they were in the jail.

Former prisoners were then asked to invite two family members (preferably of the younger generation) or a friend to the last workshop to participate in the drawing and photography process. Our hope was that this invitation would create the opportunity for a dialogue about how apartheid impacted on family structures and disrupted the possibilities of emotional stability in both ordinary and political families.

Indeed, involving friends and families of former prisoners in a project of this kind has been deeply rewarding despite the cursory nature of the interaction. The visit seemed to open potentially rewarding avenues to explore issues that may not have been spoken about in family structures before. It turned out that many of the friends and family members had never visited the site before. The workshops afforded them their first opportunity to come to this place. The visitors' very moving accounts of what it meant for them to have visited the prisons with a former prisoner gives a sense of what an incredibly rich encounter this has been.

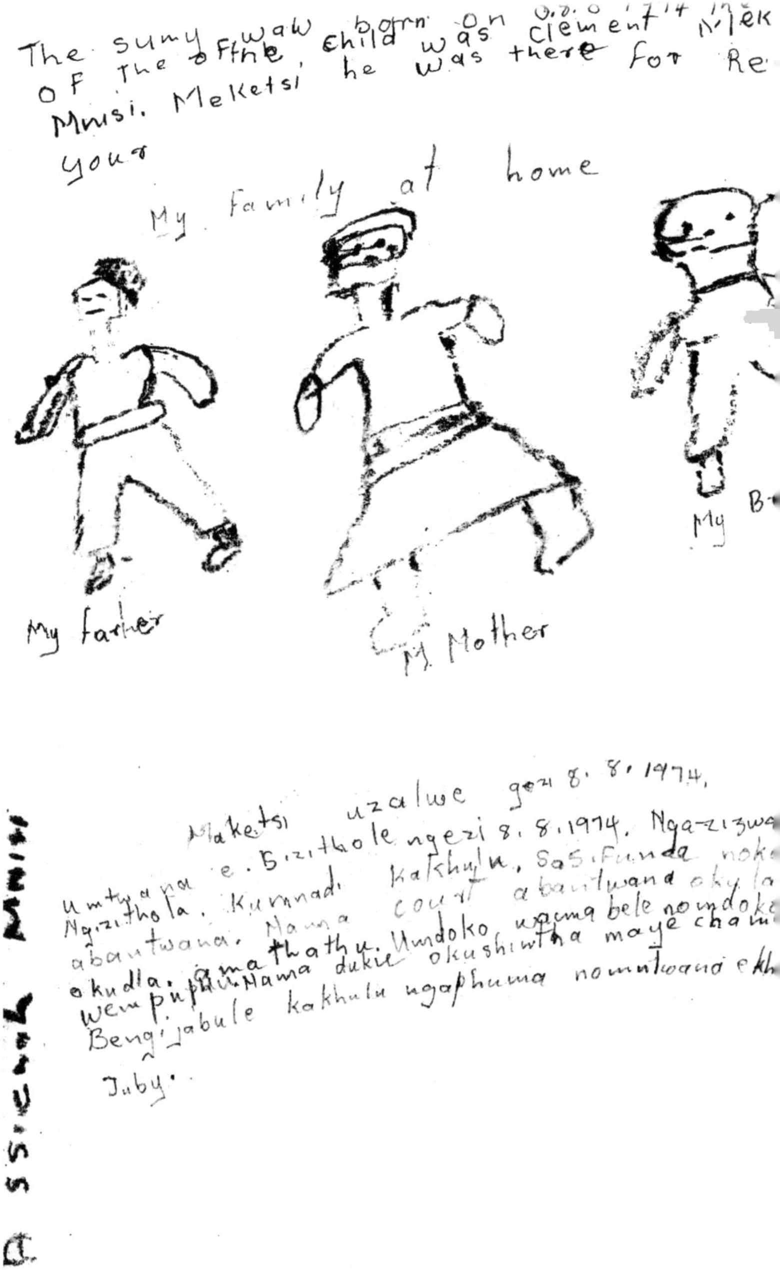

ASSIENAH MNISI'S DRAWING

LILIAN KEAGILE

This is a drawing of my siblings, my baby boy and my parents at home having supper, while I am in prison. I always imagined them enjoying being together and missing me. Mom and dad were working together, my father as a postman and my mother as a tea girl for the insurance company. All my brothers were working and Hubbly was the only one who was married. My sister took care of my son by bathing him and taking him to school. She was the one who took care of my boy from the day we came home from hospital. She thought he was her toy.

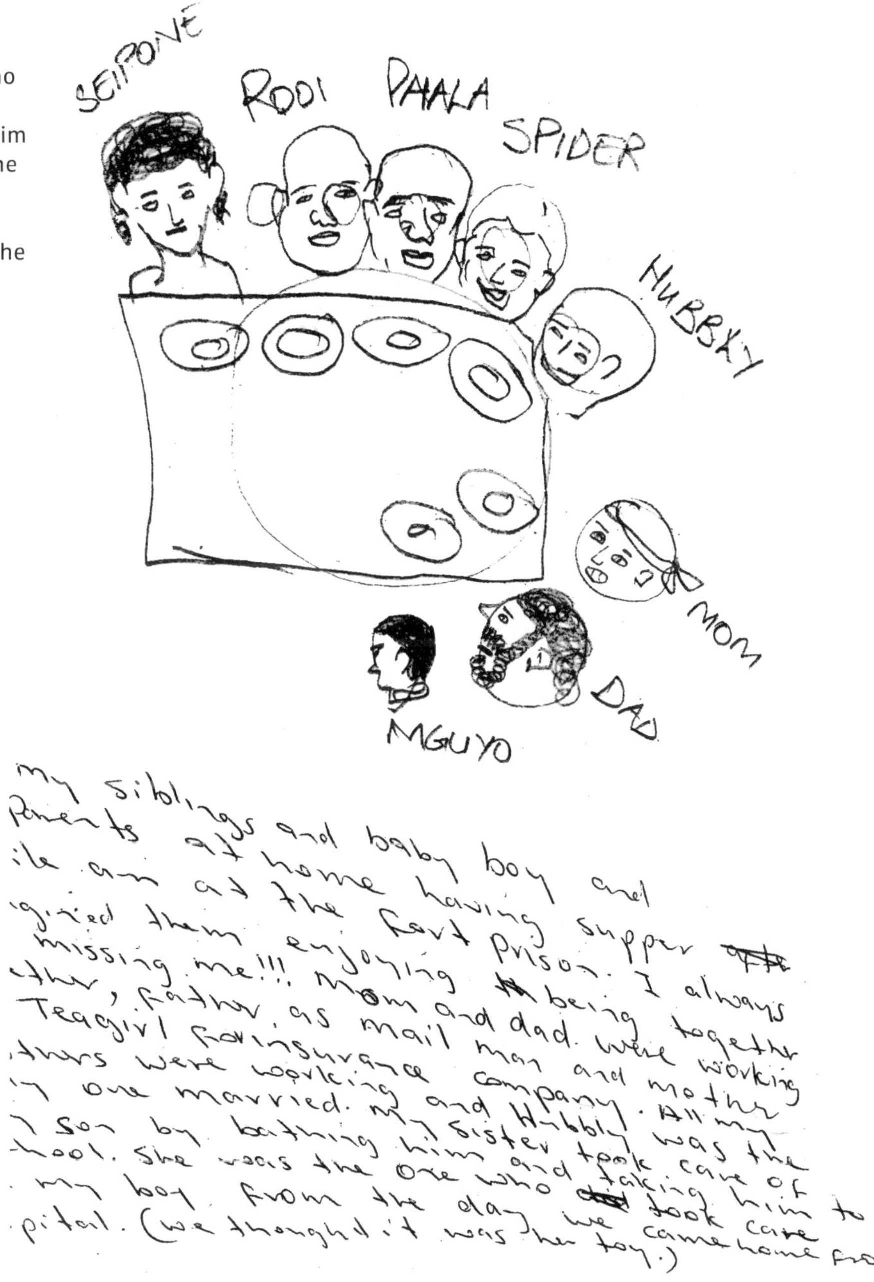

LILIAN KEAGILE'S DRAWING

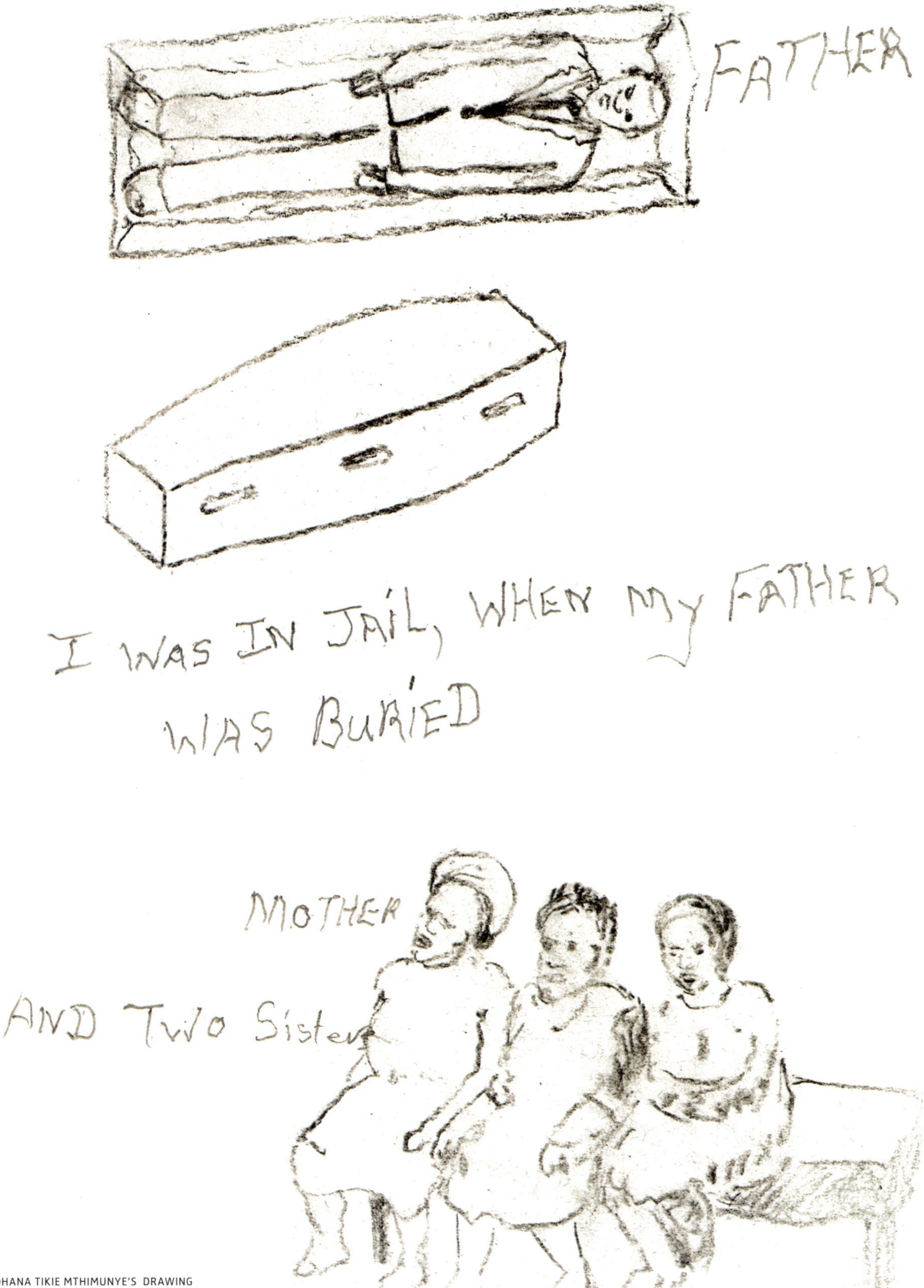

JOHANA TIKIE MTHIMUNYE'S DRAWING

JACO MALEFO
Johana Tikie Mthimunye's boyfriend

I met Johana Tikie Mthimunye after she was released and then I made her promise not to commit crime again. One day while I was at work, her mother called to say that she had gone to town with her friends to shoplift. She came home that afternoon with the stolen goods. The next day I told her that she will lose me if she goes to jail again.

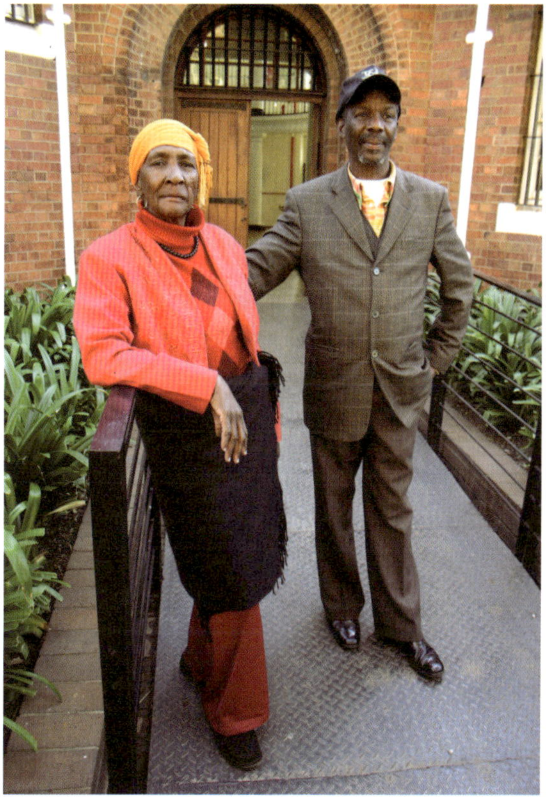

JOHANA TIKIE MTHIMUNYE WITH JACOB MALEFO (BOYFRIEND)

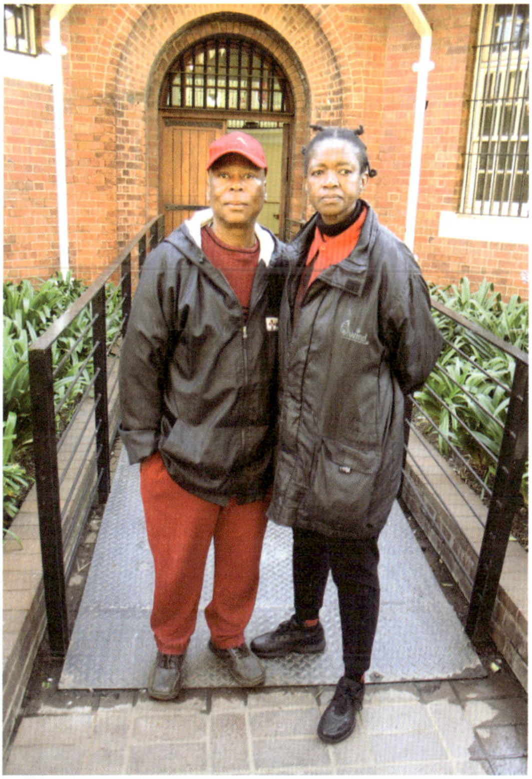

JOYCE DIPALE WITH TIEGO MASINGA (HUSBAND)

TIEGO MASINGA
Joyce Diphale's husband

To be back at Number Four reminds me of the sadness of being separated from family and friends. The idea of keeping political prisoners in solitary confinement makes families sad and worried about the health and safety of their loved ones.

105-106

NIKIWE DEBORAH MATSHOBA

The story about the house

This house is situated at the corner of Dabulamanzi and Senzangakhona. By the standards of those days, it was viewed as a mansion and a residence only for affluent people.

Outside were two back rooms known as *Mngungundlovu* and Ghetto *Mngungundlovu*. *Mngungundlovu* was bigger in size. It was like our own common room, where we played music. Gradually it became a place of political discussion, concretisation and recruitment.

This place has housed from time to time, Onkgopotse Tiro, Steve Biko, Boikwe Mafuna, Wellie Nhlapo, Thenjiwe Mtintso, Nomsisi Kraai, Mamphela Ramphele, O'Hare Ngoma and others. I remember how Jackie Selebi, quite heavily bodied would manage to squeeze under the bed during police raids.

My father was a well-known business and sportsman owning one of the prominent soccer teams, the Krugersdorp Rovers. He was also the executive of the tennis board and a member of the National African Chamber of Commerce and the first president of the Transvaal Bantu Football Assocation. My mother and I were both actively involved in the Young Women's Christian Association. Mother also served in the local Methodist Manyano (solidarity) executive. For a long time the system mistook my friends' movements, coming in and out of this home as being here for sport, church and business.

My sister Thembi and her husband, Sedupe Ramokgopa relocated to Swaziland. My younger sister, Nosipho went into exile in 1974 and my little sister Lindy was always at home with me.

This home bears memories of my brother, Blocky, who died tragically in 1967 at the age of 20. The jacaranda and palm tree that grace the yard were his creations. I missed sitting under the shade of these trees during the long spell of my incarceration in this prison and others.

It was at this house that police torches shone all around the windows at 3.20 a.m. on a cold July morning in 1976. The corner house was surrounded by about eight cars and two big police caspirs on both sides of the street. They had come to arrest 'Debs the terrorist', and brought me to Number Four, the Women's jail.

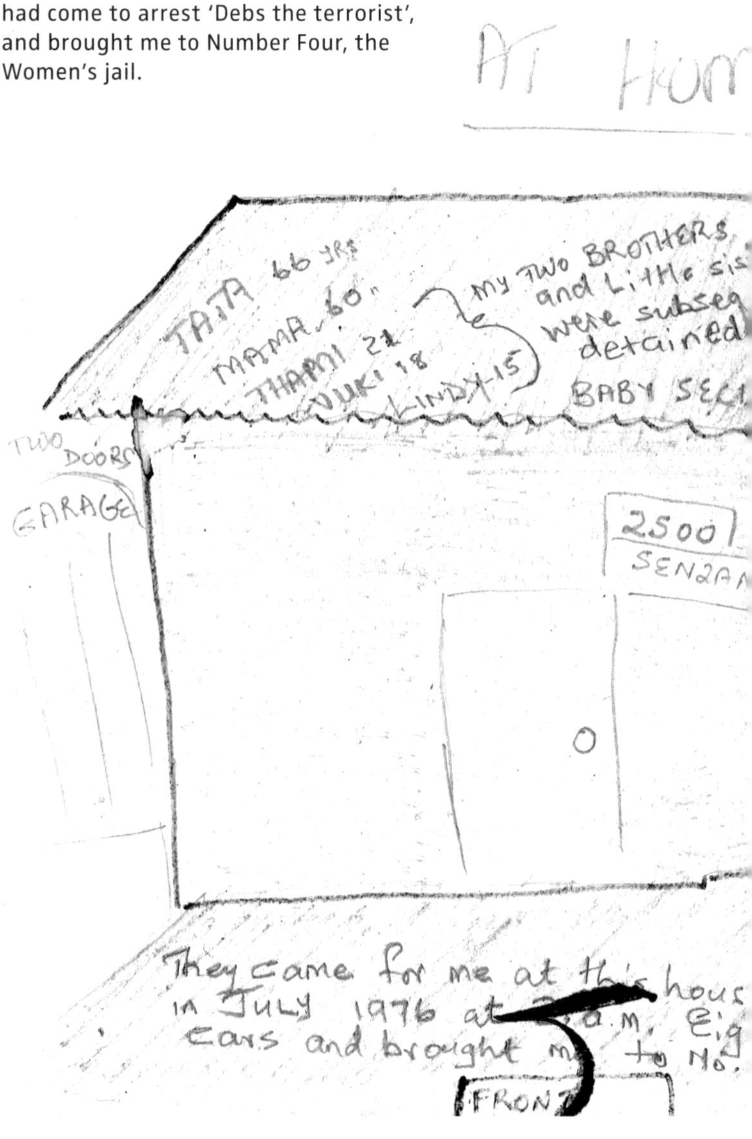

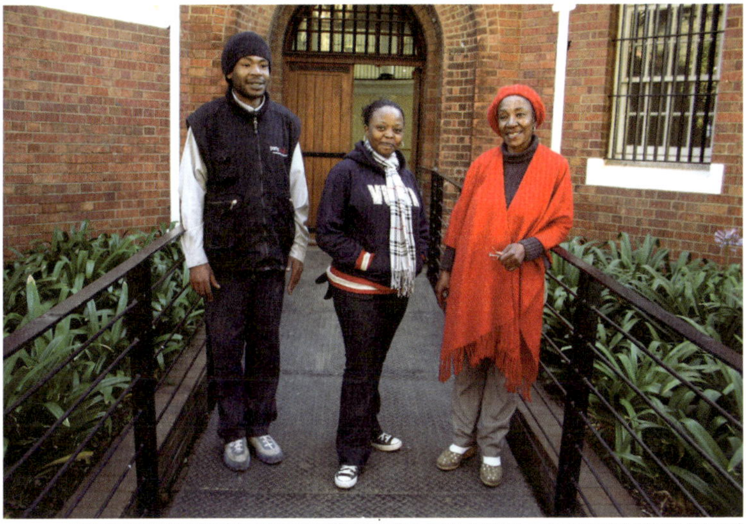

NIKIWE DEBORAH MATSHOBA WITH SECHABA TEBOGO MABALE (SON) AND NANDI HLATSHAYO (FRIEND)

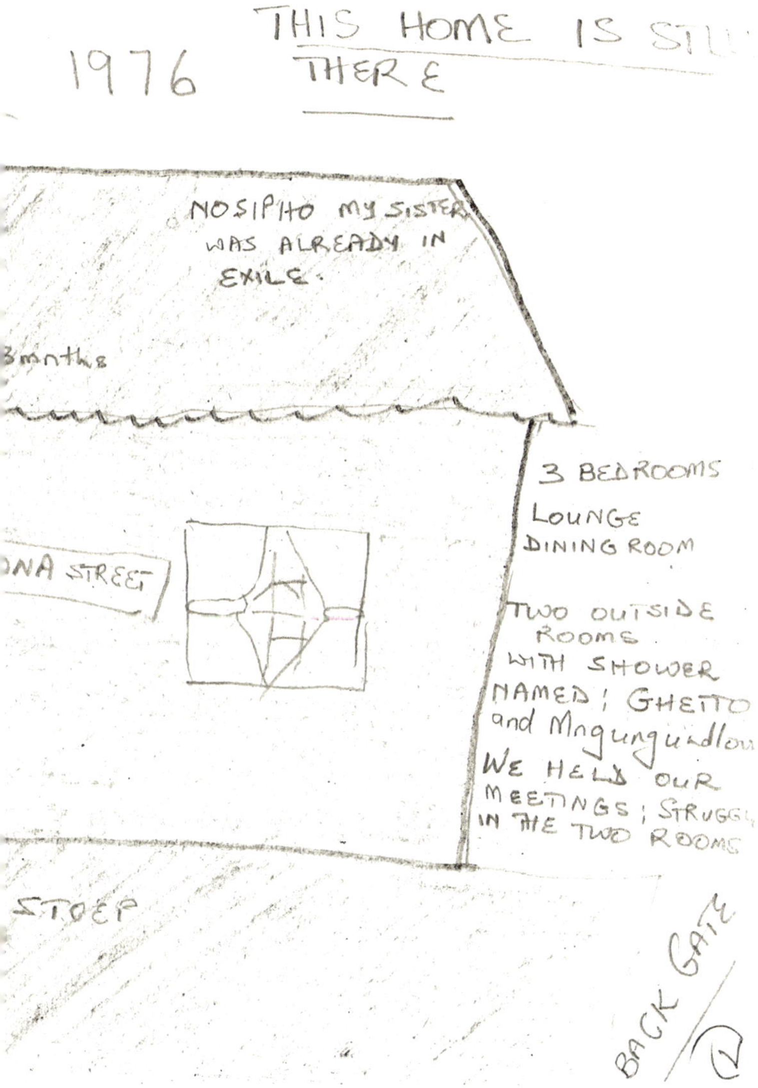

NIKIWE DEBORAH MATSHOBA'S DRAWING

SECHABA TEBOGO MABALE

Nikiwe Deborah Matshoba's son

In May 1976 I was taken along to the Black Consciousness Movement annual general meeting in Durban. By June the country would never be the same again, as townships all over the land literally burst into flames. By August, both my parents had been arrested under the Internal Security Act. My grandmother took me to Botswana. An aunt of mine, Nosipho, had fled there during the uprising. I remember seeing a light aircraft turning on the runway at Gabarone Airport. This is my earliest childhood memory. My other prominent memory is that of caravans that were for sale on Ontdekkers Drive in Roodepoort. Whenever I saw them I knew it meant we were on our way to visit my mother in Number Four. Next I remember being woken up in the dead of night by loud banging on the door by the Security Police at my aunt Thembi's house in Orlando West. This is where I would eventually spend the first five years of my life, dodging black cars and learning to *'shaya umthangalo'* (jump the fence).

107-108

NOKUTHULA TSHABALALA

Sibongile Tshabalala's daughter

My name is Nokuthula Tshabalala and I am here with my mom, Sibongile. It's my first visit here and it's very exciting because I get to see the place where my mom was kept and learn more about how they were treated here. The best experience was when I was inside one of the cells and I could feel how it must have felt. It was like I was one of the prisoners.

Whenever I hear my mother's stories, I become so emotional and it is hard for me to imagine her in this place being so young.

After all that has happened to my mother, I really think that she is a survivor. After being imprisoned for brewing beer, she still kept herself together and became stronger and that's why she is continuing with her business that was started by her mom, my grandmother. I am proud of her because today I am able to go to school. I am able to dress like any other child because of this business which my mother and gran fought for. And today I'd like to say to Mom, "I am proud of you".

NOZIPHO TSHABALALA

Sibongile Tshabalala's granddaughter

My name is Nozipho. I am a Grade 9 learner and I came here with my grandmother. I want to thank her and all the other women because we are where we are today because of their bravery and strength. They fought so that our families and friends can be free. I think they deserve a round of applause or a reward. At first it was difficult to understand the situation my grandmother was dealing with - the police coming to our home to destroy the African beer. She was only doing it so that we could buy food and stuff, and also to pay our bills.

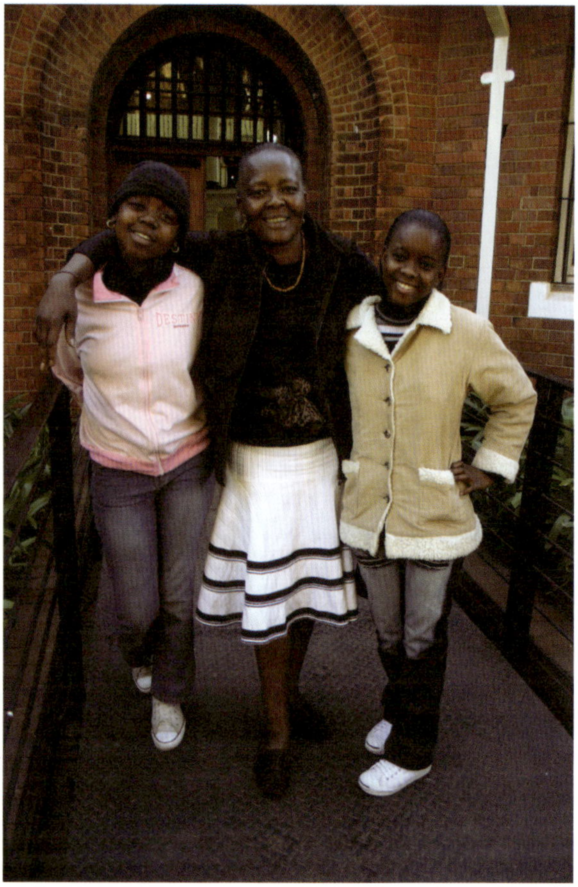

SIBONGILE TSHABALALA WITH NOKUTHULA (DAUGHTER) AND NOZIPHO (GRANDDAUGHTER)

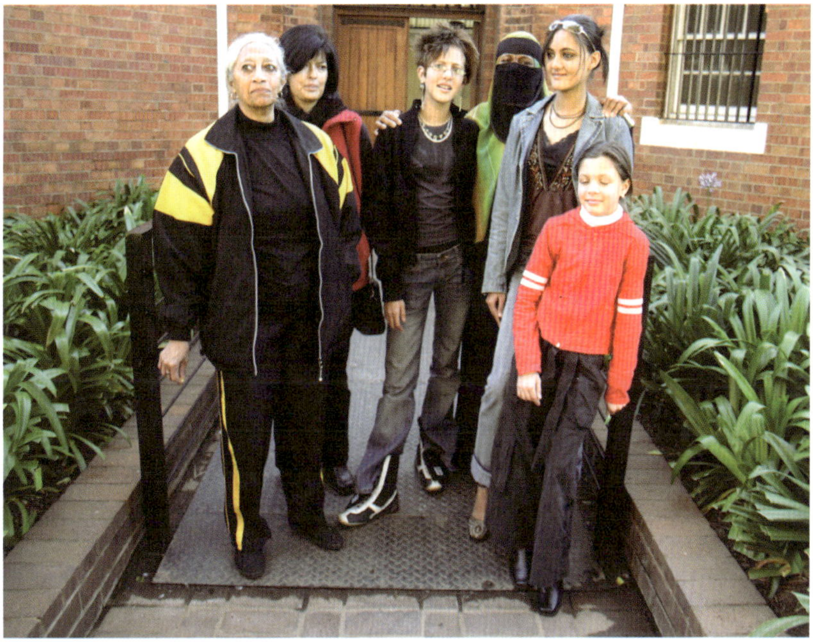

JUBY MAYET WITH NAEEMA (DAUGHTER-IN-LAW), SAFIYYA (GRANDDAUGHTER)
ZAINAB (DAUGHTER), SAMEERA AND SUMAYYA (GRANDDAUGHTERS)

ZAINAB MAYET
Juby Mayet's daughter

Coming back here to the Fort is quite overwhelming and emotional. I remember as a Standard two pupil, that every Monday and Thursday we battled to obtain permits for us to visit at John Vorster, that horrid blue building. The time we had for the visit was short and all eight of us wanted to tell Mum something at the same time. My worst moment was when they refused my little sister Natasha the right to hug Mum. Touching was not allowed but she was our mother, for crying out loud! Today I am glad it was not all in vain although we had to live without our wonderful mum, Juby. We are all very proud of her. While Mom was detained I am very grateful to her one brother, uncle Amien and sisters, Mariam, Zanna, Julie and Granny for so lovingly taking care of us and seeing to our needs.

SAMEERA KARA
Juby Mayet's granddaughter

It's very shocking to see that the prisoners used to live in such small cells. I'm very proud of my granny for being a part of the struggle so that my generation can live this free life that we are currently enjoying. My sisters and I can't imagine how it would be to live without parents like my mum and her siblings did.
I think that coming to see the cells has benefited me, and now I'll appreciate what I have even more. It was also very sad to see that the one lady could not even attend her own wedding. I'm glad I had this opportunity of walking where others walked to freedom.

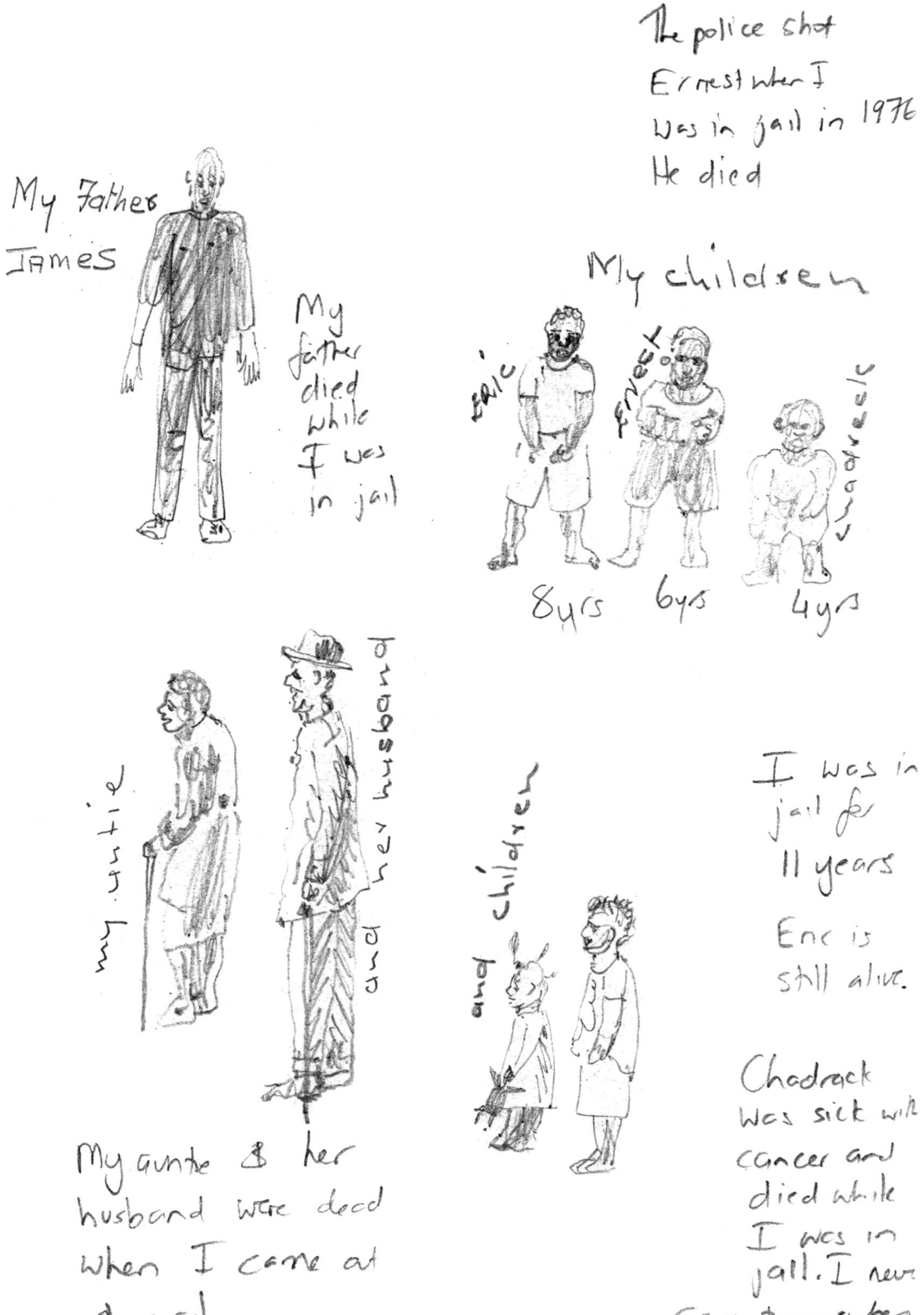

PATRICIA ALARM'S DRAWING

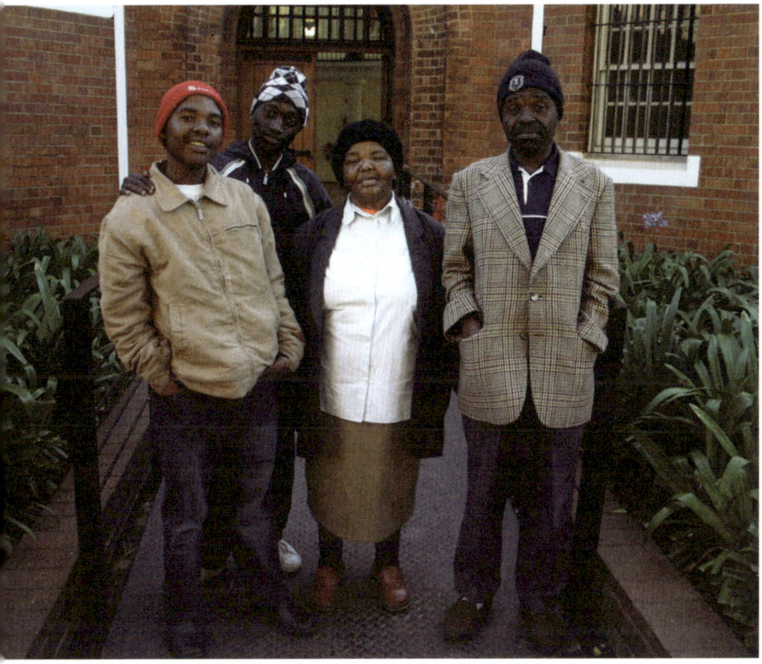

PATRICIA ALARM WITH SFISO AND OUPA (GRANDSONS) AND ERIC (SON)

ERIC ALARM
Patricias Alarm's son

First of all, thanks for bringing us here today. My mother was arrested in 1976 for political acts. She was sentenced to 11 years and only came out in 1987. I was 13 years old when she left us. When she came back we were all happy and celebrated as a family. She started telling us what it was like in jail and the way that they lived and what she got up to in jail. She is a good mother and we love her and are proud to see what she has achieved. It was good to see the cell that she used to be in. As her children, we want to learn more about what was happening before. When she was arrested we never believed she would be back. We are happy and we love you, Mom.

IRENE DUBE
Bella Dlamini's sister

During my sister's incarceration, I could not come to visit her. I was a teacher under apartheid and I was scared to come to the prison in case I was fired. Bella had a baby by the name of Sbongile, who I looked after. I was the only breadwinner. I also could not take the chance of going to Bella because if I got arrested no one could look after my mother and my other sister and brother. Bella used to send friends to come collect whatever she needed.
It was very tough during those days. My mother used to be very sickly. Her brother had left the country for political reasons, her daughter was in jail and she had a child to look after. Our mother was very depressed.

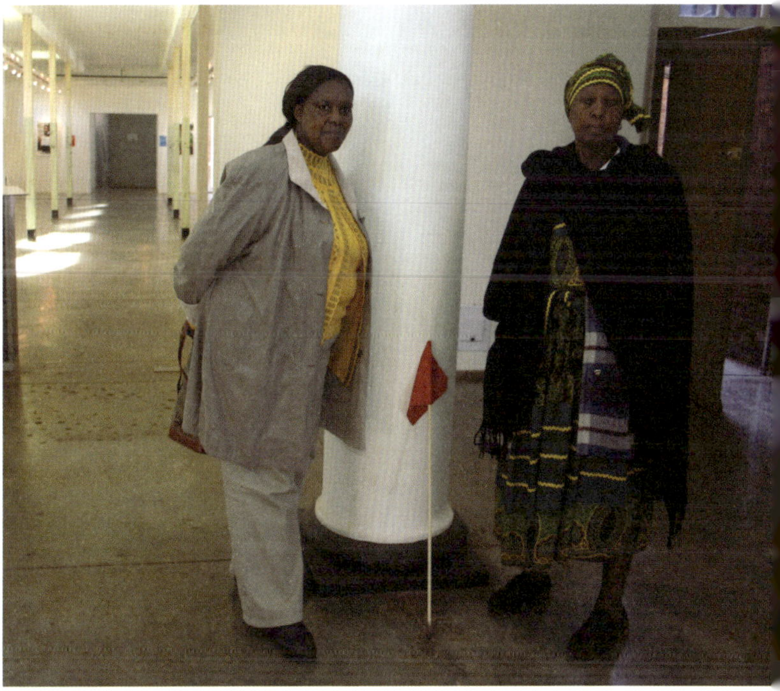

BELLA DLAMINI WITH IRENE DUBE (SISTER)

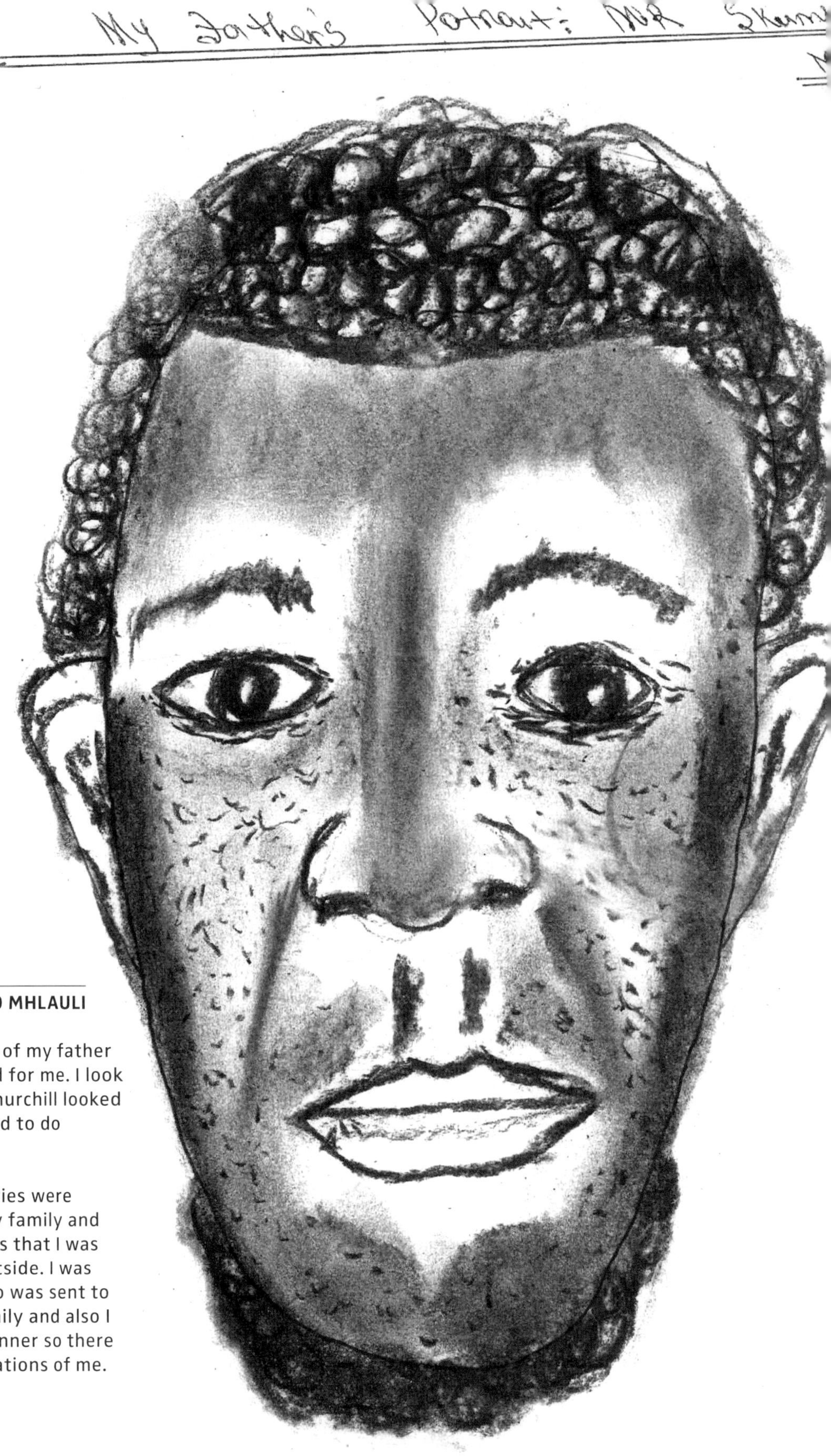

YVONNE NTONTO MHLAULI

This is a portrait of my father that Churchill did for me. I look like my dad so Churchill looked at me and started to do the drawing.

My worst memories were remembering my family and the opportunities that I was losing out on outside. I was the only one who was sent to school in my family and also I was the breadwinner so there were big expectations of me.

NANDIPHA THENA
Yvonne Ntonto Mhlauli's niece

Because I was not yet born when Yvonne was in prison here, it is wonderful for me to come here today. To know that my aunt was amongst the people who fought for us black people to stay in the inner city is a great thing, although these people are not recognised for their efforts.

SYDNEY RADEBE
Yvonne Ntonto Mhlauli's friend

My visit here brought me old memories, especially when I thought of Yvonne's arrest in 1981 when I could not freely visit her because I was afraid that my coming to this place might cause me to be arrested, as it was said, "a black man is always a suspect". I myself was active so I was not sure whether I was clean to come and pay a visit to some of our colleagues.

SIBONGILE MLINJANA
Yvonne Ntonto Mhlauli's friend

Oh when I came back to visit this place today with Yvonne, it reminded me of the time I was incarcerated here for pass laws and trespass. I was not aware of what is taking place here at Constitution Hill until Yvonne invited me back with her today. I also have mixed feelings about this place. Maybe when I come back for a second time it will be easier...

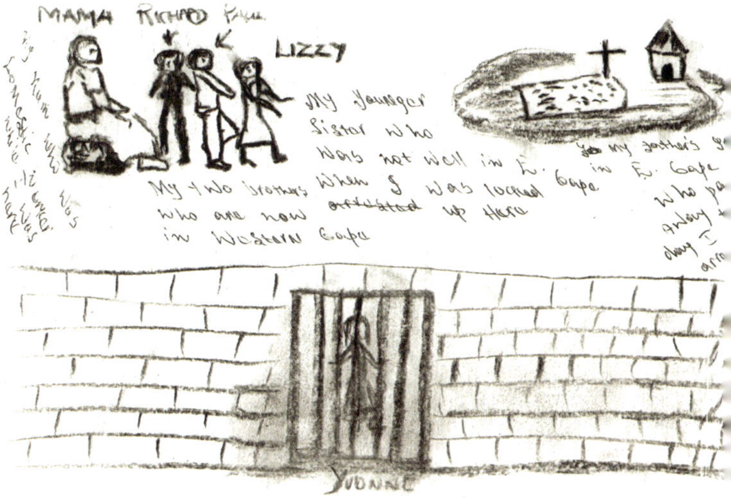

YVONNE NTONTO MHLAULI'S FAMILY DRAWING

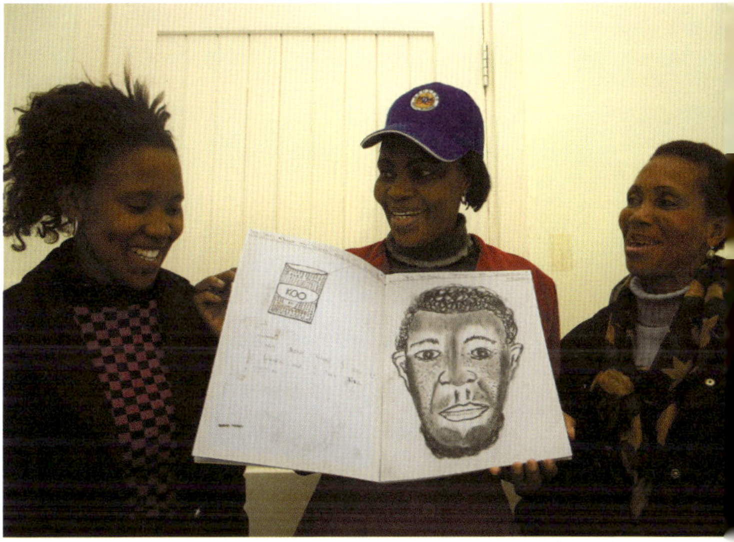

YVONNE NTONTO MHLAULI WITH NANDIPA THENA (NIECE) AND SIBONGILE MLINJANA (FRIEND)

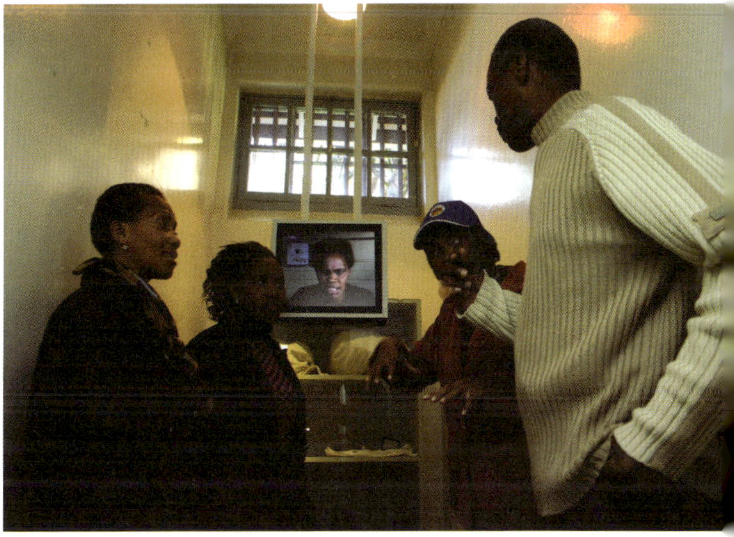

YVONNE NTONTO MHLAULI SHOWING HER NEICE AND FRIENDS HER EXHIBITION IN THE ISOLATION CELL

113-
114

JOHN MOEKETSI MAHAPA

I left my family on 21 March 1960 to take part in the call of the liberation of the African people. I was stressed to leave my happy family to venture into the unknown, though deep in my heart, I knew that this was a noble cause I was embarking on. I was happy to be reunited to my whole family after serving eight months of the three years that I was sentenced to. The happiness was short-lived because about four months later, I had to answer a call of going out for military training outside of South Africa. In 1970, I married Edith Nomsa (nee Ntuli). I have three daughters: the eldest Portia Mydubu, the second eldest, Louisa Tsunkie and the youngest, Paula. In this picture, I have drawn some of the people that kept our spirits high under the circumstances we were living under.

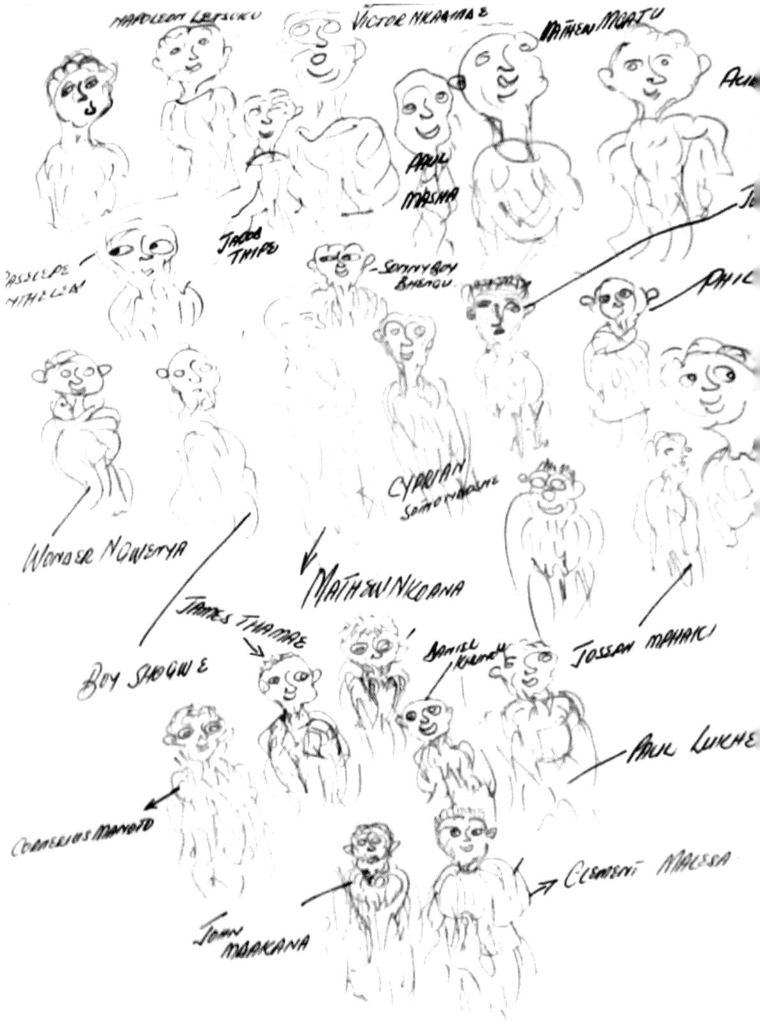

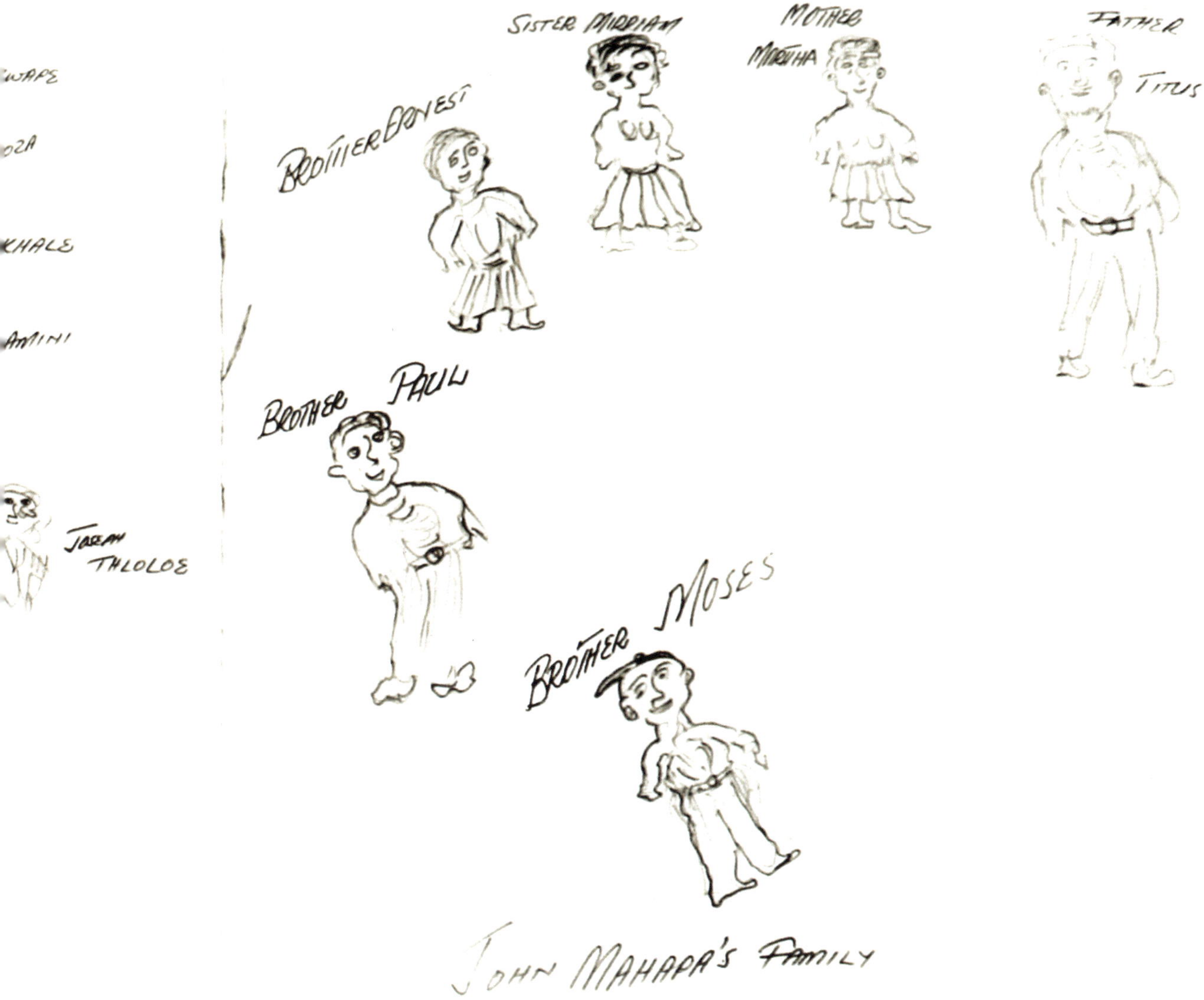

MAFORI EZEKIEL MOTIMELE
John Moeketsi Mahapa's friend

I was imprisoned here in 1960 as part of the PAC. The whole place has totally changed. It is more like a holiday resort now. The whole place was hell before these changes. My memories of the place were rekindled because some of the places are still the same. The only unfortunate thing is why the court building was built where we were kept. Why not somewhere else? The whole Fort should have been treated as a heritage site and the Constitutional Court should have been built somewhere else.

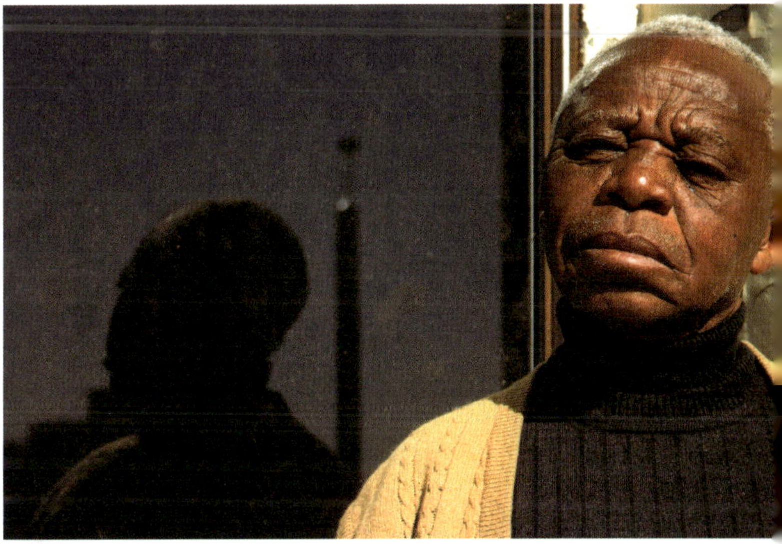

MAFORI EZEKIEL MOTIMELE (FRIEND)

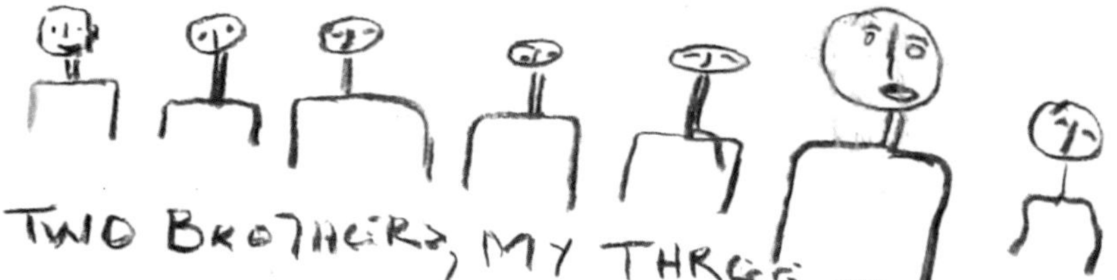

MY TWO BROTHERS, MY THREE SISITERS

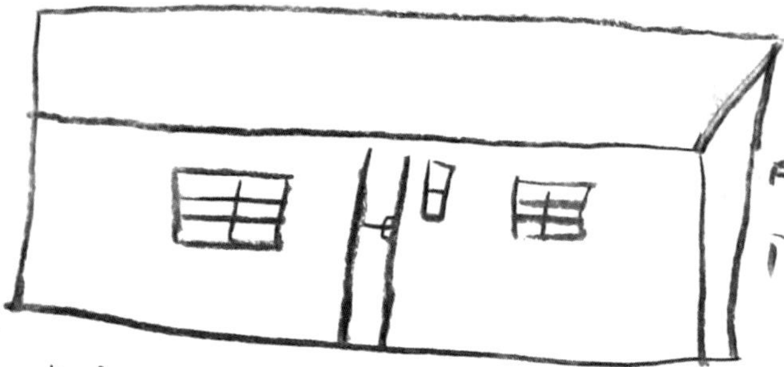

MY FARTHER AND MY NEPHEW

MY HOME IN ORLANDO

JOSEPH GOGO KHOZA

3587 MPANE STREET ORLONDO

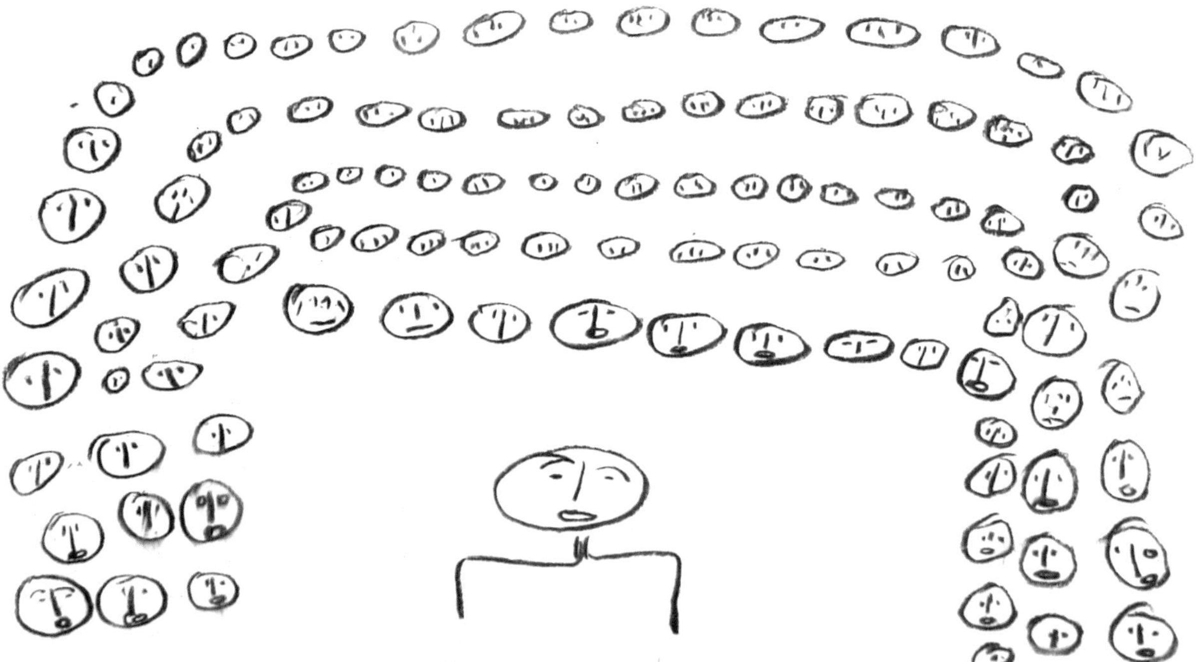

"PROF" R.M. SOBUKWE
ADRESSING US IN PRISON COURTYARD

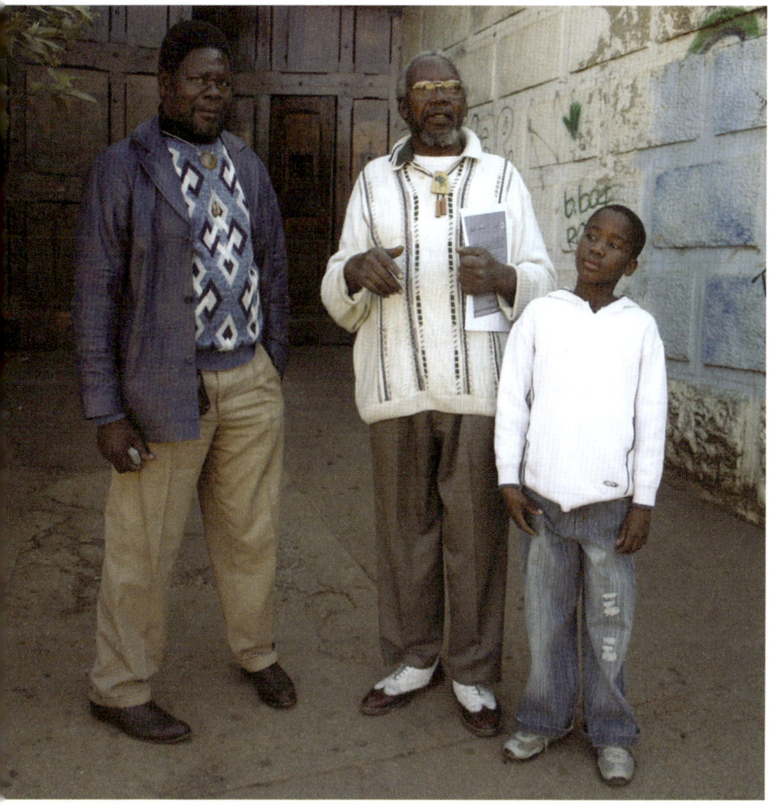

JOSEPH GOGO KHOZA WITH PHILIP KHOZA (FRIEND) AND SINQOBILE MBELE (GRANDSON)

MAGUDU PHILIPH KHOZA
Joseph Gogo Khoza's friend

I was once in section number eight for staff riding (riding on the roofs of trains) and what I have just seen is the opposite of the Fort as it was. The concept of the place is damaged but conditions are improved from what they used to be. The reception for Number Four is still like it used to be.

SINQOBILE MBELE
Joseph Gogo Khoza's grandson

My name is Sinqobile Mbele and today I went to the Fort prison with Gogo Khoza. It was tough being in this place. The prison I saw were most horrible prison I have ever seen. The locks were more harder then you think they were. They were like the locks that they used to put animals in the cage. Thank you very much.

ERIC TSHABALALA
Raymond Nene's son

I have learned about this place where people were treated like animals and how my father was one of the people locked in this living hell. In this place, people were being killed for being freedom fighters by the apartheid police. I have learned that people were treated as slaves rather then prisoners and that their rights were being violated by the police. I will never forget about how my former President, Nelson Mandela, and our freedom fighters were treated.

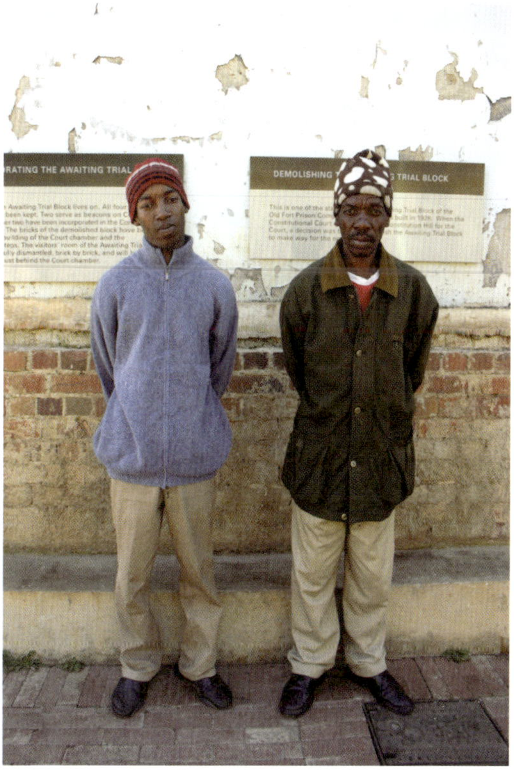

RAYMOND NENE WITH ERIC TSHABALALA (SON)

117-
118

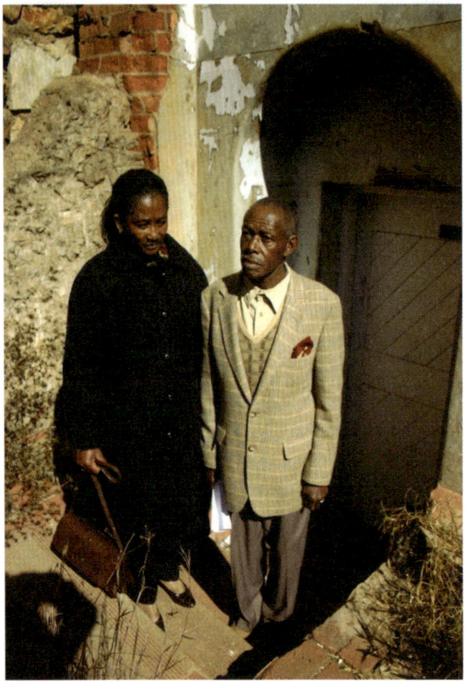

CORNELIUS MPSHE MANOTO WITH DIKELEDI SEBOTA (FRIEND)

DIKELEDI SEBOTSA
Cornelius Mpshe Manoto's friend

This was an adventurous day, an experience, imagining what it was like to be a prisoner. From the look of things, it was terrible right from the entrance. The reception they received – being naked right from the front. The toilet place looks unhygienic. The isolation room makes your body freeze, imagining a prisoner being locked up for days with no food. For me, this experience would bring memories that would make anyone want to write a book and give the history to the prisoners' families', their friends and the world.

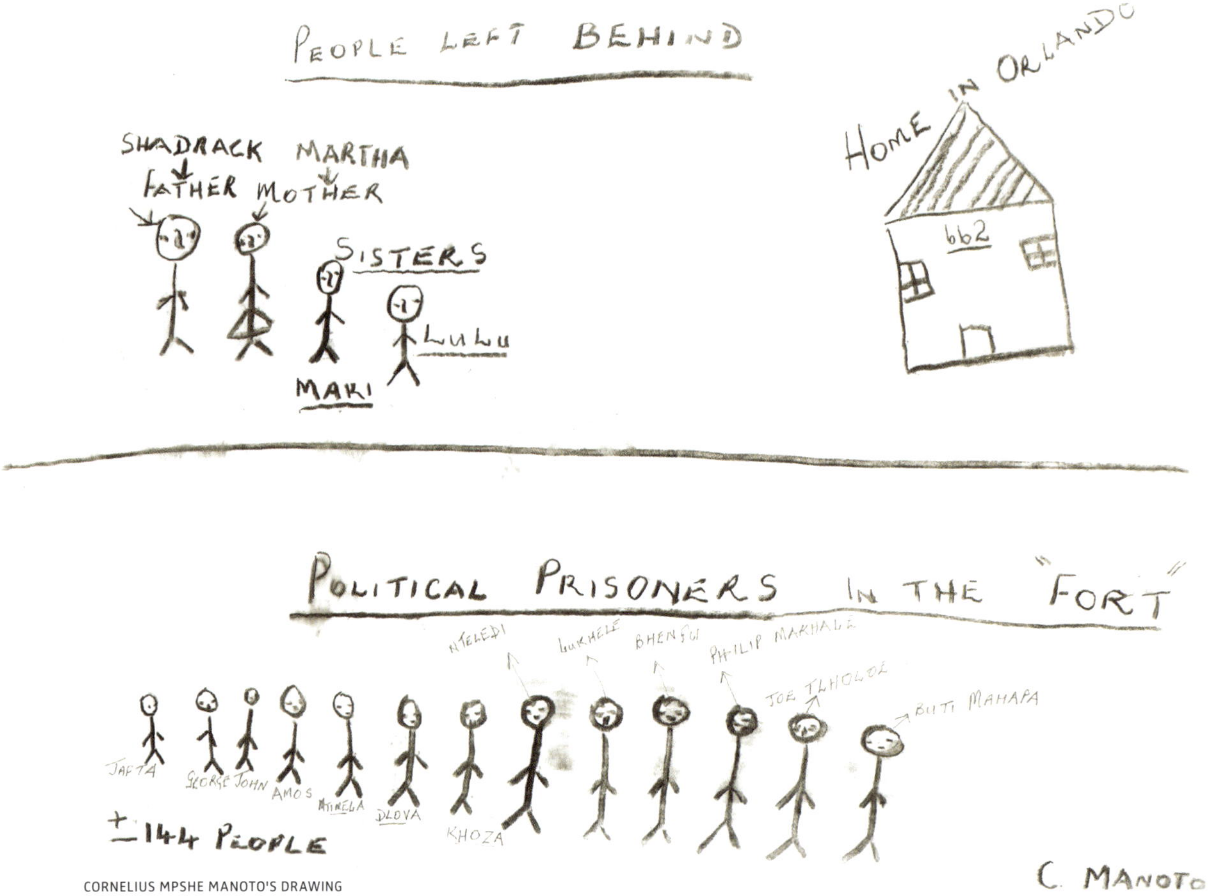

CORNELIUS MPSHE MANOTO'S DRAWING

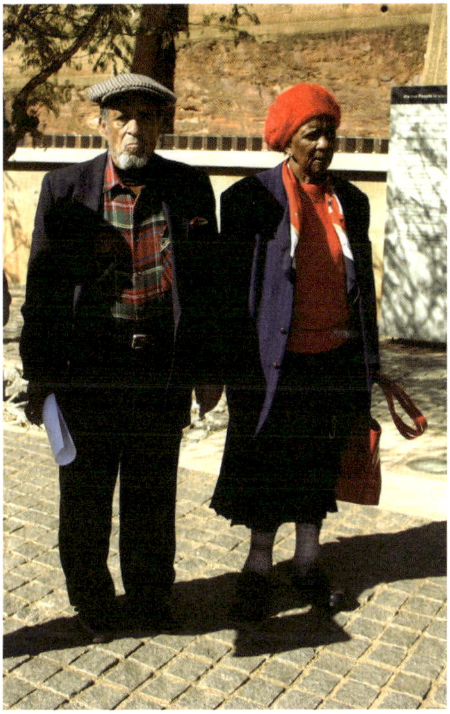

EDWARD SONNYBOY BHENGU WITH CHRISTINE BHENGU (WIFE)

EDWARD SONNYBOY BHENGU

I lost my mother on the 24th of December 1959. It was on Christmas Eve and we buried her on the 31st of December 1959. It was on New Year's Eve. Three months later, on the 21st of March 1960, I was arrested. This was under the PAC anti-pass campaign. I had left my wife with my baby daughter Maki Mabel, who was born on the 25th of July 1958. She was only a year and a half old. I was worried about them because I was the breadwinner at home and my wife was not working.

MBULELO RICHARD MAKHAPHELA

Khaya Isaac Magi's friend

I was very excited about being here today because it reminded me of how badly one was treated by the apartheid regime. I was also an ex-convict on criminal charges. It reminded me about what happened to me all those years ago. I was here in Number Four in the sixties and seventies with different charges because I did not like the Nationalist Party.

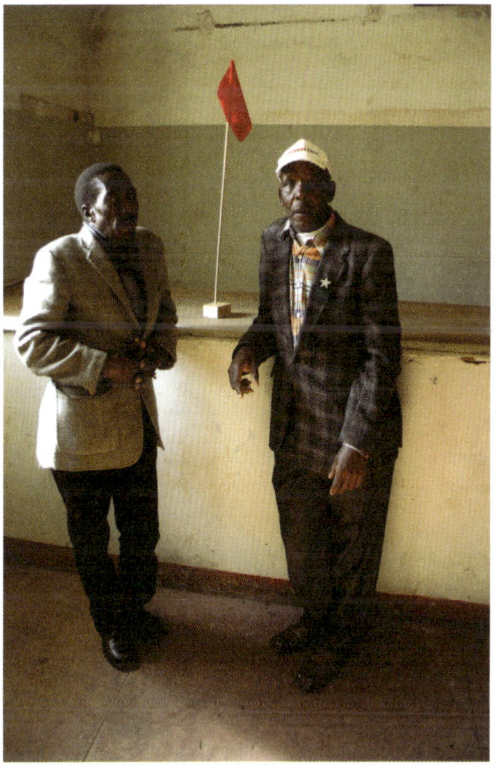

KHAYA ISAAC MAGI WITH MBULELO RICHARD MAKHAPHELA (FRIEND)

JOSEPH LUKHELE

Mehlokazulu Lukhele's son

How was our life without a father who was jailed for fighting an unjust system? My father used to be visited by either two white or black men, whom we later learned were special branch police. They would search the house and later leave.

On the 21st of March 1960, my father never came home from work. Our mother simply said, "Your father will be back". Days went by with no sign of my father. Life was hard as I was a sickly child and my mother used to carry me on her back to the Orlando clinic on foot. Some days we would only eat *umbubhudlo* (porridge mixed sugar water). We later learned that my father was arrested for contravening the Suppression of Communist Act. When other children celebrated their birthdays, we did not. On Christmas day and New Year, our neighbors would give their kids presents and would also enjoy good meals, but we would have none.

The only toy I had was a brick that I would push around as a car in our yard. Every week we would have police coming with sharp instruments and they would poke them into the ground in search of hidden liquor or banned books. We never sold liquor in our home. Even those who did, only did it to take their children to school. As blacks, we did not have bursaries or have lots of ways to get food on the table.

Every day we were harassed by those police and a car was parked in front of our house almost every day. One day my mother said she was going to take us to Mapetla at one of her aunt's places to stay until they got the house of their own.

In January 1962, Sipho, Sibongile and Fikile went to stay at Mapetla. I attended school at Donaldson Primary School in White City, Jabuvu. Life was not easy then as I had to walk from Mapetla through Molapo to get to White City for school. The school uniform we would wear with my sisters showed the hardship we went through during those seven years our father was arrested. At the back of my trousers, one would see a patch. My shoes were torn and so were my sisters'.

When my mother came to visit us we begged her to take us with back home. My mother would only shed a small tear and would tell us not to worry as everything would be all right very soon. When we got back from school, we would go to the open field with my granny to pick *morogo* (African spinach). My granny would soak it in water and cook it, we would then eat it with pap. If we could not get morogo, we would eat pap with peanut butter.

Life was now so bad in that we would see my mother maybe once a month and we were also missing my elder brother and sister. We last saw them when we left Orlando East in 1962, nearly two years before.

My father was then released from jail but he could not join us at Mapetla. After a few months we then joined both my parents and my elder brother and elder sister at our new home in Orlando West where we are staying at the present moment.

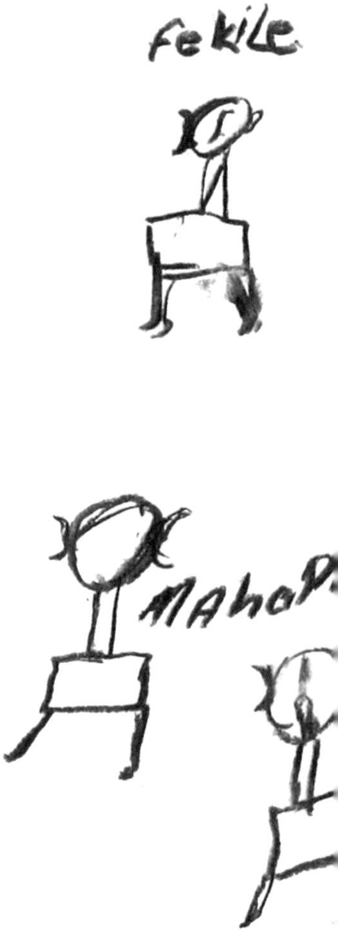

MEHLOKAZULU LUKHELE

These are my children whom I love very much. also in the picture are my sons-in-law helping at home.

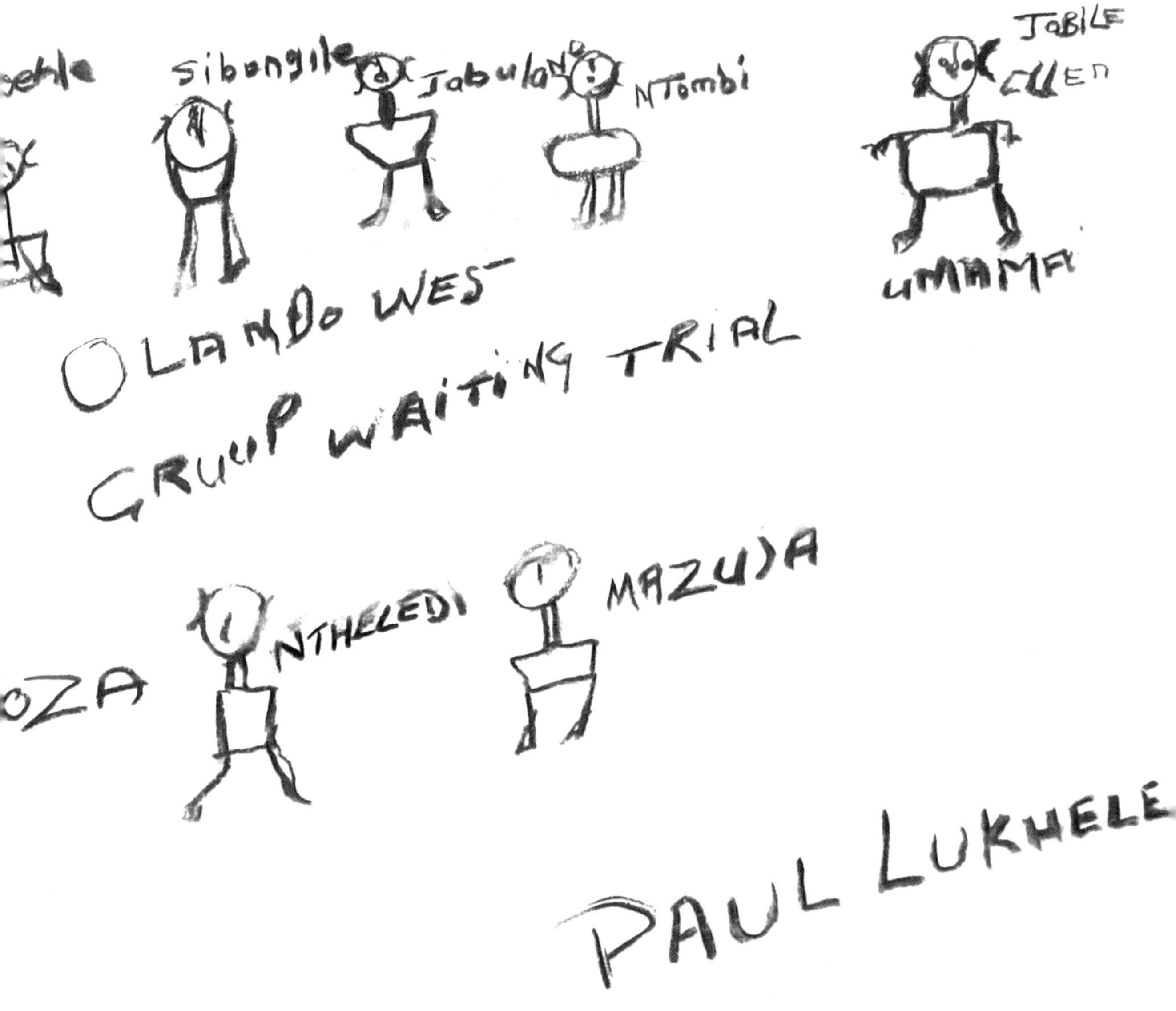

121-122 THABISO MADISOKENG

Napoleon Mazabane Letsoko's son

I am here at Constitution Hill to see and experience how my father was kept in a cell. It hurts me to see how people were kept. I saw how my father was kept in a small dark cell with no one to talk to, just the four walls and himself. When I took the photo inside the cell, I could feel the loneliness and pain, how it must have felt to be kept just like a caged animal wondering whether you will be set free. It hurts me a lot to be told how people like my father were treated unfairly and beaten by the police. The stories of unhappiness and defenseless and missing your loved ones really hurts.

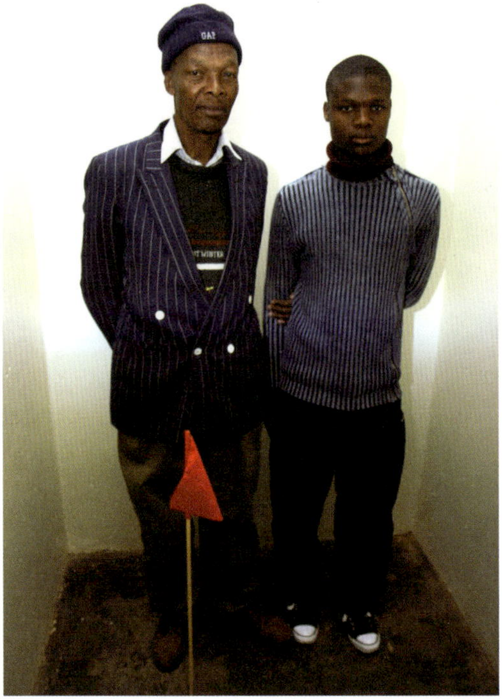

NAPOLEON MAZABANE LETSOKO WITH THABISO MODISAKENG (SON)

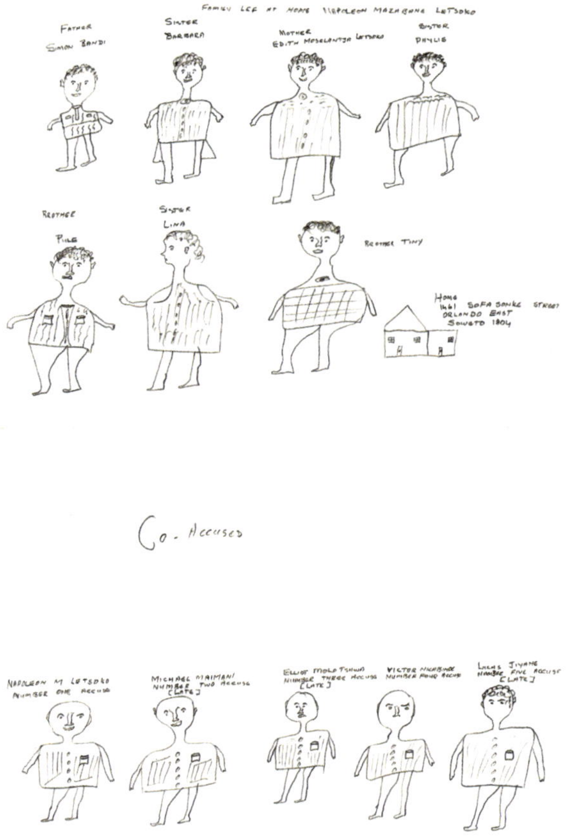

NAPOLEON MAZABANE LETSOKO'S DRAWING

NAPOLEON MAZABANE LETSOKO

While I was in jail my father two brothers and a sister passed away. When I was told about these sad tidings, I became numb and I felt rejected and lonely, regardless of the fact that I was with people in the cell. I was always lamenting. At times, I started to blame myself and say that if I had been at home, they may not have died. But in the course of time, I recovered. But just as I recovered, I received once more the news that someone else has passed away. Yet another letter. At times, I felt that I too was going to die in prison because I already had a fear that my mother would die. Who would take care of my siblings? I suffered from migraine headaches and I remember being admitted to hospital. Victor was in the hospital. I said to him, "I am tired and sick. I am giving up the struggle of fighting. The pain is agonising. Now I choose to die." Victor said, "Don't talk like that," and tried to console me. I prayed and said, "even if I walk in the path of death, the Lord is with me. And God, do not forsake me. Be with me until I leave prison and disappoint my enemy." I told this to myself and I fell asleep and when I woke up, the headache had subsided.

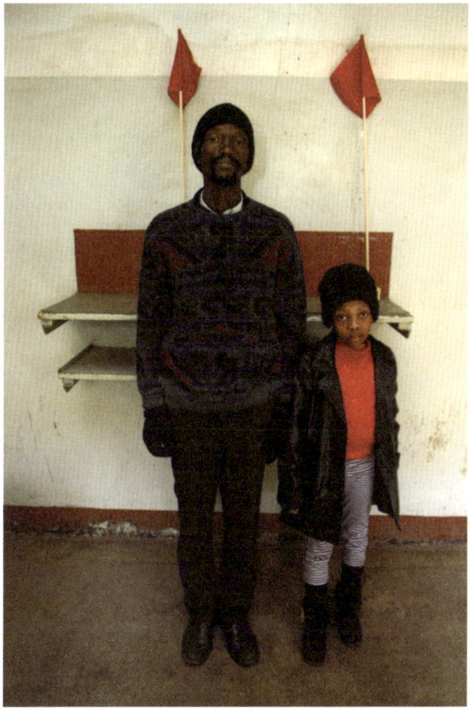

MUTHUPHEI PATRICK MUDAU WITH AYANDA MUDAU (DAUGHTER)

AYANDA MUDAU
Muthuphei Patrick Mudau's daughter

I was born in 1997 and I am ten years old. I came to visit the place where my father was arrested in 1976. It is good for me to see the place where my father was locked up. The place was too dangerous to live in. I am happy because the place has been changed so that we can learn from it. I wish for my father that God be with him so that he can never be arrested again.

MUTHUPHEI PATRICK MUDAU

This drawing illustrates my family. There is my brother Samuel, my sister Rose, my mother Violet and my father Samson. My sister Rose was the first child, I am the second and the last born being Samuel.

I had about three friends that I use to play with, namely Dumisani, Sizwe and Alphius.

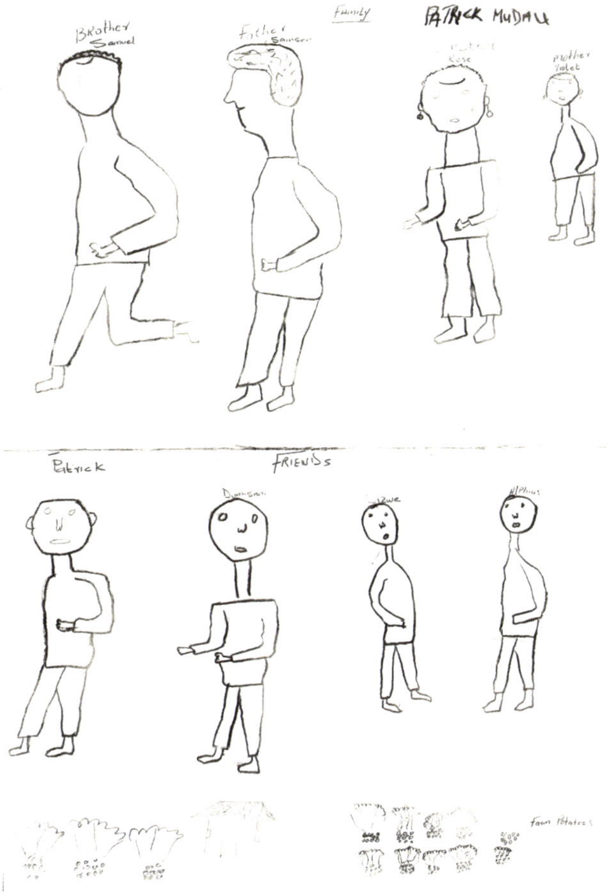

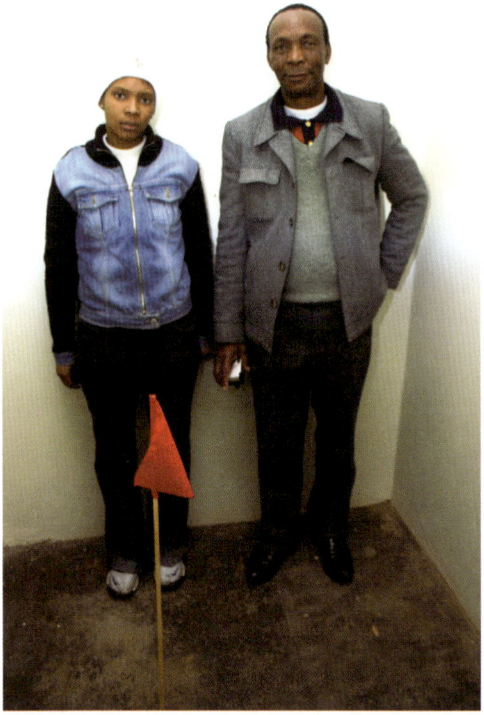

WITH NONKULULEKO NKABINDE (DAUGHTER)

NONKULULEKO NKABINDE
Sipho Victor Nkabinde's daughter

On my way here I was very excited but as a daughter, as we were shown the place where my father was kept, my heart broke. I feel bad that he lived in this place not for being a criminal but for fighting for freedom. Thanks to my dad and other former prisoners for fighting for our future. I think it is up to the future generations to embrace and be proud of what our dads and grandfathers did in the past. Though I was sad to see that other cells and parts of this place were demolished. It feels like some of their memories have been destroyed. So I am happy and sad to see this place. It is a history I will never forget. I wish people should see this place and most importantly learn the truth about our past.

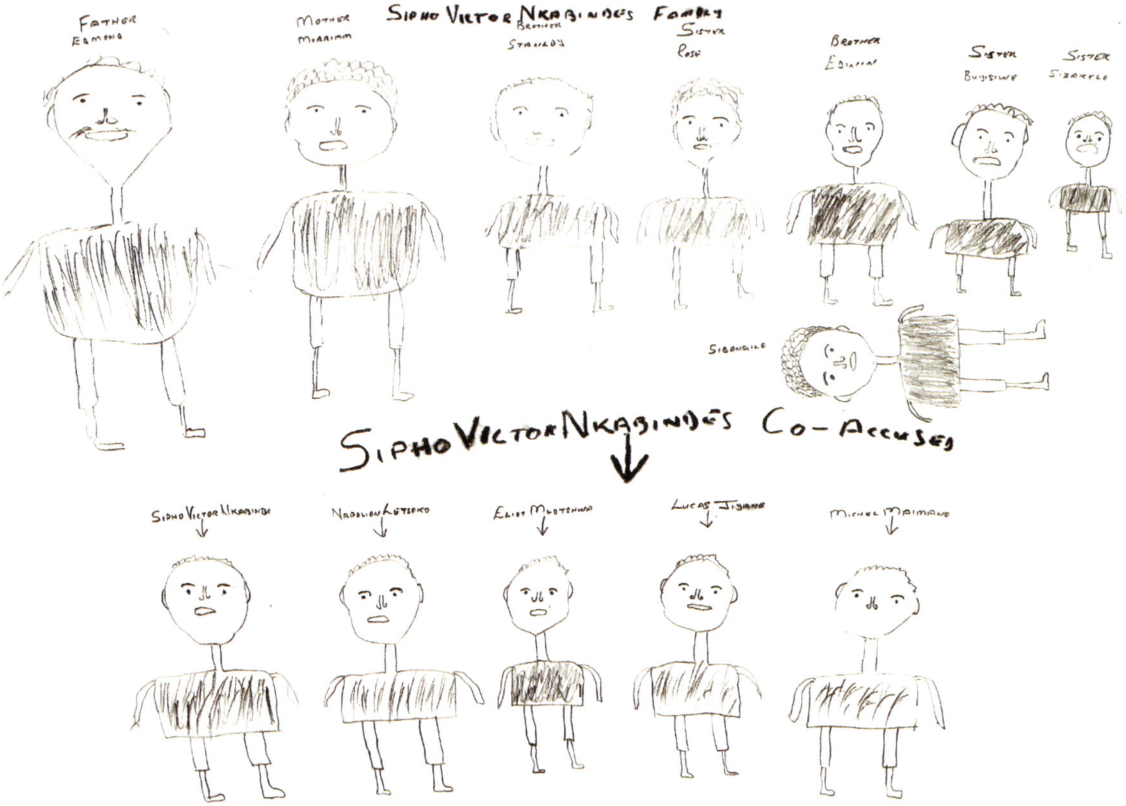

SIPHO VICTOR NKABINDE'S DRAWING

TOBBY MOTSHWANEDI
White Sesinyi's friend

I, Tobby Motshwanedi, was born in August 1939, in Munsieville. I attended school and high school in Munsieville and joined the PAC in 1960. I was arrested in 1963 and held at the Fort as an awaiting trial prisoner. I served at Stofberg prison. I am still a member of the PAC organization to this day. I saw the place has changed so much that it does not look the same. When I was here 43 years ago, I was an awaiting trial prisoner. If I can come here again, I know I could see more things that will again arouse my memory. Now I will have to bring my wife and my children on a tour, hoping that it won't be my last.

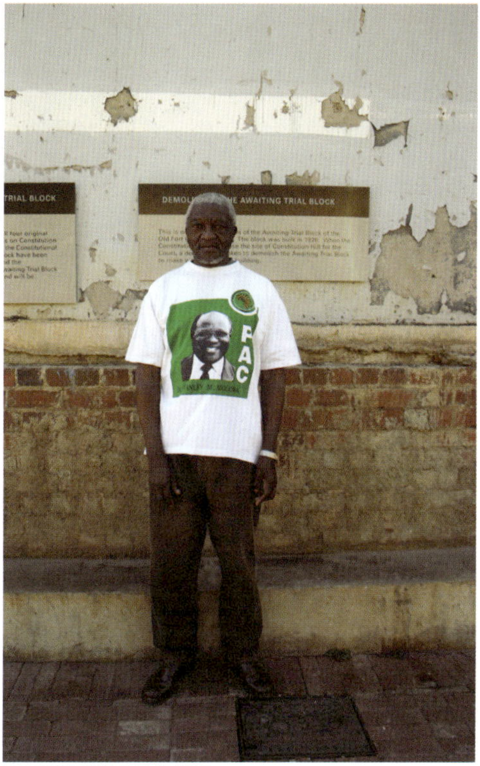

TOBBY MOTSHWANEDI (FRIEND)

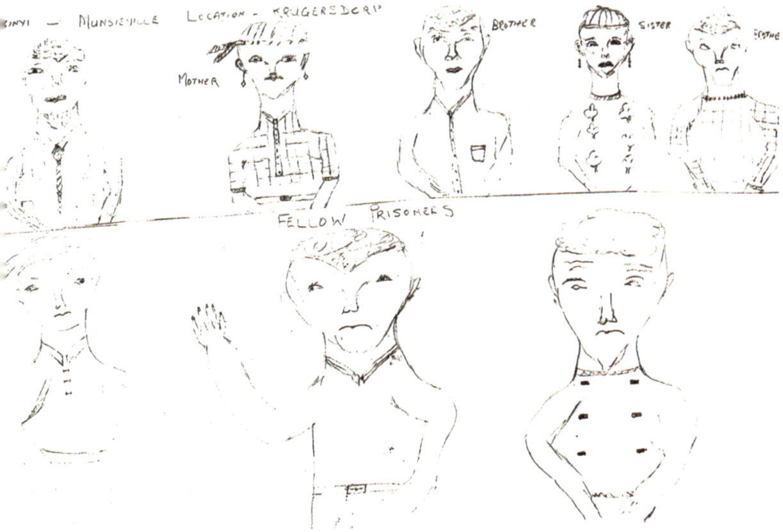

WHITE SESINYI'S DRAWING

WHITE SESINYI

The top part of the picture is about the family members I left behind when I was arrested. My father had to work hard to maintain the family, my mother had to sell liquor to help my father and my two brothers and sister left school prematurely because there was no money for their education. This made me sad and made me see the negative effects of oppression. The result was an intense hatred of the oppressor.

MAKING THE EXHIBITIONS

Over the last years of working on exhibitions in the jails of Constitution Hill, it has become clear that each exhibition offers mere fragments of insight into the experiences of former prisoners. No single exhibition can claim to represent a finite truth about its subject. This is partly because the jails operated over the course of a century and many different events occurred in each decade. It is also partly because so much time has passed since the buildings functioned as a jail and the memories of former prisoners are fragile. But these memories deepen as the process of oral history continues on site. At best, we have been able to represent conditions at a certain period, and even these, with qualifications. The exhibitions therefore have to accommodate accumulative layers of truth as they are revealed. Mapping Memory is just one of those layers. It augments what is already known, adding to the textures of the place and, most importantly, has provided for groups of former prisoners to hear an echo of what they experienced here. Parts of the exhibition are temporary and will eventually find their way into the archive, but other elements of the exhibits will form part of the permanent exhibition. The cell reconstructions show the scale and conditions of cells that have now disappeared, demolished some time after the de-commission of the prison. For former prisoners who had been housed in these cells it was very disorientating not to be able to find the spaces where their lives had been so profoundly disrupted. There was literally no place to locate memory. These prison cells had also been enforced homes and were thus important places in the memories of their inmates – despite the conflicting emotions that this evoked. The partial remaking of such spaces together with the objects and drawings that the participants have made serve as a bridge to the reconstruction of memory.

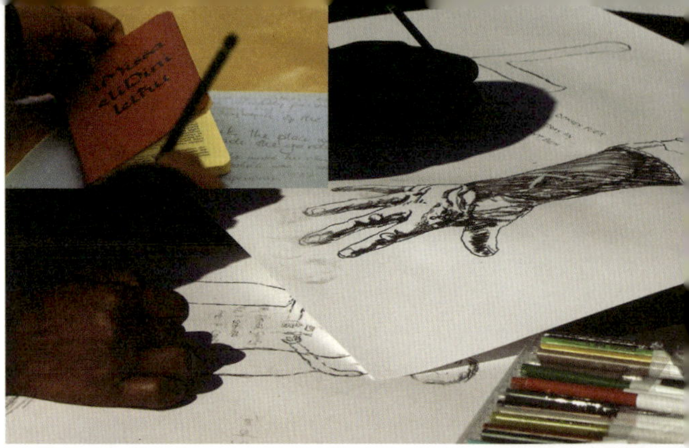

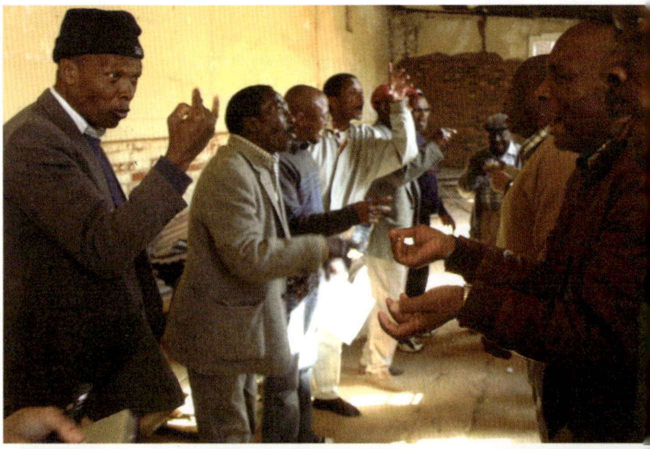

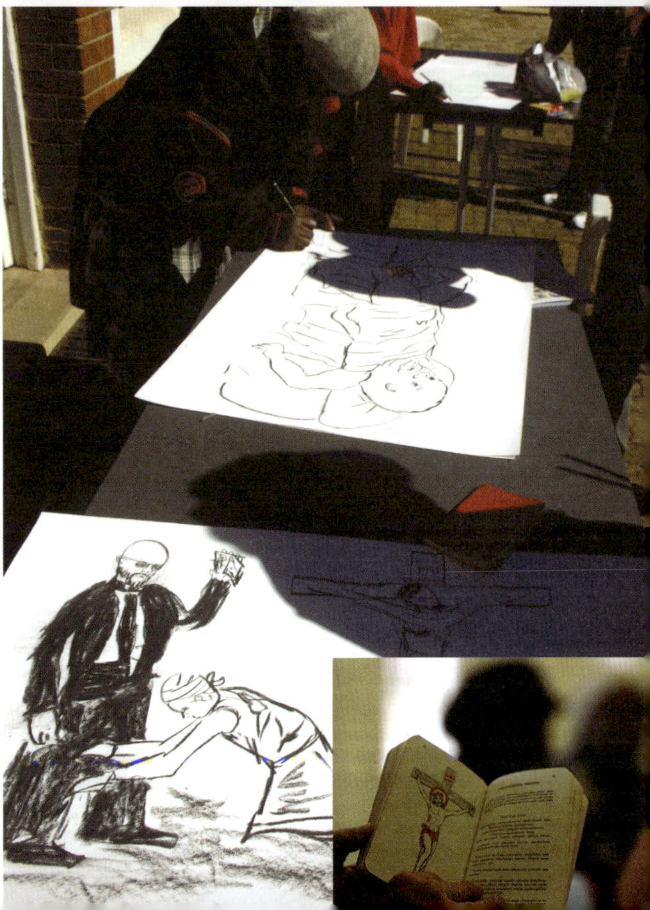

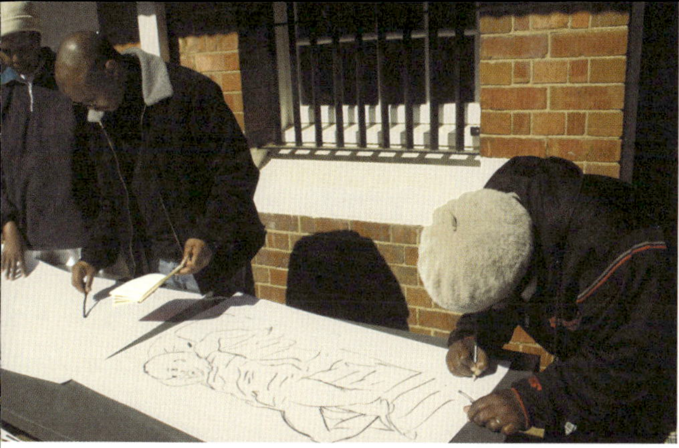
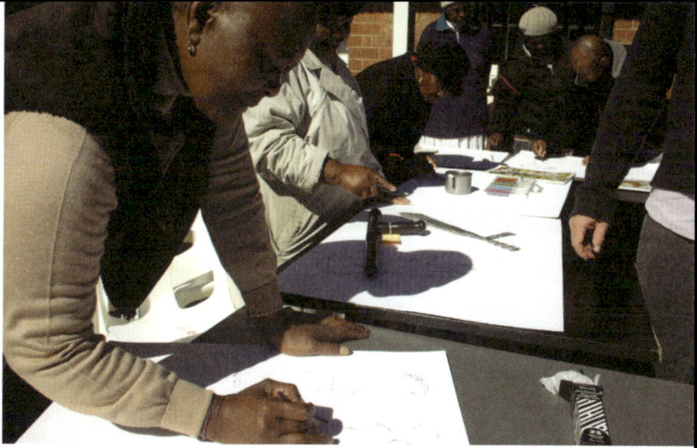
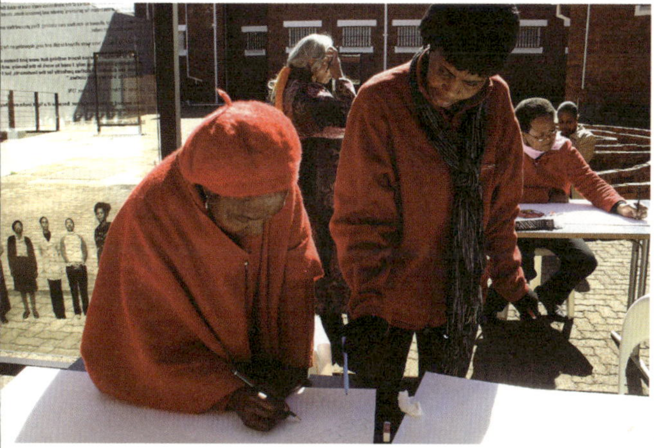
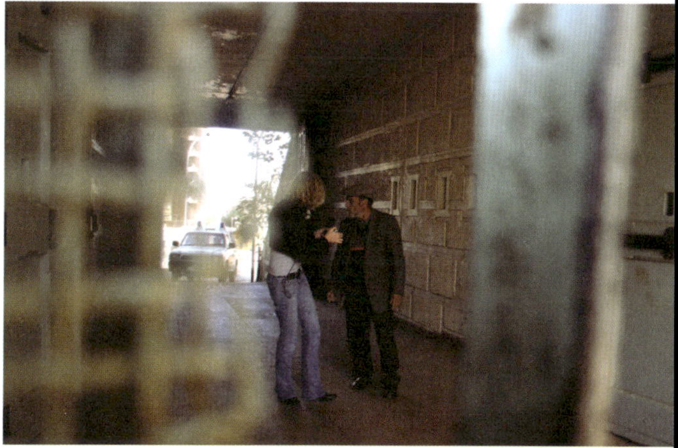
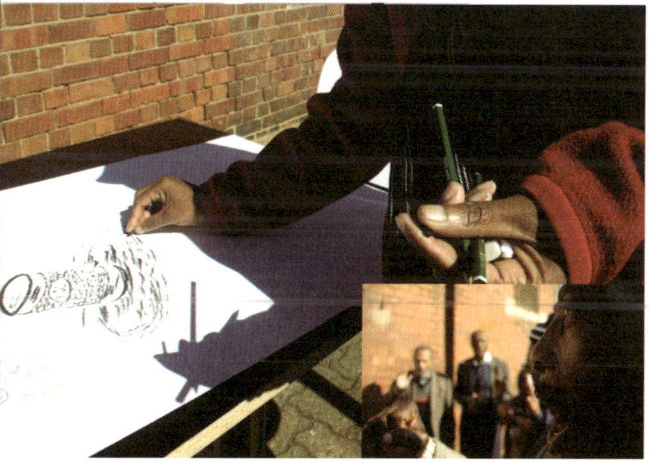
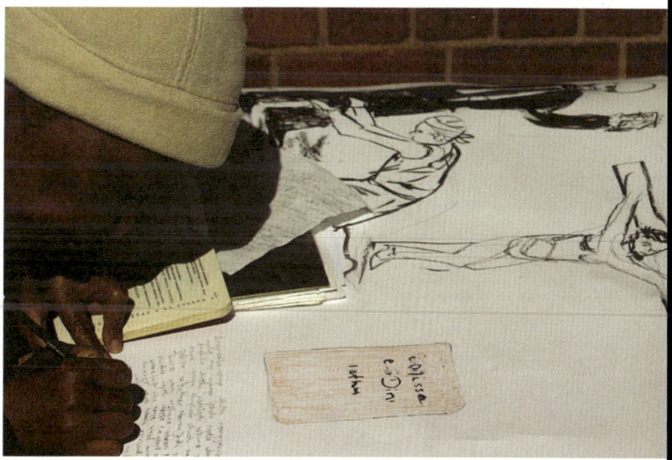
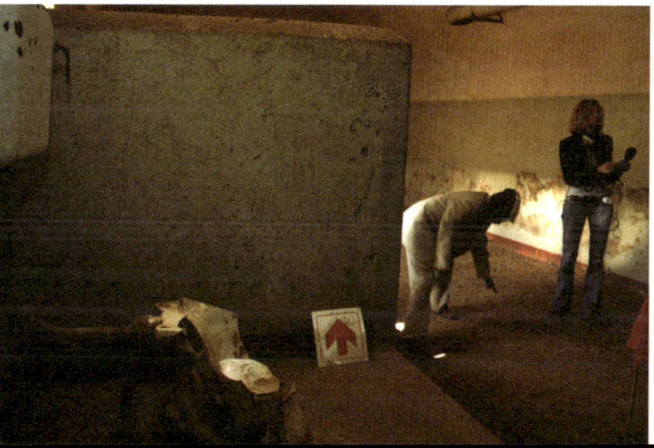
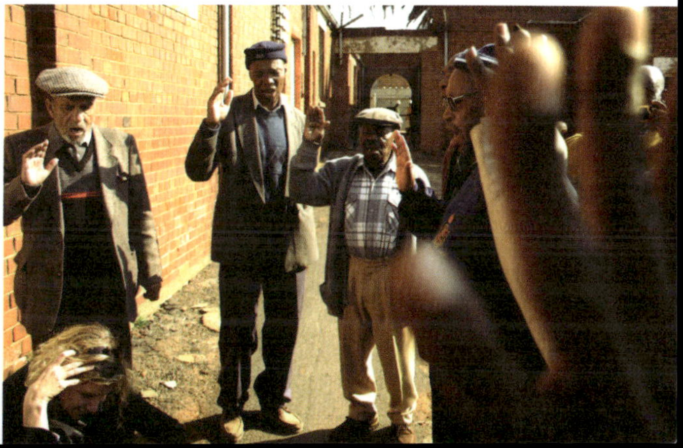

REFLECTIONS
Women Former Prisoners

ASSIENAH MNISI

I was feeling quite happy when they asked me to attend the workshops. I felt that I was learning and it was also interesting for me to listen to the other women's stories. It gave me a chance to tell my story and I felt like I am part of something good – something from which young people can learn a lot.

NIKIWE DEBORAH MATSHOBA

The workshop was different in approach. The focus here has been to relocate our memories once more.

There has been no fear, resentment and tears during this workshop. A lot of misunderstanding occurred in the past workshops; I hope that our memories are better placed now, giving us hope. There is better involvement and positive placement of the real memories. A true interaction of how the different forms of incarceration affected us, and how we related to one another, came into focus.

JUBY MAYET

I started remembering stuff I didn't even know I had stored in what passes through my mind. After 28 years I guess my memory is somewhat wobbly, but discussion and interaction with some of the other females of Sizoya Sibuye (SiSi) helps me to recall with greater clarity some of my experiences like the views and feelings I had during my time in detention at Number Four in 1978.

LILIAN KEAGILE

The first time that I returned to this jail, I was so emotional. I never used to be a crier but after coming here, I just went home and cried and cried. Maybe I was too angry to cry? I thought that I had dealt with the pain but it was clearly just deeply buried inside of me. I didn't know how much I had to deal with. Each time I came back, I had this tingling feeling under my feet and sweat in my hair.

Now, having the chance to put the pain in art form, in embroidery, feels like getting a weight off me. It helps the healing process. It surprises me. The embroidery may look bright or sad to the other person but for me it means renouncing my past and all the pain I have gone through. The good has come out. Victory!

PATRICIA ALARM

I like everything in this workshop but not the workshop before. This workshop focuses on one issue at a time, so I am not as confused as the first time. The organisers were easy to work with and they took good care of us. I wish the workshop would continue since I really enjoy the treatment from the organisers.

The workshop made me feel different about the prison, coming here 30 years ago in 1976 was not as wonderful as being here in 2006; the workshop changed my feelings about this place. Our remembrance about the prison will benefit the next generation. During the workshop I saw different expressions on my fellow former prisoners; their faces looked happier than when they were prisoners here. Seeing happy faces from my fellow former prisoners made me optimistic about the future of our country. This time there was no crying and less bitterness.

SIBONGILE TSHABALALA

By being part of this project I realised it was a wonderful thing because now we know where we come from. The first time when I came here there was sorrow and sadness. My heart has a wound that will never heal. I am glad that I am given a chance to talk about my experiences and express my feelings but I hate Number Four because it traumatised me a lot and I couldn't even finish my studies and I was in jail at the age of 14 years.

All my life I have struggled because of Number Four. My heart has a wound that will never heal. I am glad that I have been given a chance to talk about my experiences and express my feelings, but I will never forget Number Four and that is why I say that I hate Number Four.

TIKIE MTHIMUNYE

Coming back to the Women's Jail for the first time since my release was an emotional moment. I was crying because this was the very place in which I received the sad news of my father's death.

But, however, as the process continued I was relieved and relaxed. I began to easily remember almost everything that happened in my life while I was here serving nine to 15 years for shoplifting. And I even brought back the mug, spoon and the overall that I was using while I was here.

YVONNE NTONTO MHLAULI

Coming back to the Women's Jail for the above project was a wonderful time to me. I was relaxed and remembered some of the things that were not included in previous interviews and exhibitions, for example baked beans. So I am very excited about this process that nothing is left out. It was my life at Number Four.

REFLECTIONS
Men Former Prisoners

CORNELIUS MPSHE MANOTO

To undergo this process made me thrilled because now I am able to tell my memories to the public about my participation in the struggle. At least now it shows that I have created history with the information I have given forward in my participation in the struggle for the liberation of the African people.

EDWARD SONNYBOY BHENGU

It was the morning of Wednesday, 28 June 2006 and I came back here to Number Four to find that this place has changed dramatically. It is the Constitutional Court of Justice. The place is named Constitution Hill. It is very interesting to find that political activities of various political organisations have contributed to our time and the history of our suffering. I would like people to come and see for themselves the contributions made by all politicians, our comrades in the struggle.

JOHN MOEKETSI MAHAPA

My participation in this workshop was a thrill. To be with some of the former inmates at a time when I am urging the PAC members to come up with their history, which I feel will never be recorded. It would be sad when we die without reflecting what role we played in the dispensation. South African history is being distorted. With such workshops, the truth will be out and the world will be shocked to learn that the PAC also played an important role in the struggle.

JOSEPH GOGO KHOZA

We came, we saw and we learned. Memories were revived, a walk through the establishment helped to refresh our memories and lasting impressions. There should be more of the same and more time should be allocated.

KHAYA ISAAC MAGI

For me these workshops were therapeutic in a way because I got a chance to express and deal with the ghost of my past. As a lay-artist I love to share with people the events of my past and this was a great a opportunity to do that. I wish we could do it again.

MEHLOKAZULU LUKHELE

I appreciate everything we did here, I learned so much here and met so many of those I was arrested with. Thank you very much.

MUTHUPHEI PATRICK MUDAU

I was not sure how I would feel, coming back to the same place I was arrested in. I then felt very happy to be here again after seeing that the place had changed because I never thought this place would change like this. Being part of the project made me feel happy knowing that this place is here to show our young children what and how life was in the olden days.

NAPOLEON MAZABANE LETSOKO

I think that what these workshops bring into my mind is not only the sad story of the policies of the national regime, it brings back a memory that in a tunnel, there is always a light at the end. They share the same repressive policies towards other nationals of darker skin. Working together here, it does not only give hope to me of a better country, but that of the future generation who will be able to learn from what we went through and what we would like to remember is that the world changes. We are living in a dynamic world because of technology and the reconciliation that we have experienced forms a country with a strong nucleus. We have become one country regardless of whether they call it a rainbow nation. I would like to stop calling South Africa a rainbow. We are one country with one allegiance. I hope that our offspring will be in a position to applaud us and say, the old generation has left us with a heritage of coming together and solving our problems amicably without gunfire and hatred.

RASELEPE GIDEON NTHELEDI

My participation in this workshop was very interesting and helped to revive old memories of the Old Fort. It made me see how old we have grown. To see the changes that have taken place. My only regret is that this workshop should have taken place before the major alterations that happened to the cells where we stayed.

MABANA RAYMOND NENE

From the word go, the workshop has been great until now. It has brought memories of my past life and to be precise it has made a positive contribution. It helped me recall and be cleared of my past. Secondly, it gave me something to do for the past five weeks. My father was so grateful that I had something to do rather than piece jobs that I do.

SIPHO VICTOR NKABINDE

This workshop was one of the best workshops I have ever attended. I think it was done in good faith. I hope it will serve as a learning tool for other people, that our contribution to humanity is always remembered and it will have God's blessing.

WHITE SESINYI

I enjoyed working with the researchers. They gave us a chance to write our history, which will be known by every South African, African, our children, grandchildren and even tourists from all over the world. I was also happy to get a chance to write about my organisation because the media, both print and electronic, don't want to write or air PAC's positive contribution to the freedom struggle. This will mislead the youth of this country.

ZOLILE WILLIAM MGWEBA

I was introduced to Mr. Churchill Madikida, who makes incredible sculptures. He introduced me to Mr. Clive van den Berg. They told me about the former prisoners workshop. Those memories will never be erased from my mind. Because of what I have experienced here in these workshops I might forgive myself and the apartheid regime for causing the horrible memories at Number Four. I hated this place.

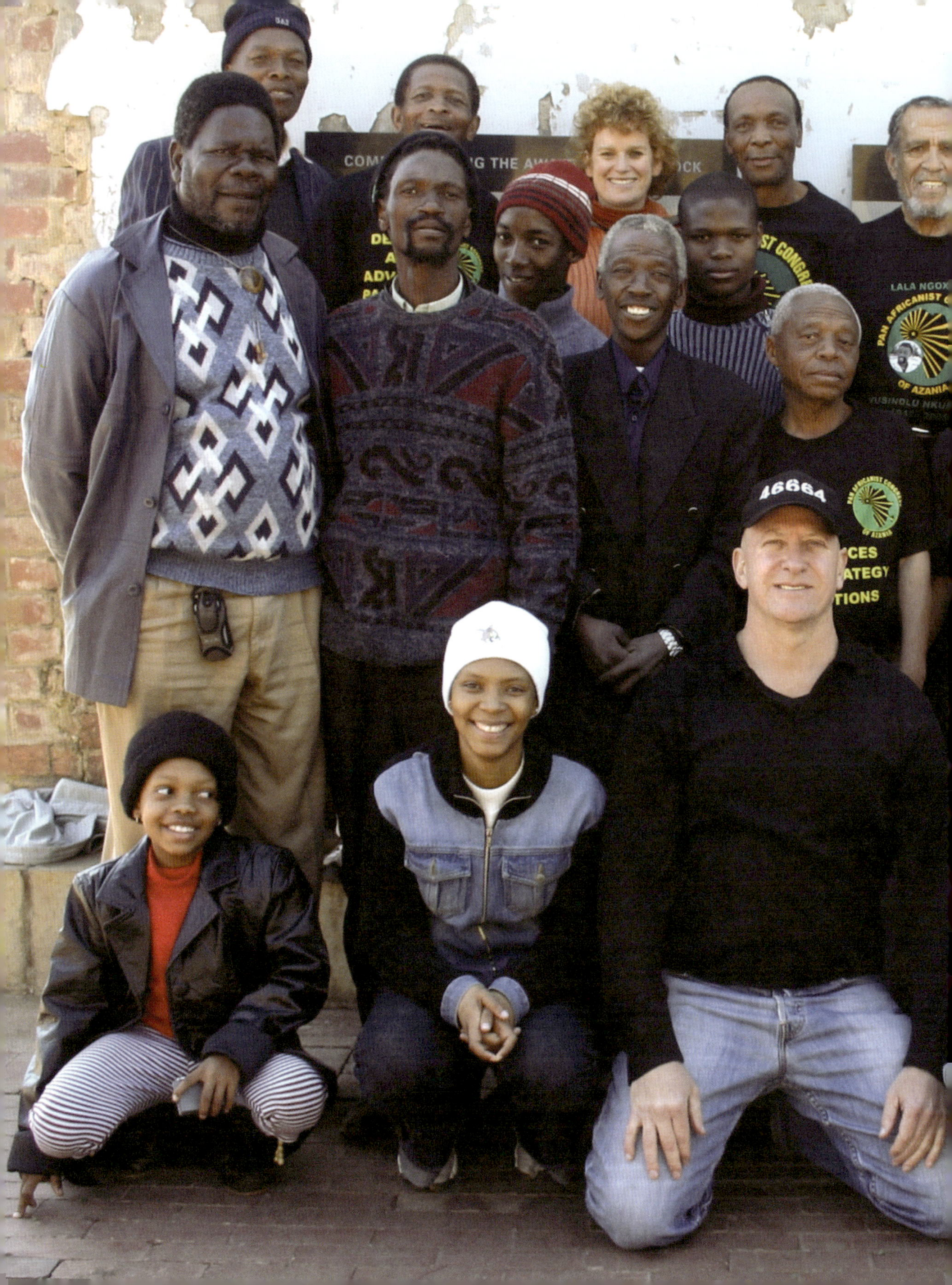
46664
OF AZANIA

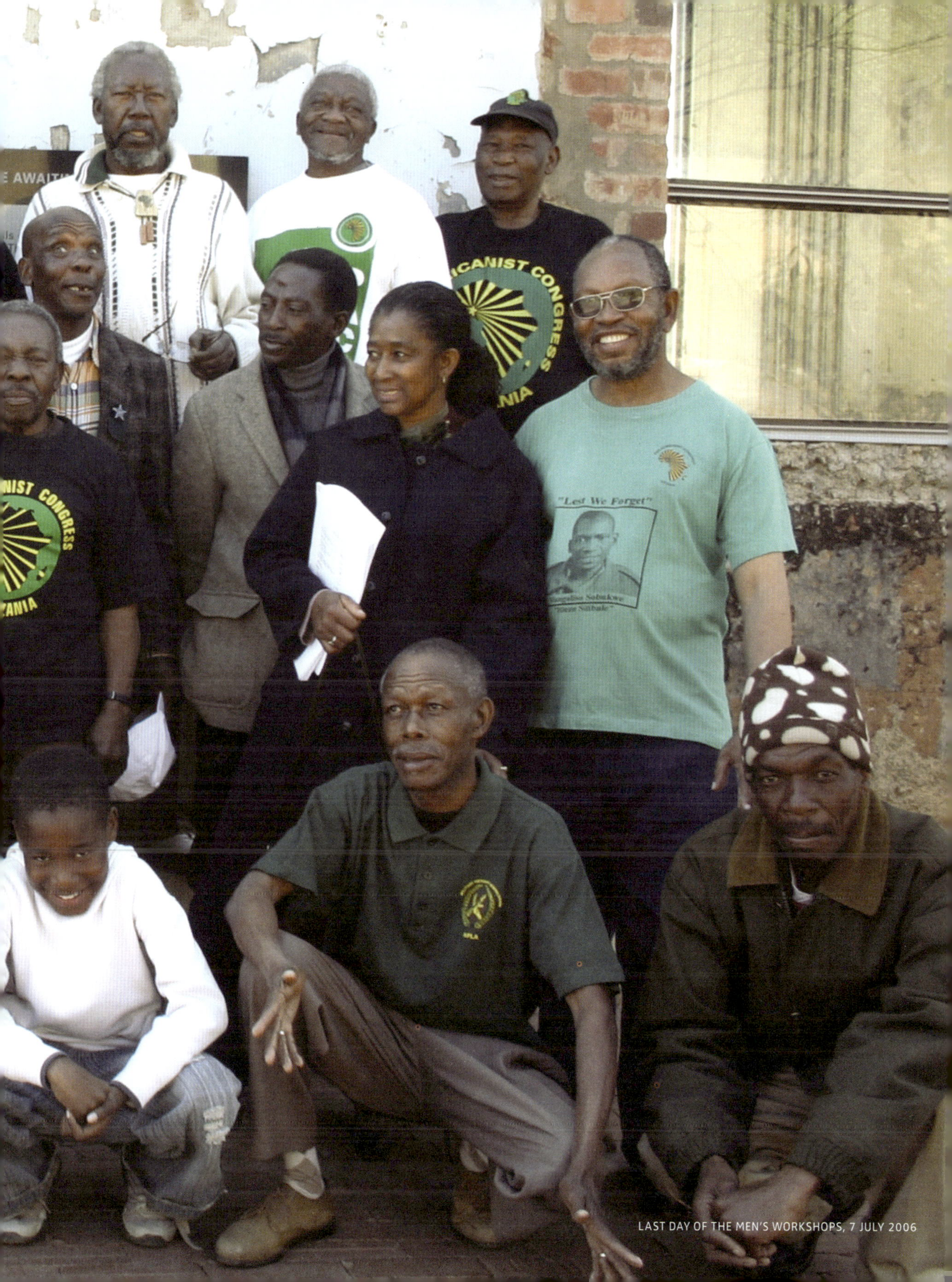

LAST DAY OF THE MEN'S WORKSHOPS, 7 JULY 2006